FAITH AND OBJECTIVITY

FAITH AND OBJECTIVITY

FRITZ BURI AND THE
HERMENEUTICAL FOUNDATIONS
OF A RADICAL THEOLOGY

by

CHARLEY D. HARDWICK

PREFACE

by

VAN A. HARVEY

MARTINUS NIJHOFF / THE HAGUE / 1972

230.01
B916YR

188605

FOR
ALLIE
AND
KEVIN AND CARY

TABLE OF CONTENTS

PART I

THE PROBLEM OF OBJECTIVITY IN THE
FOUNDATIONS OF A THEOLOGICAL HERMENEUTIC

PART II

THE PROBLEM OF OBJECTIVITY IN THE IMPLEMENTATION OF THE HERMENEUTICAL PRINCIPLES

LIST OF ABBREVIATIONS USED

BntE	*Die Bedeutung der neutestamentlichen Eschatologie für die neuere protestantische Theologie. Ein Versuch zur Klärung des Problems der Eschatologie und zu einem neuen Verständnis ihres eigentlichen Anliegens*
CF	*The Christian Faith*
DcG	*Der christliche Glaube nach den Grundsätzen der evangelischen Kirche im Zusammenhange dargestellt*
DG	*Denkender Glaube. Schritte auf dem Weg zu einer philosophischen Theologie*
I	*Dogmatik als Selbstverständnis des christlichen Glaubens* Erster Teil: *Vernunft und Offenbarung*
II	*Dogmatik als Selbstverständnis des christlichen Glaubens* Zweiter Teil: *Der Mensch und die Gnade*
ET	English translation
EoE	"Entmythologisierung oder Entkerygmatisierung der Theologie"
HSRG	"How Can We Still Speak Responsibly of God?"
DP	*Der Pantokrator. Ontologie und Eschatologie als Grundlage der Lehre von Gott*
PaP	"Das Problem der ausgebliebenen Parusie"
PuDR	"Das Problem des ungegenständlichen Denkens und Redens in der heutigen Theologie"
RF	"The Reality of Faith"
RGG²	*Die Religion in Geschichte und Gegenwart* (2nd edition)
SthUm	*Schweizerische theologische Umschau*
TdE	*Theologie der Existenz*

PREFACE

In the last decade, too many American theologians have been preoccupied with charting and interpreting in a superficial manner the movements of the newest stars in the Continental theological firmament. This preoccupation contributed much, unfortunately, to that faddism that was so characteristic of American theology in the Sixties, the period immediately following the passing of a generation of theological giants like Barth, Bultmann, Tillich, Gogarten, and the Niebuhrs. There has seldom been a period in which so many promissory notes were issued so carelessly onto the intellectual market, notes that were not, and perhaps could not, have been redeemed.

Given this temper of the times, it is difficult to account for the almost total neglect of the work of Professor Fritz Buri of Basel, whose "theology of existence" is one of the most interesting and impressive contemporary attempts to interpret the myths and symbols of the Christian faith in terms of an existentialist philosophy. Even if one were to apply that most superficial, though for many apparently decisive, criterion of "radicality," one might have expected his work to attract some sustained attention because Buri has consistently posed a radical solution to most of the hotly debated issues of the times: the problem of demythologization, the meaning of theological language, the problems raised by historical criticism, and the meaning of the historical Jesus for faith, to mention a few. But when one takes account of other more important features of his thought, the neglect of it becomes even more difficult to understand.

Consider, for example, the basic sensibility underlying and informing his point of view. It is peculiarly congenial with that sensibility characteristic of American theology in both its liberal and neo-orthodox manifestations: the drive to establish what one can theologically believe and express in a secular culture impressed by the achievements of the sciences, the concern with the results of historical criticism, with the limits of the human intellect and, above all, with the way in which the categories and symbols of the mind are conditioned by one's culture and history. Buri's thought, like that of H. Richard Niebuhr, which stamped the thinking of an entire theological generation, is pluralistic and relativistic, and it is no accident that Buri has attempted to come to terms with Niebuhr's thought in his recent writings. In short, Buri's concern is, to use a popular neologism, how "to do theology" in the modern world, and this modern world is one that most Americans will recognize to be much more like their "world" than the "world" of many of those European thinkers upon which so much attention has been lavished.

A second reason one might have expected American theologians to be concerned with Buri is that he, perhaps more than any other Continental theologian, has felt it important to read, digest, and enter into discussion with his counterparts in America. I have already noted his concern with H. Richard Niebuhr, but his recent and as yet untranslated book, *Gott in Amerika: Amerikanische Theologie seit 1960,* is a remarkable testimony to the extent and depth of his knowledge of American theology. There is scarcely a contemporary American theologian whose work is not discussed in some detail in this book – Altizer, Cobb, Cox, Fletcher, Gilkey, Hamilton, Kaufman, Lehmann, MacQuarrie, Michaelson, Ogden, Robinson, van Buren, Winter – and the bibliography in the final pages is an impressive piece of *Kulturgeschichte.*

The third and most important reason of all why it is difficult to understand the neglect of Buri's work is the range and magnitude of his achievement. He is, at this writing at least, the only radical theologian who has, as Professor Hardwick has pointed out in a recent article, advanced beyond the stages of methodological controversy and promissory notes and developed a full-blown systematic theology that attempts, on the one hand, to be consistently existentialist and, on the other, to stand in conversation with the entire Christian tradition.

It seems clear, then, that a rigorous and thorough assessment of Buri's achievement is long overdue, and it is a happy fact that Professor Hardwick, a young theologian at American University in Washington, D.C., has now provided it. The significance of Hardwick's accomplishment is two-fold. First, he has not written a superficial introduction to Buri's thought but, on the contrary, interprets it against the background of the most profound currents of Protestant theology since Schleiermacher. Second, Hardwick carries on a running debate with his subject over the latter's basic premise regarding the necessity of translating all objective theological statements into statements regarding human existence. Hardwick argues, if I understand him, that Buri's method makes a distinctive Christian theology impossible because when Buri tries to specify what is unique in the Christian self-understanding according to the hermeneutical principles derived from existentialism, the actual content that emerges is nothing more that a restatement of the basic, formal principles of existentialist philosophy.

This brief statement of Hardwick's argument scarcely does justice to its richness, and whether he is correct or not can properly be left to the reader to judge. But if he is correct, then the possible conclusions that can be drawn are of the greatest importance for Protestant theology. One possible conclusion has, of course, already been drawn by Barthian theologians such as Helmut Gollwitzer. It is that an existentialist theology is incapable of doing what any adequate Christian theology must do if it is to retain the name of Christian, namely, make sense out of the uniquely Christian language about the being and existence of a personal God. Another possible conclusion is similar but leads in a quite different direction. It is that if one does observe the limits of human knowledge and does translate Christian symbols without remainder into existentialist philosophy, then there can be no essential difference between a theology of existence and a philosophy of existence, and Christian symbols may be regarded as merely one culturally relative form of expression of basic anthropological truths. A third possible conclusion is the one Hardwick draws, but it would only spoil the matter were I to attempt to rehearse it for the reader here. But for anyone who takes the pains to read the following pages carefully, I can promise that he will be driven to consider the most fundamental issues confronting contemporary Protestant theology.

Van A. Harvey
Department of Religious Thought
University of Pennsylvania

FOREWORD

This book represents the first comprehensive study of Fritz Buri in any language. It is the product of a conversation with Buri stretching over a period of eight years. Despite the critical position toward his basic methodological distinctions to which I finally came, Buri has never suspended the conversation nor has he ever ceased to encourage my independence of thought. When I first studied with Buri in Basel, I was graciously invited to live in his home, and during this time, I was made to feel a part of his family. In the intervening years when much of our conversation has had to continue at a distance, Buri has never failed to respond to my written communications, and he has been of inestimable assistance in helping with the very difficult problems of bibliography and sources. So, it is with very great pleasure that I take this opportunity to express my thanks to Professor Buri and to his wife, Elsa. I have every confidence that Buri will accept this study not so much as a rejection of his position as the fulfillment of his teaching, and that, of course, is the greatest honor a student can give to those from whom he has learned. Consequently, this book itself stands as a testimony to Buri's conception of theology, namely, that in the final analysis authentic theology reaches its terminus not in objective results but in *Kommunikation* reaching out *von Glaube zu Glaube.*

Although it concentrates on many technical aspects of Buri's position, the informed reader will recognize another, much larger conversation of which this book is also a part. Here the names of Rudolf Bultmann, Gerhard Ebeling, Heinrich Ott, Schubert Ogden, Van Harvey, Thomas

J. J. Altizer, William Hamilton and Paul van Buren come most immediately to mind. In particular, I should like to mention two additional authors whose work came to my attention too late to incorporate in any integral way into the study. These are Langdon Gilkey with his *Naming the Whirlwind: The Renewal of God-Language* and Robert N. Bellah with his *Beyond Belief: Essays on Religion in a Post-Traditional World*. While there are many points of difference between the last chapter of this book and themes developed by these authors and while I would undoubtedly develop the last chapter somewhat differently today, I, nevertheless, regard my own work as a contribution to the discussion of problems and themes which these two men have begun to elaborate with great distinction. I also regard them as offering some of the most promising suggestions for ways out of the impasses of radical theology. This book is an effort to elaborate some of the philosophical foundations on which these continuing discussions might profitably proceed.

This book is, finally, an expression of an entirely different series of conversations which, if only indirectly visible in the study itself, have still been very much present during the various stages of its composition. I speak here of all of those persons and agencies which, through their support, encouragement, and forebearance, have made my scholarly development possible. The debts which a young man carries are heavy indeed, and as I bring this work to completion, I feel them with particular urgency. If I cannot repay these debts, it is nevertheless with great honor that I take this opportunity to acknowledge them.

From my undergraduate days at Southern Methodist University, my thanks go to W.B. Mahan who first taught me to love philosophy and to Van A. Harvey and Schubert M. Ogden who first taught me to love theology. In a perhaps surprising reversal, Dr. Mahan indelibly impressed on me (and on many generations of students) that *scientia* in philosophy is foolishness if its goal is not *sapientia*. From Harvey and Ogden, I learned from the outset that the *sapientia* to which theology aspires is worth loving only if it is disciplined by *scientia*. I count it the highest privilege to have learned these lessons at the feet of these men even if their ideals are only inadequately realized in my work. From Drew Theological School I must especially thank John Dillenberger, Ray Hart, and Will Herberg and from the Department of Religious Studies at Yale University, where my graduate studies were completed, Julian Hartt, David Kelsey, and Hans Frei. In particular I wish to express my gratitude to Professors Kelsey and Frei who guided me through the earlier version of this study as a Ph.D dissertation and who demonstrated a kind of selfless devotion to their students out of all proportion to what might be expected from their duties. Among my colleagues in the Department of Philosophy and Religion at The American University, I wish especially to thank Harold A. Durfee and David F.T. Rodier for invaluable editorial assistance in the later stages of revision.

My parents could never quite understand how a boy from the cow country of New Mexico could get involved in such esoteric things as philosophy and theology, and I am not sure they understand it to this day. But they never stood in my way in any fashion and never asked that I do anything but express my excellence as a person according to my best lights. My appreciation for this gift from my parents grows with each passing year, and it gratifies me to be able to voice my thanks publicly.

To my wife, Allie, and to my children, Kevin and Cary, my debts and my thanks are beyond expressing. But they already know and will understand, each in his own way, the dedication to this volume.

My thanks also go to the following institutions without whose support and encouragement my work would have been immeasurably more difficult if not impossible: to The Fund for Theological Education for a year in their Rockefeller Brothers Trial Year in Seminary program; to the Danforth Foundation for the unparalleled opportunity to participate for eight years in their "relationship of encouragement," a relationship which went considerably beyond financial aid in both depth and breadth; to Drew University for assistance in supporting a year of study abroad with the William S. Pilling Travelling Fellowship; to Yale University for a Graduate Fellowship; and to The American University for a 1970 summer research grant which made the final revision possible and for help in defraying typing and copying expenses.

Washington, D.C.
February, 1971

INTRODUCTION

When Rudolf Bultmann first made his demythologizing proposal in 1941, he commented that demythologizing was no peripheral issue to be addressed and solved by a single effort but was a task that would "tax the time and strength of a whole theological generation."[1] Bultmann's prophecy has surely proved true, for almost all post-war theology has, in one way or another, revolved around the various issues initially suggested by his proposal. Indeed, it would be no exaggeration were some future historian to designate the post-war theological period as "the era of demythologizing."[2] Yet in a peculiar sense, this whole discussion has been foreshortened, for with the single exception of Fritz Buri, in particular his massive *Dogmatik als Selbstverständnis des christlichen Glaubens*[3] now nearing completion, the project to which Bultmann called the

[1] Rudolph Bultmann, "New Testament and Mythology," in Hans Werner Bartsch (ed.), *Kerygma and Myth*, tran. and ed. Reginald H. Fuller (New York: Harper Torchbooks, 1961), p. 15. (Cf., Hans Werner Bartsch, (ed.), *Kerygma und Mythos,* Vol. I (Hamburg: Herbert Reich Evangelischer Verlag, vierte erweiterte Auflage, 1960), p. 26.)

[2] This is not to say that all post-war theology has been a discussion of Bultmann's demythologizing proposal directly but that the wide variety of issues discussed may be interpreted in terms of the ramifications of the problem first focused clearly by Bultmann. In this broad sense, it includes the new interest in hermeneutics, the death of God movement and other forms of radical theology, as well as the attempts to give a theological interpretation to secularization. Viewed from this perspective, a surprisingly large amount of recent Roman Catholic theology can also be brought under this rubric.

[3] Fritz Buri, *Dogmatik als Selbstverständnis des christlichen Glaubens. Erster Teil: Vernunft und Offenbarung. Zweiter Teil: Der Mensch und die Gnade* (Bern: Verlag Paul Haupt, 1956 and 1962 respectively). Hereinafter references to these volumes will be abbreviated simply by the volume number and the appropriate page numbers.

next theological generation has issued in no major work of synthetis. True, controversy over demythologizing has raged without end, methodological problems have been debated, and promissory notes of various kinds have been issued in abundance, but Buri alone has taken upon himself the task of erecting the full-blown theological edifice based on the method of existential interpretation which seems required by Bultmann's comment.

Demythologizing articulates the absolutely central problem for contemporary theology since it brings to expression the demand that in our time the intelligibility of faith requires the hermeneutical reconstruction of the foundations of faith from the ground up. From this perspective, demythologizing stands in the background of that broader movement of radical theology which has come into world-wide prominence in the decade of the '60's. If the demythologizing proposal has this centrality in the present theological situation, then it must be extended beyond the confines of biblical theology and methodological controversy and into the full scope of a systematic theological vision embracing all of the tradition. Buri's achievement is to have essayed this task and to have accomplished it with extraordinary methodological self-consciousness. Furthermore, his undertaking represents an appropriate radicalization of Bultmann's initial program because his proposal to demythologize the entire Christian theological tradition and to interpret it existentially is an attempt to carry out existentialist interpretation without the "remainder" of an undemythologized core which makes Bultmann's position internally inconsistent.[4] For this reason, Buri's work is a genuinely radical theology, his *Dogmatik* being the most significant statement the movement of radical theology has yet received.

If for no other reasons than these, Buri's thought deserves and requires the attention the contemporary theological community is increasingly giving it. But there is a more substantive and less topical issue behind these comments. The problem raised by the demythologizing controversy and by radical theology is finally one of language and meaning, and this in nothing less than the most fundamental sense. When, that is, the full

---

[4]For this criticism of Bultmann, cf., Fritz Buri, "Entmythologisierung oder Entkerygmatisierung der Theologie", in H. W. Bartsch (ed.), *Kerygma und Mythos*, Vol. II (Hamburg: Herbert Reich Evangelischer Verlag, 1952); Schubert M. Ogden, *Christ without Myth* (New York: Harper and Row, Publishers, 1961); and William O. Walker, Jr., „Demythologizing and Christology", in *Religion in Life*, XXXV, No. 1 (Winter, 1965-66). Hereinafter the essay by Buri will be abbreviated as EoE. For Buri's lesser known statement of the same argument, cf., Fritz Buri, "Theologie und Philosophie", in *Theologische Zeitschrift*, 2 (1952), pp. 116-134.

weight of the demand that led to the demythologizing proposal was realized, then it became evident that a great deal more was at stake than
finding imaginative, modern reinterpretations of such concepts as sin,
faith, resurrection, worldliness, otherworldliness, redemption, etc. It also
became evident that these concepts could not be understood until the
question of language and meaning was extended to those most basic
theological concepts and assumptions which constitute the horizon of
theology's very possibility, to the concepts, for instance, of revelation,
knowledge, being, event, history, world, transcendence, and even to the
assumptions lying at the basis of language itself. This is the reason why
the latest phase of the demythologizing controversy has become a debate
over hermeneutics and why hermeneutics has come to mean in this context not just the rules for particular theological interpretations but the
horizon within which any such rules are possible at all.[5]

The discussion of these issues has gone in many different directions,
but in the background, a single epistemological issue has been continually present. For purposes of convenience here, this issue may be termed
"the problem of objectivity."[6] There is, of course, a great deal of controversy over precisely what the problem is, and these different nuances of
interpretation determine the configuration of the problem in any particular theological position. But it cannot be denied that the question of the
objective status of theological language has been the central methodological issue of post-war theology. On the one side, there have been defenses
of the inviolably objective character of theological language[7] while, on
the other side, the demythologizing position, which has issued into radi-

---

[5]Cf., James M. Robinson, "The German Discussion of the later Heidegger", in *New
Frontiers in Theology*, Vol., I, *The Later Heidegger and Theology*, James M. Robinson
and John B. Cobb, Jr. (eds.) (New York: Harper and Row, Publishers, 1963) and Idem,
"Hermeneutic Since Barth," in *New Frontiers in Theology*, Vol. II, *The New Hermeneutic*, Robinson and Cobb (eds.) (New York: Harper and Row, Publishers, 1964).

[6]In the following, this phrase will function as a *terminus technicus* to designate a wide
variety of issues. The phrase is more awkward than one would prefer, but there is need
for a single shorthand reference for a preoccupation that has indeed characterized recent
theology, even though the actual perception of the issue and the meaning of its terms
varies with each author and the systematic demands of his position. One purpose of this
study is to clarify precisely what range the problem of objectivity and objectification can
have if it is of theological concern. Consequently, the meaning of the phrase and its
terms will receive more and more precise definition as the discussion proceeds.

[7]The most explicit statement of this position is, of course, Karl Barth's doctrine of revelation, especially as this is articulated in the first three half volumes of his massive
Die Kirchliche Dogmatik. A modified version of Barth's position, argued directly against
demythologizing and radical theology is Helmut Gollwitzer's *Die Existenz Gottes im Bekenntnis des Glaubens* (München: Chr. Kaiser Verlag, 1963); ET *The Existence of God
as Confessed by Faith*, tran. James W. Leitch (London: SCM Press Ltd., 1965).

cal theology, has assumed either that uncritical assumptions about theological objectivity must be reconstructed or that objectivity itself must be totally transcended. In both cases, an answer to the question of the nature of theological language and meaning has been taken to involve a position on the status of objectivity in theological language. Nevertheless, in the final analysis, the status of objectivity (and non-objectivity) in the demythologizing position has remained ambiguous and unclarified. Despite the pervasiveness of the problem in the literature, mention of it usually occurs in asides, as though its meaning were self-evident, or in contexts where it is subordinated to some substantive hermeneutical issue of primary concern to the author. There are few detailed discussions of the problem itself in which its full dimensions are laid out and in which the limits it imposes on theological formulation are specified with precision.[8]

---

[8]An exception to this is Poul Henning Jørgensen's *Die Bedeutung der Subjekt-Objektverhältnisses für die Theologie. Der Theo-Onto-Logische Konflikt mit der Existenzphilosophie* (Hamburg: Herbert Reich Evangelischer Verlag, 1967) which attempts a comprehensive discussion of the issue as it has appeared in the most important spokesmen. In certain respects, Jørgensen's argument is similar to the present study, namely, that the various ways in which objectivity is problematic for theology must not obscure the fact that the content of faith becomes ineffable, i.e., incapable of theological specification, if it cannot be acknowledged that there is some sense in which theological language itself is appropriately objective — and this in both an epistemological and an ontological sense. (Cf., Jørgensen, pp. 94-112.) As he states this in a brief formula: "Sie [i.e., Existenzphilosophie] hat allen möglichen Grund, gegen die absolute *Dominanz* des Subjekt-Objektverhältnisses zu protestieren, und *das* ist ihr grosses Verdienst, aber sie hat kein Recht, Überlegungen über die mögliche *Inhärenz* des Subjekt-Objektverhältnisses in den existentiellen Verhältnissen zu leugnen, dass ein dialektisches Verhältnis zwischen diesen und dem Subjekt-Objektverhältnis bestehen kann." (*Ibid.*, p. 168.) Jørgensen makes this point in the context of a larger argument, however, to the effect that the use made of the problem of objectivity in existentialist theology can be reduced to the position of idealism and that, in turn, the religious significance of idealism is indistinguishable from classical mysticism. As a consequence of the slant this larger argument gives his total position, the alternative Jørgensen would propose seems extremely confused. He acknowledges that objectivity is in some respects a relevant theological issue, and he even goes so far as to state explicitly his sympathy with the need for reconstruction which lies behind demythologizing and radical theology. (*Ibid.*, p. 445) But his own proposed solution is scarcely distinguishable from Barth's, for he argues that objective thinking and speaking are legitimate in theology because God has chosen to make himself available to man objectively (i.e., God's self-manifestation takes the form of a freely chosen self-objectification); the form of God's giving himself is itself gracious since he makes himself present to man in the only way in which man can receive him, namely, in the subject-object structure of all human thinking and doing. (Cf., *Ibid.*, pp. 408-412, 425 f.) This is, of course, a tenable position given certain theological perspectives, but in the context of Jørgensen's discussion of the contemporary debate, it is too cheap because it does not really take seriously the problems which first elicited the concern with objectivity, Jørgensen, for instance, seems totally unaware of the hermeneutical

This cannot be said of Buri, however. Buri explicitly takes the relationship between objectivity and non-objectivity as the formal principle of his system,[9] and throughout he gives the problem the sustained analysis it requires if it is to have both this importance for his position and the prominence accorded it in radical theology in general. Thus, at the same time that Buri has extended the demythologizing proposal into the scope of a full systematic theology, he has also addressed himself directly to the basic epistemological issue that has characterized the entire position. This explicit preoccupation with the problem of objectivity makes Buri's theology a particularly good test case of the adequacy of the kind of theology that has been evolving during the post-war period.

The following study will focus on these two concerns which define Buri's importance for the contemporary theological situation: (i) the extension of demythologizing into the full range of a radical systematic theology which (ii) acknowledges the central methodological importance of the problem of objectivity for determining the nature and limits of theological language. It will be assumed that the program of demythologizing and existentialist interpretation, taken in a broad sense as characterizing the wide spectrum of positions that have developed from Bultmann, does in fact define the only viable path for contemporary theology to follow. It is assumed, therefore, that the promise, of the even broader movement of radical theology can best be realized by carrying the demythologizing proposal to completion. No attempt will be made to justify the legitimacy of this type of theology as such.[10] It will simply be taken for granted that contemporary theology stands in a crisis that can be met only by the most far-reaching hermeneutical reconstruction of theological foundations. And of course, radical theology, including demythologizing, represents those theological positions which have reached consensus on this point however different they may be in other respects.

---

obscurity of an appeal to God's self-objectification as a warrant for theological objectification. When the problem of objectivity first became a problem because of the hermeneutical obscurity of such claims, it is scarcely a solution to dissolve the problem by appealing back to the hermeneutically unreconstructed claim. Consequently, despite many helpful analyses in this exhaustive work, it does not advance very far the hermeneutical discussion as it appears in radical theology.

[9]Cf., I, pp. 441 f.

[10]Two important critiques which proceed in terms of a more external approach and start from entirely different theological assumptions are: Gollwitzer, and Hermann Diem, *Theologie als kirchliche Wissenschaft : Handreichung zur Einübung ihrer Probleme.* Band II. *Dogmatik: Ihr Weg zwischen Historismus und Existentialismus* (München: Chr. Kaiser Verlag, 1955); ET, *Dogmatics,* tran, Harold Knight (Philadelphia: The Westminster Press, 1962).

Given this latter, unargued assumption, however, the question of the epistemological horizon within which reconstruction can take place does become crucial. This horizon has been largely defined by a critical position on objectivity. The purpose of this study is to explore the methodological adequacy of this problem by focusing on Buri's theology. The conclusion toward which it will move is that Buri's highly self-conscious attempt to found a systematic theology on this problem fails to establish the adequate conditions for the radical reconstruction of theological language. If this contention be accepted while continuing to agree with the program of developing a radical theology in the demythologizing tradition, then it becomes evident that quite different methodological conditions are necessary to carry it through to completion. It should be clear from what has been said previously that this conclusion will in no way derogate Buri's importance for the contemporary theological situation since his is the most ambitious, imaginative, and radical statement to come out of the demythologizing controversy. But it will mean that the problem of objectivity is not in its present form an adequate epistemological basis to ground the broad hermeneutical reconstruction which is necessary.

It cannot be denied that the problem of objectivity has received a wide variety of formulations. It will be held here, however, that the basic theological force of the problem is identical throughout and can be stated in a fairly straightforward manner. But in order to articulate this position, it will be necessary to develop an extended and complex analysis of the ramifications of the problem in Buri's theology. It may be helpful at the outset, therefore, to give a blunt statement of the thesis to be argued and to show why the theological dimension of the problem is unitary and straightforward. This can be accomplished by a brief account of the historical background of the problem in Kant and Kierkegaard.

The constructive side of demythologizing has always been more or less explicitly identified with a method of existentialist interpretation, and it is, of course, through the influence of existentialism that the problem of objectivity has come into prominence in contemporary theology. The roots of the problem, both philosophical and theological, are to be found in Kant and the Kantian heritage in the nineteenth century. Kant's importance for the delineation of the problem of objectivity in existentialist theology occurs at two points.

First, Kant's criticism of the cognitive status of metaphysical claims was based on the synthetic powers of the human mind in the constitution of all legitimate objects of cognition. The most obvious result of this

conception of the phenomenality of knowledge was to challenge the traditional understanding of the knowledge of God which has presupposed
a philosophical justification of metaphysical principles. Behind this assumption, at least in the main line of Christian theism, was the further
assumption that God is a being related externally to finite substance and
knowable as such, and the traditional grounds for knowledge of this God
were called into question by Kant's epistemology.

But another, more subtle result followed from this epistemology. Since
the only objects of knowledge are the particular items of sensible apprehension and since reality as known is partially constituted by the structures of the mind, the transcendence of God must be conceived more radically than traditional theology had found necessary. God must be
"non-objective" not merely because he is never given as a phenomenal
object. Also it is now necessary so to conceive his transcendence that his
sovereignty is not made questionable by the control and manipulation
inevitably implied in the synthetic capacities of human rationality. The
danger of such control and manipulation, had, of course, always been recognized, but traditionally it was a problem that could be avoided by the
disciplined use of human rationality. Now it became a problem embedded in the structure of rationality itself. God cannot be an "object" and
he is, therefore, "non-objective" and "non-objectifiable" because otherwise he would be subjected in principle to the constituting powers of
mind. God must be fully transcendent not merely to the world but to the
mind and its capacities as well. In both of these senses of "non-objective"
the knowledge of God became problematic after Kant, and it is this
problem context which has determined the repeated efforts over the last
two hundred years to rethink the nature of faith (or religion) and the
status of theological language.

Second, Kant's epistemology also raised questions about the "objective"
status of assertions concerning the self. His understanding of the transcendental function of mind in the constitution of reality meant that the status of assertions about the person or subject making assertions about objects must be different from the status of assertions about the objects
themselves. It was at this point that the difference between subject and
object began to assume momentous proportions. The intrinsic self, if it
can be conceived at all, must be conceived as other than and transcendent to any determination of it as an object. This hiatus between subject
and object became especially important when Kant extended it to his
practical philosophy by locating freedom and moral responsibility in this
transcendent dimension of the self. It is especially in terms of freedom

and responsibility that the idea of the "non-objectivity" of the self has become important for existentialist thought.

The consequence of these two points for theological existentialism seems to lead to a serious tension. On the one hand, in opposition to the idealist tradition, existentialism has fairly consistently followed Kant in rejecting any possibility of a concrete knowledge of an internal relation between absolute being and the finite mind. In this respect it has insisted on the non-objectivity and non-objectifiability of God. On the other hand, it has also insisted that the religious dimension of human experience occurs only in the non-objective dimension of the self. This has meant that all theological assertions, especially those about God, must be strictly relational, that is, must essentially involve the self because "God in himself" is not given as a cognitive object and because the religious significance of any subject matter derives solely from its appropriation by the non-objective dimension of selfhood. Thus, the problem of objectivity as it follows from Kant forces an emphasis on the transcendence of God to the point of his total otherness while the same problem demands and understanding of faith which forces an absolutely indissoluble relation between God and self, at least in terms of the cognitive status of theological assertions. The way this is put characteristically is to say that one cannot talk about God without talking at the same time about the self.[11] Then the primary methodological problem is to show how this can be achieved in such a way that God really remains God and man remains man.

This tension is saved from becoming a total contradiction because the focus of relation occurs in the non-objective dimension of the self. In order to see what this means, it is necessary to note that the concept of the self's non-objectivity allows "non-objectivity" to refer both to the being of the self and to the nature of assertions about that being. To say that the self is non-objective is to say, according to the existentialists, that the self is a self-making being ontologically unformed apart from the *acts* of self constitution. What the self is is not given apart from what the self becomes. Such acts are non-objective because the existential self always transcends what can be said objectively about it. No par-

---

[11]This, of course, is not and need not be taken in a Feuerbachian sense. To say that one can speak of God only by speaking at one and the same time of man does not entail that one is, therefore, speaking only about man. It is, however, this internal tension which the problem of objectivity introduces into theology that makes Feuerbach's thesis a plausible solution. For this reason, it may be argued that even though existentialist theology is not forced into Feuerbach's logic, it does have the burden of showing how it can avoid his conclusion.

ticular self can ever be entirely captured, for instance, by what the biologist, the historian, the psychologist, or the sociologist says about it. This
double meaning of "non-objectivity" makes it possible for existentialist
theology to claim that the relational character of theological *assertions*
does not assume the internal relation of an *ontological prius*. The reason
is that the relation which theological language must always assume is not
itself an ontological given but is established ever anew by the transcending, non-objective act. In this way, it is at least theoretically possible to
preserve the transcendence and freedom of God as well as the givenness
of revelation (though the givenness will be non-objective and, thus, strictly correlated with the act of the self) while also claiming that one cannot
speak of God without at the same time speaking of the self. For the
same reason, the reference of theological assertions to the self need not
necessarily lead to a Feuerbachian anthropologizing of theology.

But at a purely formal level, the separation of subject and object does
lead to a serious problem if thought through to the end. The difficulty
with saying that statements about the intrinsic or transcendental self have
a different status from statements about objects is that, once one has recognized the phenomenal character of consciousness, then *all* statements
about anything are objectifying. If the self as act is non-objective, then it
seems necessary to say not merely that statements about the self have a
different status from statements about objects but that *no* meaningful
statements can be made about the non-objective dimension of the self at
all. When the religious dimension of human experience is located entirely in the non-objectivity of the self, the status of theological statements,
which must of necessity be objective, becomes problematic. It was Kierkegaard who picked up this implication of the subject/object hiatus and
pushed it to its ultimate conclusion. And it is Kierkegaard who has been
of decisive influence on the conception of the problem of objectivity in
existentialist theology.

Although Kierkegaard continued to accept a more or less traditional
Lutheran account of the actual doctrinal content of the Christian faith,
he radicalized the problem of the appropriation of this content in faith
through his definition of truth as subjectivity in his philosophical writings, especially the *Concluding Unscientific Postscript*.[12] He thereby gave
the fully existential statement of the Kantian problem of subject and object. By sharply distinguishing the subjective problem from the objective

---

[12]Søren Kierkegaard, *Concluding Unscientific Postscript*, tran. David F. Swenson and
Walter Lowrie (Princeton: Princeton University Press, 1941), pp. 177 f., 180-183, 185,
206, 248, 251, 306.

problem, he introduced an unbridgeable chasm between the objectivity of a result yielded by disinterested reflection and the subjectivity of realizing the truth in one's own existence. As Henry E. Allison has aptly put in, the purpose of Kierkegaard's theologizing was "not to convince the reader of a philosophical or religious truth, but to prevent him from theorizing, even in an 'existential' sense about Christianity, and instead to help him to come to grips, in the isolation of his own subjectivity, with the question of what it means to become a Christian."[13]

Kierkegaard maintained this sharp cleavage between objective and subjective truth by relegating objectivity entirely to the realm of possibility and by seeing subjectivity entirely at the point of actuality. By this he meant that rationality or objective reflection can never determine more than a series of possibilities; they can never determine the actuality of any existing individual – including, incidentally, the reflecting individual who envisions the set of possibilities. As a consequence, any result of disinterested reflection is no more than a process of approximation to the actuality of concrete existence, and the gulf between objective possibility and existential actuality can never be bridged by mediation.[14] It can only be crossed by a leap between logically different realms. In existentialist parlance the concept of *Existenz,* taken over from Kierkegaard, has come to denote the actuality of existing in contrast to the realm of objective possibility. The term means that the self must be understood entirely as a mode of realization, a process of becoming, and not as a given reality comprehensible in terms of a cognitively structured world of objects. Existence is non-objective because its reality is given solely in the concrete particularity of an individual act of self-definition. Its non-objectivity again has a double sense here referring both to a mode of being and a mode of consciousness. As a being, the existential or intrinsic self is not an object but a subject, and as a subject, it can in no way be reduced to an object. Consciousness, at least in terms of cognitive specification and the use of language, is seen as the objective determination of subject matter apart from the subjective reality of the intrinsic self. Since such determination is impossible for actual existence, the intrinsic self is non-objective. It can never be reduced to the level of abstract possibility appropriate to consciousness. Objective statements ei-

---

[13]Henry E. Allison, "Christianity and Nonsense," in *The Review of Metaphysics,* XX, No. 3 (March 1967), p. 433.

[14]Cf., Kierkegaard, *Concluding...,* pp. 267-307, and Louis Mackey, "Kierkegaard and the Problem of Existential Philosophy," in *The Review of Metaphysics,* IX (March and June 1956).

ther about existence itself or about the content of existential acts of appropriation (about, e.g., the content of the Christian faith) can never touch the actual concrete realization of existence.

When faith is defined existentially and is thereby understood as a mode of existence and not as an assent to doctrine and when the subject matter of theology is limited to statements about the existential self, the problem becomes whether theology is any longer possible at all.

Kierkegaard solved this problem by redefining the theological question as the question *how to become a Christian* and then subordinating theological methodology to this question. The problem of objectivity thereby became the fulcrum point, for in that case everything depends on existing in the truth and on bringing the reader to such existence rather than on determining a certain objective content of the Christian message. This gave rise to Kierkegaard's distinctive theory of theological language, the theory of indirect communication. As Allison notes, the problem of communication in such theology

is grounded in the recognition of the different goals of objective and subjective reflection. Objective reflection . . . is concerned only with results, i.e., with the attainment of a body of authenticated truths. As results they can be directly communicated in a series of propositions. The subjective thinker, on the other hand, is not concerned with the acquisition of a given body of truths, with "finding something out," but with "existing in 'the truth'," appropriating it existentially. This different goal demands a different type of reflection, "the reflection of inwardness, of possession, by virtue of which it belongs to the thinking subject and no one else." This uniquely personal quality of subjective reflection brings with it two consequences which determine the problem of existential communication. First, since the subjective thinker is concerned with the task of living in the truth he is constantly in the process of becoming. "Subjective truth," e.g., religion, faith, is not the sort of thing which one can simply acquire once and for all, but rather it requires a continual effort at re-appropriation. Thus, "subjective truth" can never be a permanent acquisition in the form of a result . . . . Second, the reflection of inwardness demands a "double reflection," both an intellectual reflection which leads to recognition and an existential reflection which leads to appropriation. "In thinking," Climacus writes of the subjective thinker, "he thinks the universal; but as existing in his thought and as assimilating it in his inwardness, he becomes more and more subjectively isolated."[15]

The consequence is that subjective thought cannot be communicated directly because to do so would be to present it as a result which would thereby contradict its existential character.[16]

[15]Allison, pp. 456 f. The quotations cited are from Kierkegaard, *Concluding...*, pp. 67 f. and 68 respectively.
[16]Cf., Allison, pp. 457 f.

Despite the importance of Kierkegaard's conception of language for the genre of general religious writing, it is doubtful that it can serve as a model for the theological task as such. That task is to provide a systematic statement of the content of the Christian faith. It may be argued, in fact, that at the level of theology, indirect communication presupposes this conception of theology since the problem of how to become a Christian assumes the content of the Christian faith. The more traditional understanding of the nature of theology must, in any case, be normative for demythologizing because precisely what is at stake in such theology is the hermeneutical horizon for reconceptualizing the *content* of the Christian faith. If this is the case, however, then is it legitimate for the existential analysis of objectivity to assume such prominence in this theology?

Here it will be helpful to make a terminological distinction between "existential theology," which refers to Kierkegaard's method of indirect communication, and "theology as existentialist interpretation' or, more simply, "existentialist theology," which refers to Buri and the demythologizing theologians who attempt to rethink the content of faith. The crucial interest for existential theology is the problem of how to become a Christian. Given the understanding of communication necessitated by this interest, the problem of objectivity must become decisive, but on this basis alone it becomes impossible to carry out the proper task of theology. In contrast, theology as existentialist interpretation consists of a particular method for interpreting the content of the Christian faith. It proposes to interpret the meaning of all theological statements in terms of the understanding of the self which arises out of existential theology. But *qua* theology and not proclamation, its mode of communication is precisely the objective mode rejected by the subjective thinker. Its primary problem is not to elicit the act of existence itself but to interpret theological statements in terms of the act of existence. As such, it provides results of thought for theological consideration. Its interpretations, that is to say, result in *objective doctrinal proposals*.[17]

---

[17]It is now possible to explain the terminological distinction between "existential" and "existentialist" as it will be used henceforth. "Existential" refers to *existentiell* or, in other words, to the non-objective self-understanding actualized by an individual in the here and now. "Existentialist" refers to the objectifying, philosophical or theological attempt to think about *existentiell* states. Because existential theology must speak in objectifying categories and yet has as its task the confrontation of the individual in the here and now with the problem how to become a Christian, its means of communication must always be indirect. Existentialist thought takes over the concept of the non-objectivity of existence from existential thought. But its purpose is not to create *existentiell* ac-

Obviously, the problem of objectivity, its nature and its methodological limits, is more ambiguous in existentialist theology than in Kierkegaard's straightforward position. On the one hand, there must be an abiding connection with existential theology since the non-objectivity of existence provides the hermeneutical basis for understanding faith, the God-man relation, and the function of theological language. On the other hand, existentialist theology must develop a position on the problem of objectivity that does not force it into the mode of indirect communication. It is necessary, consequently, to develop a conception of theology which acknowledges its proper task while also admitting the proviso of an existential analysis of objectivity. Such a proviso may be stated by saying that the concept in terms of which the content of the Christian message is to be interpreted is a concept of the self defined by non-objectivity. Theological statements are to be interpreted as applicable solely to the self in its "to be" and not as referring to any kinds of given states of affairs independent of this non-objective act of self-definition. What follows from this proviso is not merely that theological statements must be interpreted in terms of the non-objective dimension of the self but also that the statements made about this dimension must themselves take account of the proviso. That is, statements about the non-objective self, which are themselves objective, must, if they are to be adequate, make clear that they describe a process of becoming and are not descriptions of given modes, states, or feelings. By some such proviso as this, the existential character of existentialist theology can be preserved without also forcing the conclusion that the status of non-objectivity in his hermeneutical principle prevents the theologian from entering the realm of objective description when he moves to the task of stating the content of faith.

Although Kierkegaard could not agree with this argument, he gives a precise equivalent to the proviso when he says that "when subjectivity is the truth, the conceptual determination of the truth must include an expression for the antithesis of objectivity."[18] For Kierkegaard this "conceptual determination" meant that even the articulation of existential truth (e.g., the statement "truth is subjectivity") must be so presented that it cannot be taken as a result but throws the reader back upon the inwardness of his own existence. When the concern is properly theological and is separated from the problem of how the content is appropriated in

---

tualizations of existence. One of the results of its objectifying analysis is, however, to assign responsibility for the individual's *existentiell* condition precisely to him.

[18]Kierkegaard, *Concluding...*, p. 182.

faith, "conceptual determination" can mean something else. It can mean that the existentialist interpretation is constantly guided *in its objective descriptions* by the proviso that these descriptions apply to the non-objective, existential process of becoming and must not be taken as descriptive of given states in the self. Furthermore, it states that to be conceptually adequate to their "object," such descriptions must themselves "include an expression for the antithesis of objectivity." That is, they must continually be qualified so as to point to the non-objectivity of their actualization.

Without allowing some such distinction as this between the non-objectivity of existence (or faith) and the objectivity of theological description, it is difficult to see how theology is possible at all given the aims of demythologizing and existentialist interpretation. The purpose of the following analysis of Buri is to clarify this issue. It will become evident that there is indeed a confusion between the implications the analysis of non-objectivity has for understanding the nature of faith and the implications it has for properly conceiving the status of theological language. And despite certain differences which derive largely from the more self-consciously systematic character of his writing, Buri's confusion here is representative of a confusion which runs throughout existentialist theology. This confusion causes such theology to tend in the direction of becoming equivalent to indirect communication with the result that faith becomes ineffable. It becomes possible on these terms, that is, to say only *that* faith occurs but not *what* its content is. This does not occur in Kierkegaard for the simple reason that the traditional, orthodox content never became hermeneutically questionable for him. His only problem was the problem of appropriation. But where this content can no longer in any way be presumed, this confusion cannot but vitiate the theological task.

There have been, of course, countless criticisms of the existentialist position on the problem of objectivity. Almost without exception, however, these criticisms have, either consciously or unconsciously, qualified the foundations of a genuinely radical theology by identifying the preservation of some form of objectivity with the preservation of some hermeneutically unreconstructed core of the tradition.[19] The analysis and criticism here

---

[19]This is the problem with Jørgensen's study, (Cf., *supra*, note 8.) But it is a common error. It occurs whenever a writer agrees, on the one hand, that there is a necessity to make the gospel intelligible and living for modern man and then, on the other hand, exempts some portion of the traditional gospel from this rethinking or even uses this exempted portion as the basis for the so-called translation. Examples of such exemptions

will attempt to remain at a formal, methodological level precisely in order to avoid such special pleading. The concern will be to examine the
extent to which the problem of objectivity is and is not useful as a hermeneutical device establishing the nature and limits of theological language for a radical theology. There is no desire to challenge the idea of
a radical theology as such. When it becomes clear that the typical em-
ployment of the problem of objectivity is confusing, then it may be
possible to envision a quite different hermeneutical horizon within which
a radical theology can be developed.

Some thinkers, including apparently Buri and other existentialist theologians in places, would object at this point that it is illegitimate to distinguish between existential theology and theology as existentialist interpretation. They would argue that once the subjective problem of how to
become a Christian has been recognized, then theology as such must be
assimilated to existential theology. From this point of view, to quote
Allison again, the purpose of theology "is not to convince the reader of a
philosophical or religious truth, but to prevent him from theorizing, *even
in an 'existential' sense* about Christianity, and instead to help him come
to grips, in the isolation of his own subjectivity, with the question of
what it means to become a Christian."[20] Agreement with the force of this
remark is what creates the confusion over the problem of objectivity
among the existentialist theologians.

The argument of this study (as well as the viability of a genuinely radical theology) depends on there being an alternative to this Kierkegaar-
dian conclusion. Admittedly the subjective problem is the true "existen-

---

are appeals various writers make to the particularity and exclusiveness of the Christ
event, to the concept of God's "mighty acts in history," to the concept of "covenant,"
or to various theories of revelation as God's self-manifestation. It cannot be said in advance that the advocacy of a radical theology in and of itself requires the rejection of
any of these concepts. That is not the point. It is, rather, that none of them can be
used until precisely the hermeneutical foundations of these more or less „final" theological concepts are themselves completely rethought and, therefore, translated. It is the failure to conceive the hermeneutical problem radically enough that causes the above confusion, and this confusion always ends in some form of special pleading. Perhaps the
most striking example of this special pleading is Harvey Cox's enormously influential but
only superficially secular or radical *The Secular City* (New York: The Macmillan Co.,
1965). For an extremely well stated criticism of Cox on this point, cf., Langdon Gilkey,
Naming the Whirlwind: The Renewal of God-Language (New York: The Bobbs-Merrill
Co., 1969), pp. 25 f. The best American attempts to avoid this confusion and to rethink
the hermeneutical problem to its ground in a truly radical fashion are probably Gilkey
and Ray L. Hart, *Unfinished Man and the Imagination* (New York: Herder and Herder,
1969).
[20]Allison, p. 433. My italics.

tial" problem. But it is a problem of living, a problem every man must confront in the isolation of his own soul, and not a properly theological problem. Of course, the theologian in his "theorizing," must make clear that the subjective problem is the truly important question of which men ought to be aware, and he must make clear that theorizing itself can become a way of avoiding this question. But this does not detract from the fact that theology proper is a pre-eminently theoretical undertaking and that, unless it lapses into the mode of indirect communication which cannot articulate the content of faith, its clarification of these things is also theoretical. Taking this position need not reduce theology to "gross objectivity" and nothing else. The proviso still makes clear that the objective articulation of the content of faith does not reduce faith itself to an objective theory. If this argument is correct, then the theologian is simply not forced to choose between "the Hegelian both/and whereby the individual finds himself in the infinite after forgetting himself in the finite" and the "existential either/or wherein the forgetfulness of self, characteristic of speculative thought, is viewed as a fantastic flight from one's existential situation."[21]

[21]*Ibid.*, p. 435.

CHAPTER I

THE PROBLEM OF OBJECTIVITY IN THE GENESIS OF BURI'S THEOLOGY

Neo-orthodoxy rested much of its claim to be a major theological movement on its decisive repudiation of nineteenth century liberalism. Although this claim appeared credible twenty years ago, it has become increasingly apparent in recent years that neo-orthodoxy was really a historically conditioned parenthesis within a line of development continuous with the nineteenth century.[1] The contemporary movement of radical theology represents in this sense a return to many of the themes, if
not the tenor of thought, in nineteenth century liberal theology. This is
true despite the equal emphasis that must be placed on the distinctive
features of any truly twentieth century theology: the tempering by the
historical events of the twentieth century, the greater theological self-consciousness, the promise but also the horrors and the perils of post-war,
post-industrial society. The same must be said of Buri. He has absorbed
the twentieth century theological revolution as deeply as anyone, and his
thought is unintelligible apart from understanding his appropriation of
twentieth century philosophy and theology. But unlike many of his con-
temporaries, Buri has never believed that a decisive break with nineteenth century theology is either necessary or possible. He is and always
has been a basically liberal theologian. Buri has always fought for a
truth, therefore, which younger or newly converted radical theologians
are only just now discovering.

This means that his thought is defined by the tension that characterized
all the great liberal theologians in the nineteenth and early twentieth
centuries. On the one hand, liberal theology has always been concerned
to maintain the integrity of the Christian faith. It has never wanted to
retreat from the affirmation that there is a unique Christian contribution
to the understanding of human life and destiny. On the other hand, it

[1]Cf., Peter L. Berger, *The Sacred Canopy* (Garden City, New York: Doubleday and
Co., Inc., 1967), pp. 105-171, esp. pp. 154-171.

has always been concerned not to allow this affirmation to compromise the allegiance it has felt any modern man owes to the modern understanding of man and the world and to the methods and results of scientific knowledge. This has occasioned the tension that liberal theology, at least in its more honest moments, has recognized that there is a disjunction between what the theologian must say in his systematic work as a modern man and much that the New Testament and the Christian tradition have affirmed as integral. Liberal theology, as a result, has never seen any *easy* way of honestly avoiding philosophical or cultural reduction of Christian assertions. The crucial problem for liberal theology, therefore, is to work out a way of saying that the two views, Christian and cultural, are distinct yet not in conflict so that they can be positively related.

This tension characterizes Buri's thought, and it provides a way of understanding the development from his early thought to his present mature position. His mature thought, represented by his *Dogmatik als Selbstverständnis des christlichen Glaubens,* is an attempt to solve the problem of tension in liberal theology. Between his present position and his earlier thought, there was a transition, though not a revolutionary break,[2] which occurred in the years 1950-54. It was marked by a growing awareness that his earlier position could not maintain the integrity of the Christian message and could not bring it to adequate expression. At a methodological level, this awareness was made possible by his deepened understanding of the problem of objectivity, which he acquired from Karl Jaspers, and by his development of the closely related concept of "self-understanding," which he appropriated from Rudolf Bultmann and which has since defined the title and focusing theme of his dogmatics.

A. CONSISTENT ESCHATOLOGY AND PHILOSOPHY OF RELIGION: BURI'S EARLY POSITION

Buri's earliest position was an attempt to articulate the dogmatic significance of the "delayed parousia" and the thesis of "consistent eschatology" set forth by Albert Schweitzer and Martin Werner. As an historical thesis "consistent eschatology" is of mainly negative force. It argues that Jesus's message and the hopes of the primitive Christian community were defined by a highly realistic eschatology. This eschatology expected

---

[2]Cf., Fritz Buri, *Gott in Amerika: Amerikanische Theologie seit 1960* (Bern: Verlag Paul Haupt, 1970), pp. 245 f.

the imminent return of the messiah on the clouds of heaven to usher in a new aeon beyond the present world. The continuing course of history proved this expectation illusory. The delay of the parousia, Schweitzer and Werner argue, caused an extraordinary crisis in the life of the early Church. Werner has gone further and argued that the whole history of Christian doctrine and of the life of the Church can be told as the story of the single continuing attempt to avoid the implications of the delay of the parousia. Christian theology, therefore, has been nothing more than a massive attempt to "de-eschatologize" the fundamental doctrine of the original Christian message in order to avoid the fearful consequences that seem to follow from holding to a "consistent eschatology". But if this historical thesis is correct then the history of Christian thought is a huge aberration, and the Christian tradition is a *problemgeschichtlichen Zusammenhang*.[3]

Consistent eschatology is mainly negative because if it is a true thesis it seems to make theology both impossible and unnecessary. If Jesus based his message on an illusion which the course of history has quite simply proved false, does not a theologically consistent eschatology mean the demise of the Christian faith as such? It was just this question of what to make dogmatically of a consistent eschatology that preoccupied Buri from the time of his doctoral dissertation in 1934.[4] As he asked in a significant, later article: "How do we preach a Jesus who was deluded in relation to the central moment of his message, namely, concerning his immediately expected parousia?"[5]

To answer this question and to remain a Christian theologian is difficult if not impossible. But despite his allegiance to the Christian faith, Buri's thinking at this time was dominated by what has been pointed out as the second pole of tension in the liberal theological mind. He was concerned with the demand for utter clarity and honesty that arises out

---

[3]Fritz Buri, "Das Problem der ausgebliebenen Parusia", in *Schweizerische theologische Umschau*, 16 Nr. 5/6 (Oktober/Dezember 1946), p. 101. Hereinafter this article will be cited as PaP, and the *Schweizerische theologische Umschau* will be abbreviated as *SthUm*.

[4]Fritz Buri, *Die Bedeutung der neutestamentlichen Eschatologie für die neuere protestantische Theologie. Ein Versuch zur Klärung des Problems der Eschatologie und zu einem neuen Verständnis ihres eigentlichen Anliegens*. Dissertation, University of Bern (Zürich: Niehans, 1934). Hereinafter abbreviated as BntE.

[5]PaP, p. 99. "Consistent eschatology" is an ambiguous term because it is used by Werner and Buri both to designate the historical thesis and to characterize the theological position they propose on the basis of the historical thesis. When the phrase is used below, it should be held in mind that for Buri it also refers to a theological posititon as well as an historical argument. It means *"the dogmatic significance* of a consistent eschatology."

of the development of modern, scientific methods of knowledge.[6] In his mind, the results of historical-critical scholarship were particularly important. Such results may be highly damaging to prejudices the Church holds dear, but it is time, Buri would say, that theologians woke up to their responsibility as modern men to acknowledge without qualification the results of modern paths to knowledge. Just as the results of the modern search for knowledge have forced men in other disciplines to surrender deeply held viewpoints, so must the theologian acknowledge these results in his own discipline. Buri felt that there has been too much special pleading in modern theology. Failure to acknowledge this responsibility to the modern world, no matter how painful it is, can only result in making the Church an isolated enclave of superstition.

To the extent that the consistent eschatology thesis shows that almost the whole history of Christian thought is a monstrous case of special pleading, its case against Christian theology must be faced, even if its results are solely negative and destructive. Buri incorporated this demand for honesty directly into his own interpretation of one aspect of the dogmatic significance of the delayed parousia. Whatever else consistent eschatology may mean, it at least signifies that

what is settled once and for all through the non-eschatological course of history is the impossibility of grounding on this eschatological mythology a *Heilsgeschichte* which will include real history. The process of continuing de-eschatologization which was already started in the New Testament and which can be demonstrated in the whole history of dogma up to the present ... makes every biblically grounded salvation history untenable in the long run.[7]

This demand that theology must face the situation of modern man and the results of modern scholarship is still one of Buri's primary concerns, and it is what allows his present theological program to be characterized as the first liberal dogmatics in thirty years.[8]

Buri was particularly concerned to counter contemporary interpretations of eschatology, especially in dialectical and neo-orthodox theology. He described these views as an *überzeitliche Deutung* of eschatology.[9] After Schweitzer and Wrede rediscovered the significance of eschatology in the New Testament, it was impossible for contemporary theology to avoid taking it into account. But Buri argued that the way it was gener-

[6]Cf., *ibid.*, pp. 115 f.
[7]*Ibid.*, p. 117.
[8]This is the description of the publisher placed on the dust jacket of the first volume of Buri's *Dogmatik*.
[9]PaP, p. 97 *et passim*.

ally accounted for failed to do justice to the significance of the delay of the parousia.[10] Eschatology became a central motif, but attempts were made to interpret it variously in a "trans-temporal" manner. By this Buri meant the attempt to ground the abiding significance it was now said to have for every moment of faith in some trans-historical, supernatural realm. Representative here was the manifesto of contemporary theology, Barth's *Römerbrief*, where eschatology was seen as the crisis situation of faith as such.[11] While trying to preserve the supernatural character of biblical eschatology, such interpretations fail to maintain the linear nature of the biblical understanding of history for which eschatology is the realistic, if supernatural, culmination of a linear temporal process. Buri thus argued that the *überzeitliche Deutung* is really only another attempt to avoid the consequences of the delayed parousia and results in nothing different from the flight from time and history which has characterized Christian theology since the inception of the de-eschatologizing process. Contemporary theology is nothing but the final phase of that process.

Buri agreed that the meaning of eschatology must be one that is present for faith in every moment, but he argued that it must not be time and history negating. He set the dichotomy, "either historical existence or consummation beyond history," and argued that the two were in no way compatible.[12] If Christian faith is to have any meaning, it must speak to man's situation here and now by placing him in that situation in a meaningful way rather than drawing him out of it. If eschatology is meaningful, it must be a mythological expression for a particular dialectic in terms of which man can confront his present historical situation. He explained this dialectic in terms of the will toward the fulfillment of life and the realization of meaning in the face of those forces in reality which seem to contradict them. As he said:

> In our real situation of the actual reality of God's creation, the essential content of eschatology, the will toward the fulfillment of life and the realization of meaning, can be recognized as grounded in reverence before the mystery of creation. The eschatological event is present in every moment where one acts in concrete decision out of reverence before the mystery of creation. The stance of man corresponding to the truth content of eschatology cannot for us consist in waiting for an imminent catastrophe breaking in in a supernatural way.[13]

---

[10]Cf., *ibid.*, p. 107.
[11]Cf., e.g., Karl Barth, *Der Römerbrief* (München: Chr. Kaiser Verlag, 1924, dritter Abdruck der neuen Bearbeitung), p. 484.
[12]*BntE*, p. 19.
[13]*Ibid.*, p. 168.

Buri insisted that the confidence which the eschatological vision incorporates cannot be articulated as a fully rational vision of reality. The dialectic of eschatology must be accomplished in every individual life in the face of an ultimate confidence in the mystery of creation; but precisely because creation is a mystery, this confidence can receive no rational grounding. It can be worked out in no universal world-view but only in the concreteness of every individual life.[14] Buri proceeded from this point to make his own constructive proposal in terms of Schweitzer's philosophy of reverence for life.

At this time, however, Buri had found no suitable way to articulate his own interpretation of eschatology. He was trying to interpret eschatology, and thus the Christian faith, in terms of *Lebensvollendung* and *Sinnverwirklichung* in the present situation of man. But lacking an appropriate methodological basis for integrating his understanding of the results of the historical-critical method with the traditional affirmations of the Christian tradition, he tended to fall into that cultural and philosophical reduction of the Christian faith which has always been the danger of liberal theology. His interpretation, like Schweitzer's, was an independent philosophy of religion attached only indirectly to biblical eschatology and the Christian faith. The biblical mythology provided the imagery illustrative of a philosophy of religion which could be developed quite independently. This meant, of course, that the realistic and truly Christian eschatology had to be abandoned, the images remaining only as symbolic material for a different vision of reality altogether. In view of Buri's other liberal concern, that of remaining faithful to the truth of the Christian faith, the options thereby posed became stark. A truly historical understanding of the original claim of Christianity *must* hold a realistic, literal view of eschatology; a truly modern philosophy of culture seeking to incorporate the truth of Christianity cannot. Buri thought at this time that he could mediate between these options but only by giving priority to the philosophy of culture side. In his doctoral dissertation he wrote:

For us, in the first instance naturally, nothing depends on whether the opinion represented in this chapter concerning the formulation of the echatological will toward the fulfillment of life . . . also really corresponds to New Testament eschatology. When the question of truth is at stake, what is biblical or non-biblical is no criterion . . . . To be sure, we arrive *in another way* at the assertion of the biblical character of our views. For us New Testament eschatology is not the norm, but,

[14]Cf., *ibid.*, pp. 166-172.

seen in terms of its essential content, it proves to be appropriate to the norm. *The norm, however, is grounded on knowledge of the experience of reality.*[15]

What brought Buri to a deeper understanding of the tension within a liberal theology which wants to do justice to the Christian affirmation was not, at least at first, the insight that the direction in which he was going could not but end in a cultural and philosophical reductionism. He genuinely believed not only that he was giving the only viable interpretation of eschatology but also that it was in basic accord with the perduring significance of the Christian faith – seen, however, not as an authoritative revelation but as the formative cultural phenomenon in the West. The change in his thought came about because he began to feel that the kind of interpretation he was giving was not methodologically adequate to the nature of religious phenomena. Reflection on methodological issues then led him to an understanding of the contribution of the Christian faith to the understanding of man and his destiny which allowed him both to affirm the original and lasting significance of the Christian message and to avoid having to articulate that contribution through a cultural and philosophical reduction. These methodological reflections center on the two major themes of his present system, the problem of objectivity and the concept of faith as a self-understanding.

B. OBJECTIVITY AND SELF-UNDERSTANDING: THE TRANSITION TO BURI'S MATURE POSITION

The turning point in Buri's work came with the realization that his position amounted to nothing more than a philosophical world-view, even if not a speculative one. Such a position myopically narrows the content of religion to a philosophically defensible intellectual statement. It thereby fails to understand both the nature of faith and the relationship between the modalities of the religious life and the content of religious assertions. Buri came to believe with the existentialists that an interpretation of the content of religious assertions can be intelligible only if it finds some way to take account of the appropriation of that content in faith itself. The appropriation in faith is integral to the very meaning of the content.

As Buri's position developed into its present form, he found Karl Jaspers' understanding of *Existenz* and his analysis of the subject-object

[15]*Ibid.*, p. 171. My italics.

structure of consciousness increasingly helpful in bringing this idea to complete expression.[16] Initially, however, it was Bultmann's programmatic essay on demythologizing that showed him the possibility of a new orientation. After the publication of this essay in 1941, the influence of Bultmann's ideas gradually began to appear in Buri's writings. In 1943 in an essay on the problem of predestination, Buri began to speak of the "existenzielle Wahrheitsgehalt" of doctrines, and he proposed to adopt the method of "*existentiell* interpretation."[17] According to Buri, such an interpretation in the instance of the doctrine of predestination will mean the "reduction *(Rückführung)* of its mythology to the understanding of existence which therein comes to expression and, from this point, the renewed critical use of the mythological symbols as a designation of one's own understanding of existence."[18] Three years later in his essay on the delayed parousia he again returned to this theme. Consistent eschatology is important because the delayed parousia places in question "the traditional dogma of a saving history" which is the erroneous meaning traditional Christianity gave to the New Testament message. By clearing the air of a false interpretation, the delayed parousia also makes possible an interpretation of the Christian message which can take account of and incorporate precisely the fact that the parousia did not occur. It opens the way for the "comprehension of the particular understanding of existence which comes to expression through the historical disavowal of the primitive Christian expectation of the parousia."[19] Here Buri began to use the phrase "expression of existence" to designate how mythological doctrines must be interpreted.[20]

---

[16]The influence of Jaspers on Buri has been decisive and pervasive. He stands to Jaspers much as Bultmann stands to Heidegger. Jaspers will not, however, be discussed in any great detail below. This is partly because to do so would turn this study into a much different kind of work, a study, e.g., of the relation between philosophy and theology in Buri. But it is also not necessary. In the first place, as with Bultmann's appropriation of Heidegger, the influence of Jaspers on Buri is not a point by point correlation but an overall perspective sharing certain fundamental philosophical concepts, arguments, and points of view. (This point is argued in relation to Bultmann by Gerhard Noller, *Sein und Existenz: Die Überwindung des Subjekt-Objektschemas in der Philosophie Heideggers und in der Theologie der Entmythologisierung* (München: Chr. Kaiser Verlag, 1962).) In the second place, at those points where Jaspers' detailed influence on Buri is most obvious (e.g., in the analysis of the subject-object structure of consciousness and of the nature of the existential self), Buri argues his own case, and his arguments can be evaluated on their own terms.

[17]Fritz Buri, "Das Problem der Prädestination," in *SthUm*, 13, Nr. 3 (June 1943), pp. 57 f.

[18]*Ibid.*, p. 58.

[19]PaP, p. 118.

[20]*Ibid.*, p. 119.

The meaning of these technical terms is far from clear in Buri's writings at this time. He seemed himself not entirely clear of their nature and scope. What is clear is that existential philosophy had begun to suggest to him a procedure by means of which he could interpret the rich religious significance of mythological imagery which heretofore he had only been able to reject as conceptually illusory. And Bultmann's method of existentialist interpretation provided a model for applying existentialist analysis concretely to the content of the Christian message. In this way Buri began to break with the philosophy of religion approach which had earlier appeared to him as the only option once the realistic eschatological vision had been understood and rejected. The further development of his thought is marked by the progressive clarification of these technical terms into an acceptable methodology. But this clarification also led him to break with consistent eschatology.

In 1946 he was happy to affirm the statement Oscar Cullmann had made pejoratively that his theology consisted of a "combination 'of this Bultmannian demythologizing with M. Werner's de-eschatologizing'."[21] He did not realize, however, that the adoption of existentialist interpretation would lead him to see consistent eschatology as far too restricted an historical base on which to erect a full theology that does justice to the Christian affirmation. The transitional period of his career saw him preoccupied with the attempt to work out the implications of the two methods, demythologizing and consistent eschatology, and the end of that period came when his deeper understanding of the implications of existentialist interpretation led him to reject the position of consistent eschatology. But these implications also led him to a criticism of Bultmann and to a consequent clarification of the direction a more consistent application of existentialist interpretation would have to take. By working through these two foci of his transitional period, he arrived at a point where he was ready to present a mature and encompassing articulation of the Christian faith.

Through this criticism of Bultmann and his own radical proposal – for "dekerygmatizing" Buri recieved some recognition in the English speaking world and gained the reputation of being the *enfant terrible* of continental theology.[22] He criticized Bultmann for holding on to a mythological remainder in his argument that authentic existence (i.e., faith) is a possibil-

---

[21]*Ibid.*, p. 117. Cf., Oscar Cullmann, *Christus und die Zeit: Die urchristliche Zeit- und Geschichtsauffassung* (Zollikon-Zürich: Evangelischer Verlag A. G., erste Auflage, 1946), p. 25.

[22]Cf., EoE and Buri, "Theologie und Philosophie."

ity in fact only through the kerygma of God's decisive act in Jesus Christ. Buri correctly saw this as an inconsistency in Bultmann's method. Bultmann proposed a thoroughgoing demythologization and an exhaustive existentialist interpretation. He said that myth was an inadequate vehicle for communicating the proper intention of the Biblical writers, for, in attempting to articulate the source and goal of human life, myth falsely objectifies the non-objective reality of both God and self. It reduces the transcendent to an object in space and time, and it treats the self in a purely external way as an object or thing. Nevertheless, legitimate motives seek expression in myths. Beneath their objective form, they give expression to various possible modes of existence by means of which men can and have understood themselves in their world. Bultmann used the word "self-understanding" to designate this existential way of being. A self-understanding is a non-objective actualization of the self in the concrete events in which the self not only decides who it is but *is* who it is. In proposing to interpret mythological statements existentially, Bultmann was forced to argue that all such statements must be understood entirely in terms of the *existentiell* self-understanding that comes to expression through their inadequate objective form. This means that demythologizing must be exhaustive because the meaning of mythological concepts is exhausted by the content they have in the *existentiell* act in which the self-understanding comes to expression. To leave some content external to this *existentiell* reality of faith is to fall back into that inadequate understanding which created the problem of mythological language in the first place.[23]

Bultmann executed this program brilliantly with such mythological concepts as resurrection, eschatology, sin, etc., but Buri saw that when he came to the Christ event, he stopped short and made this existential reality for faith dependent on a single, purely external, and non-*existentiell* event in the past. Bultmann's argument was that authentic existence is not a simple human possibility because the arrogance of sinful man condemns the search for authentic existence to continual reassertions of that arrogance. He claimed that only some event from outside can free man from this vicious circle. That event is God's decisive act in Jesus Christ, and apart from this event there is no possibility of authentic existence. Buri argued that this claim violates Bultmann's program because such an event must be located in a single event in the past which is independent of faith. As such, it is an objective, mythological event on Bult-

[23]Cf., Bultmann, "Neues Testament und Mythologie," pp. 21 f. (ET, pp. 9 ff.), *et passim.*

mann's own terms. Consequently, it cannot be brought into agreement with his other claim that the sole reality of mythological expressions must be located in the existential reality of faith.

Buri agreed that authentic existence is not a simple human possibility. It is not something man attains through his own self-assertion but something for which he is freed. He argued, however, that the restriction of the condition of this occurrence to a single, non-*existentiell* event of the past is itself a piece of arrogance on the part of theologians.[24] If existen-tialist interpretation is to be consistent, the occurrence must be an *existentiell* event now in the immediacy of faith, and such a present reality cannot intelligibly have its condition limited to a single, non-*existentiell* event in the distant past. Referring to Bultmann's claim that man must understand his existence as a gift if he is to escape the *Verfallenheit* and *Eigenmächtigkeit* of inauthentic existence, Buri asked: "Does Bultmann then have no awareness that today Karl Jaspers speaks of the gift character of authentic existence and legitimately uses the concept of grace for it?"[25]

Buri drew the conclusion that demythologizing can be made consistent only if it proceeds to "dekerygmatizing." By this he did not mean that the Christian theologian and preacher would cease using the Christian kerygma. He simply meant that the mythological content of the kerygma cannot be exempted from demythologizing and existentialist interpretation. All mythological assertions must be interpreted in terms of the existential possibilities of gifted existence present in any situation. The mythological concepts do not express an objective view of the cosmos which first makes possible existence as grace. Rather, they give expression to a non-objective (i.e., *existentiell*) understanding of actualized existence which is possible at every moment. This is a reversal which is decisive for Buri's later position. As he expresses it here:

Now we no longer need a myth of salvation in order to attain to the reality of salvation; rather, from the experienced reality of salvation, we are in a position to understand the mythology of salvation.... The event of salvation does not consist in a once-for-all saving event in Christ as Bultmann emphasizes.... It consists, rather, in the fact that men can understand themselves authentically in the way that comes to expression in the myth of Christ.[26]

A dekerygmatized understanding of the New Testament is nothing more than a fully consistent realization of Bultmann's program. The

[24]EoE, p. 94.
[25]*Ibid.*
[26]*Ibid.*, p. 97.

New Testament mythology can be interpreted as giving expression to the existential self-understanding which is a possibility both in principle and in fact for all men in every time. As Buri articulated "the significance of the Christ myth as an expression for a particular kind of self-understanding":

> With Bultmann we likewise see the essential content of this myth in that freedom *(Freiwerden)* from the world and from ourselves through surrender to that power which confronts us in the foundering of our care *(Sorgen)* and our desire to manipulate and control *(Verfügenwollen)*. It is an inner freedom which is anything but a flight from the world and a satisfaction with self. Rather, it is an openness *(Offensein)* for the world and for surrender to what confronts us in it. Insofar, however, as precisely this liberating *(freimachende)* possibility is experienced as a gift which is not at our disposal and as grace despite all our own resolution and action involved in it, there is disclosed to us therein the ultimately mysterious ground of all being as love – in order to show itself in this disclosure now all the more as a mystery. For we do not construe from this a universal teleology *(Zweckbestimmtheit)* – as an earlier liberal theology did which Bultmann correctly criticized. All the less do we erect a kerygma here of the once-for-all saving act of God. Christ is a reality, has entered flesh to die and to rise again, only there, but there again and again, where we enact to our salvation that mysterious crisis of the awareness of being in fallenness to care *(Sorge-verfallen)* and in being-able-to-become-authentic *(Eigentlich-werden-können)* in love. In this sense the apostle Paul lived his own existence as kerygma. "We always carry in our body the death of Jesus so that the life of Jesus may be manifested in our flesh" (2 Cor. 4:10).[27]

The positive thrust of Buri's desire to adopt the method of existentialist interpretation thus came to fruition in his dekerygmatizing proposal. His later thought is an attempt to carry through the program adumbrated there in relation to the full range of Christian doctrinal and confessional statements. This must be said because Buri later left the impression that he had drawn back from the dekerygmatizing program. In the preface to the first volume of his dogmatics, he states: "I am glad today that I have not begun my dogmatics under the sign of 'dekerygmatizing' – or even of the earlier onesidedness of 'de-eschatologizing' . . . . ." (I, p.3.) And later at the 1964 consultation on non-objective thinking and speaking in contemporary theology at Drew University, he said that dekerygmatizing was only "a 'fighting slogan' against what in my opinion was a false use of the kerygma."[28] Statements such as these have led

---

[27]*Ibid.*, p. 99.
[28]Fritz Buri, "Das Problem des ungegenständlichen Denkens und Redens in der heutigen Theologist," in *Zeitschrift für Theologie und Kirche*, 61, (Nov. 1964), p. 360; ET, "The Problem of Non-objectifying Thinking and Speaking in Contemporary Theology," tran.

to the supposition that Buri was withdrawing from the radicality of the dekerygmatizing proposal. In view of the direction his later thought has taken in relation to consistent eschatology, they have led many in the liberal movement in Switzerland to the conclusion that Buri has retreated in his later years to a modified orthodox position.[29] This supposition is false, however, for it ignores not only the deepened understanding of the whole notion of existentialist interpretation which makes his mature thought a far more impressive achievement than anything so far produced in the consistent eschatology movement but also the full context in which he qualified the dekerygmatizing proposal.

Immediately following the statement quoted from the preface to the first volume of his dogmatics, he goes on to say that he "would just as little want to surrender what is indispensably designated by these catch-words." (I, p.3.) And the above quotation from his Drew address makes it clear that dekerygmatizing still applies to a task necessitated by a false understanding of the kerygma for which he criticized Bultmann and which he now has extended to any form of *Heilsgeschichte*.

When Buri's theory of myth and symbol is examined below, it will be necessary to look more closely at the continuity between the dekerygmatizing proposal and his present system. Here it simply needs to be emphasized that his later thought is a basically consistent, though far more mature, implementation of the approach proposed in the dekerygmatizing essay. The reason he did not develop his theology specifically as dekerygmatizing lies in the fact that, as he said, dekerygmatizing is a polemical or "fighting" term having a mainly negative force. Its purpose is to highlight an interpretation of the kerygma incompatible with existentialist interpretation. He still holds to the view expressed by its negative force, and there is nothing in his later thought to contradict it.[30] As a positive characterization, however, it would be misleading since properly understood Buri still wants to interpret doctrines as having a fundamentally kerygmatic significance. *All* doctrines are kerygmatic because they

H. H. Oliver in *Distinctive Protestant and Catholic Themes Reconsidered*, Robert W. Funk, ed., (in association with Gerhard Ebeling) (New York: Harper Torchbooks, 1967), p. 142. Hereinafter abbreviated as PuDR.

[29]Cf., Ulrich Neuenschwander, "Zu Buris *Dogmatik als Selbstverständnis des christlichen Glaubens*", in *SthUm*, 26, Nr. 5/6 (Dez. 1956), pp. 118 f. For Buri's responses to the criticisms of his liberal Swiss colleagues, cf., Buri, "Freies Christentum — noch oder wieder Avantgarde?" in *SthUm*, 27, Nr. 3 (June 1957), pp. 49-59, and "Abschied von der Umschau," in *SthUm*, 28, Nr. 6 (Nov./Dez. 1958), pp. 129-133.

[30]When asked by the author during a conversation in 1963 about his apparent retraction of the dekerygmatizing proposal, Buri responded that far from retreating from it, he considered his present *Dogmatik* a radicalization of that program.

give expression not to an objective view of the cosmos but to a non-objective possibility of existence. "Kerygma" may still be used as long as its association with a mythological world-view is broken and it is interpreted exhaustively in terms of the understanding of existence to which it gives expression. Dekerygmatizing refers, therefore, only to a false understanding of kerygma. Furthermore, dekerygmatizing as a description of an entire theology would lack the greater hermeneutical comprehensiveness Buri believes the concept of "the self-understanding of the Christian faith" to have.[31] It was on the question of hermeneutical comprehensiveness in the implementation of existentialist interpretation that Buri was led to see the basic incompatibility of this method with the consistent eschatology position.

Reflection on the method of existentialist interpretation led Buri to deepen his thinking in relation to two themes, the problem of objectivity and the historicity of human existence. This led him, in turn, to question whether the consistent eschatology of Schweitzer and Werner could serve as the adequate basis for a full-blown systematic theology which would do justice to that side of the tension in liberal theology desiring to hold fast to the Christian affirmation.

From his earliest writings, Buri had strongly emphasized the limited character of knowledge and was sceptical about the adequacy of any objectively expressed religious or cosmic world view to the concrete life of the religious man. By an "objectively expressed religious or cosmic world view" is simply meant the attempt to articulate a vision of things entire which has a truth value independent of the relation a man takes to it. The rejection of this approach arises out of the influence Kant's understanding of subject and object had on theology. Karl Jaspers gave an existentialized version of Kant's position by reinterpreting the limits of knowledge in terms of the subject-object structure of consciousness and by giving an embodied interpretation to the transcendental self in terms of the existential concept of *Existenz*. Jaspers was thereby enabled to interpret the metaphysical assertions of the entire philosophical tradition sympathetically in terms of their existential content while at the same time criticizing their objective form for an illicit transgression of

---

[31]Cf., the preface to the English translation of Buri's *Theologie der Existenz*: Buri, *Theology of Existence,* trans. H. H. Oliver and Gerhard Onder (Greenwood, S.C.: The Attic Press, 1965), p. xii. (The original German edition is: *Theologie der Existenz* (Bern: Verlag Paul Haupt, 1954).) Hereinafter the German edition will be abbreviated as *TdE* with the English pagination given following ET. Where the citation is to the preface of the English edition which was written especially for the translation, it will be cited as ET, *TdE,* the reference to the translation given first.

the subject-object structure of human consciousness. Appropriating Jaspers' position allowed Buri to see the relevance of the problem of objectivity not merely to the Kantian problem of the limits of knowledge but to the very life of faith itself. He saw that the reason why objectively expressed positions are irrelevant to the life of faith is that the actualization of that life is a non-objective enactment of man's being in its transcendental and transcending capacity. Faith itself is a way of being, a self-understanding. To interpret objectively articulated myths or speculative world views as an expression of self-understanding is to interpret them in terms of a non-objective dimension of the self.

This insight led Buri to a deepened understanding of man's historicity. He was now able to see that all objective attempts by man to define his place in the cosmos, the ultimate source and goal of his existence, were not as he had earlier thought, merely historically relative expressions of outdated visions of reality that can now be dismissed. However much they might be this, they are also expressions in a concrete situation of man's non-objective acts of self-actualization, and they can be interpreted as such. Man's historicity is not defined merely by the relativity of his objective opinions; it is defined as well by the unconditioned and non-objective enactment of various self-understandings, and many of his objective assertions can be interpreted as giving expression to this historicity.

Because it takes account neither of the problem of objectivity nor of man's historicity, consistent eschatology cannot be combined with existentialist interpretation. Buri came to see that consistent eschatology is itself an objective theory which gives an objectifying interpretation to the primitive Christian expectation. Because it can see religious possibilities only in terms of objective visions of reality, it gives an objective interpretation to primitive Christian beliefs and then feels it possible to dismiss them as having been objectively disproven by the course of history. But such a view takes no account of the historicity of all religious perspectives. It fails to see, according to Buri, that all religious statements give expression to possibilities of non-objective modes of existing which can neither be "proven" nor "disproven" on objective grounds. It does not matter if the objective and realistic meaning was the one in fact held by the early Christian community. In addition to this, the objective mythology also gives expression to a possible non-objective self-understanding, and this is what is theologically significant. The insight allowed Buri for the first time to turn away from the method that depended on recovering the "messianic self-consciousness of the historical

Jesus" as the way to discover the truth contained in the New Testament and to appropriate instead the insights of form criticism.[32] He was able, that is, to see the significance of the view that holds that much of the New Testament iself represents not material for historical and biographical re-construction but the proclamation of the early Church giving expression to its self-understanding. His understanding of the problem of objectivity in relation to the historicity of human existence allowed him to come his present position that faith is not "a psychological-historical phenomenon" which can be recovered merely on the basis of an objective understanding of the historical-critical method.[33]

Buri's rejection of consistent eschatology was based on methodological issues, but the results of this change in his thinking were of momentous significance for substantive issues surrounding the tension in the liberal theological mind. As noted, consistent eschatology is basically an historical thesis having mainly negative force. According to it, the New Testament faith and the Christian tradition are an aberration. The only hope of preserving "the Christian faith" is in throwing out its tradition and constructing an independent philosophy of religion which can use New Testament imagery for illustration and thereby give it a symbolic significance. Once Buri freed himself from the restriction of this view, the method of existentialist interpretation allowed him to see the kerygmatic significance of the entire Christian tradition. The whole tradition has a kerygmatic importance when "kerygma" is taken to have the significance of proclamation, i.e., existentially interpreted, the significance of expressing a possibility for a non-objective self-understanding. Buri still accepts the consistent eschatology thesis as an historical hypothesis,[34] but he now sees that no objective historical thesis can be "the single key for understanding the Christian tradition."[35] Thus, it was the break with consistent eschatology which allowed Buri to give the mature expression to his thought found in his dogmatics. He has now found it possible to move back into the full length and breadth of the Christian tradition and to bring to it a depth of appreciation and understanding that, for all its

[32]Cf., ET, *TdE*, p. xiii.
[33]*Ibid.*
[34]Cf., II, pp. 430 f. In one of his most recent and important books, Buri has returned to a strong statement of the consistent echatology position for the first time in twenty years, but he reappropriates it only as an historical thesis which can serve as a heuristic basis for eliciting an existentialist interpretation of the fundamental theological motifs in the Christian tradition. Cf., Buri, *Der Pantokrator: Ontologie und Eschatologie als Grundlage der Lehre von Gott* (Hamburg: Herbert Reich Evangelischer Verlag, 1969). Hereinafter abbreviated as *DP*.
[35]ET, *TdE*, p. xiii.

critical perception, has none of the arrogance of the typical consistent eschatology views.

The last phase of Buri's transitional period was his *Theologie der Existenz* which appeared in 1954. This book is a brief sketch of a complete systematic theology. In it every traditional doctrine is presented historically, criticized in view of the problem of objectivity, and then interpreted existentially in terms of human historicity. Already here Buri shows the openness to the full tradition which is the significance of his break with consistent eschatology. Only at two points does his later thought represent an advance over this position and a deepening of his views. In the first place, despite his openness to the tradition in *Theologie der Existenz*, he still shows himself under the influence of consistent eschatology in the chapter on Christology. His doctrines of man, sin, and soteriology are all developed independently of Christology, and the latter doctrine serves only as an illustration for an understanding of existence as grace which is developed independently out of other doctrines.[36] Here he is still adhering to the philosophy of religion approach characteristic of consistent eschatology. His dogmatics shows a far more integrated understanding of doctrines. He has seen that from the perspective of the non-objectivity of self-understanding no independent philosophy of religion can give expression to the content of doctrines but that they must receive expression and interpretation solely in terms of the mythological imagery of the self-understanding of faith itself.[37] He has also seen that within the Christian self-understanding every doctrine must be Christologically interpreted in terms of the "being in Christ" of that self-understanding.[38] In the second place, the crucial hermeneutical concept of this work is the philosophical concept of *Existenz* taken over from Jaspers. This concept still stands in the background of all Buri's thought. But he has again seen that from within the Christian self-understanding, it is not the concept of *Existenz* that is hermeneutically comprehensive but the "self-understanding of the Christian faith."[39]

The significance of each of these changes is that they make Buri's later thought a far more integrative solution to the tension of the liberal theological mind. These changes focus on the critical appreciation of the problem of objectivity and the historicity of the objective expressions of

---

[36]Cf., *TdE*, pp. 55, 72-93 (ET, pp. 46 f., 62-83).

[37]It will become apparent below that at at least one point this must be qualified, for Buri finds it necessary to develop a systematic principle of existence as grace in order to have some basis for interpreting the Christian self-understanding.

[38]Cf., II, pp. 38-40.

[39]ET, *TdE*, p. xii.

human existence to which he gradually came during the transition period. The problem of objectivity provided an epistemological stance in terms of which Buri could maintain a critical self-consciousness toward both the objective assertions of the tradition that require reformulation and the reformulations themselves. In his earlier phase, Buri had had no choice but to substitute unacceptable traditional positions with reformulations which were more acceptable to him but were epistemologically on the same level as the rejected assertions. The result was a one-sided solution to the problem of liberal theology. Combined with the problem of objectivity, the historicity of human existence enabled Buri to continue to acknowledge the relativity of religious assertions in the history of thought without therefore having to reject such assertions as a consequence of their relativity. It became possible, that is, to *interpret* traditional theological assertions instead of merely criticizing or replacing them. In this way and unlike his earlier position, it has become possible for Buri to move back into the Christian theological tradition, to affirm the distinctive understanding of human life and destiny that does come to expression in *this* tradition, without, however, having to retreat from his ongoing concern to find a new hermeneutical foundation to articulate this understanding intelligibly to modern man.

In the concluding pages of the first volume of his *Dogmatik*, Buri summarizes the conclusions of over four hundred pages of prolegomena by stating the two principles of his system. Here he shows how the methodological preoccupation with the problem of objectivity and the historicity of human existence come together in the concept of self-understanding, the hermeneutical center of his theology.[40] Buri's concern is to find principles which make a scientific theology possible.[41] They must be principles which are methodologically neutral and which thereby facilitate interpretation without presupposing a dogmatic position taken in advance. He, therefore, rejects traditional principles (e.g., justification by faith and *sola Scriptura* or canon, confession, and the teaching office of the church) because far from being methodologically neutral, such principles are themselves the expression of a particular self-understanding. They cannot, consequently, serve as methodological principles for the in-

---

[40]Cf., I, pp. 439-443 *passim* in the discussion which follows.
[41]Buri uses the concept of *Wissenschaft* in the broad German sense to mean any methodologically self-conscious discipline which is prepared to submit both its methodology and its conclusions to public discussion and confirmation. Taken in this sense, theology can claim to be a science.

terpretation of self-understandings. In contrast, Buri's formal principle becomes the dialectic of objectivity and non-objectivity. Instead of expressing a self-understanding, its formality provides the basis for interpreting any possible self-understanding. As will become clear below, this dialectic involves an analysis of the limits of knowledge. As a consequence, it provides the theologian with a critical posture for understanding the inadequacy of both a falsely objective interpretation of theological assertions and falsely objective polemical attacks on them by so-called "enlightened" self-consciousness. At the same time, this dialectic acknowledges the non-objective act of self-definition (i.e., self-understanding) which cannot be reduced to an objective assertion but which may come to expression in and through such assertions. It is, thus, also the hermeneutical basis for interpreting objectively expressed doctrines as expressions of self-understanding though it itself is not an expression of a self-understanding.

Having a formal principle of this generality frees Buri to adopt an equally broad and neutral material principle, namely, "the self-understanding of the Christian faith." He is able, that is, to take as the provenance of his theology not a particular confessional position but the entire history of the theological tradition. His understanding of the historicity of objectively expressed theological assertions makes this possible, for with the formally neutral concept of self-understanding, the entire theological tradition becomes accessible not as conflicting objective positions but as modal variations of the historistic actualization of the distinctively Christian self-understanding.

It is evident now that the dialectic of objectivity and non-objectivity, Buri's version of the problem of objectivity, involves a theory of the nature of theological assertions. By means of this theory, Buri purports to offer a viable solution to the tension in the liberal theological mind. The failure of the liberal tradition as well as his own earlier failure Buri locates in an insufficiently radical grasp of the hermeneutical problem, the problem of the nature of theological language itself. He claims to have made the attempt to think this problem "to its ground" and to have worked out a satisfactory solution in his mature position through an intensive and highly self-conscious use of the dialectic of objectivity and non-objectivity. The story of his development is the story of his increasingly more subtle grasp of the hermeneutical problem. The result is not a more radical theology since his entire career has been defined by the issues of what is now called radical theology, but it is a radical theology which can claim to be Christian. At the same time that the dialectic of

objectivity and non-objectivity has enabled Buri to radicalize the hermeneutical problem of liberal theology, it has also enabled him, at least in
principle, to develop a radical theology in intimate continuity with the
distinctive claims of the Christian tradition itself. The task here is not to
question the legitimacy of such a program as such. It is, rather, to examine the ramifications of Buri's hermeneutical principle of objectivity
and non-objectivity throughout his system in order to see whether it is in
fact an adequate theory of religious assertions for such a theology.

PART I

THE PROBLEM OF OBJECTIVITY IN THE FOUNDATIONS
OF A THEOLOGICAL HERMENEUTIC

CHAPTER II

THE THEOLOGICAL PROBLEM OF
OBJECTIVITY AND NON-OBJECTIVITY

The continuity between contemporary existentialist theology and nineteenth century liberal theology arises from a common awareness that the traditional ways of stating both the pretheological witness of faith and the theological articulation of that witness are made *fundamentally* problematic by the most ordinary outlook on himself and his world any modern man must have. The problem is misconstrued by more orthodox thinkers who attempt to reduce it to the perennial "scandal" of accepting the Christian gospel. There is a scandal, of course, but it is an existential scandal. As the liberals and radical theologians see it, the problem is the more fundamental one of the very intelligibility of the Christian message itself such that the legitimate scandal cannot even make an appearance.[1] Hence, the concern is to develop a theory of theological language allowing the distinctive word of Christianity, its legitimate scandal, to find expression without requiring what is, in effect, a sacrifice of the intellect.

Among existentialist theologians there has been general agreement that the crux of the problem arises from a falsely objective understanding of religious assertions and that a solution can be achieved if faith and its content, which is articulated by religious assertions, are understood to be non-objective. There is widespread disagreement and considerable lack of clarity, however, concerning how to incorporate non-objectivity into a theory of theological language. Most of this unclarity centers on the answers given to two questions: (i) what do "objectivity" and "non-objectivity" include and exclude and (ii) is it possible to construct a language involving the non-objectivity of faith and its content that does not overlap at crucial points with some of the features of an objectifying language one wants to avoid.

[1] Cf., e.g., Bultmans, "Neues Testament und Mythologie," pp. 21 f., 48 (ET, pp. 9 f., 44).

Buri's contribution at this point is paradoxical. On the one hand, he has attempted to bring clarity into the discussion through a sustained analysis of the nature and limits of objectivity and non-objectivity. Out of this analysis, his own position emerges as a distinctive alternative in the contemporary spectrum. On the other hand, precisely the greater clarity and the distinctive character of Buri's position make evident that, at root, the theological problem of objectivity and non-objectivity revolves around a single set of related issues, despite the diversity of points of view in the discussion. As a result, the problematic character of Buri's position, which it is the burden of this study to demonstrate, highlights with particular sharpness the central question concerning the hermeneutical foundations for any radical theology. Since Buri is to be given this paradigmatic significance, it is important to see his theory against the background of the contemporary discussion. This can be done most effectively not by discussing a series of individuals in detail but by constructing a typology of meanings objectivity and non-objectivity have come to have.[2]

A. OBJECTIVITY AND NON-OBJECTIVITY IN THE CONTEMPORARY DISCUSSION

The most important of these meanings can be included under a typological distinction between (i) different kinds of cognitive encounter with reality and (ii) the subjective forms of these encounters.

(1) A theme running throughout existentialist literature, sometimes explicitly stated, sometimes assumed, is that man's fundamental cognitive encounter with reality has a twofold form.[3] One of these is termed "exis-

---

[2] For the twofold type which follows, the author is indebted to distinctions made by Schubert Ogden in his essay, "Theology and Objectivity" (in Schubert M. Ogden, *The Reality of God* (New York: Harper and Row Publishers, 1966), pp. 71-98.) Ogden develops a fourfold typology, but only the first two of these are used here. His last two types are intimately connected with a thesis he is arguing in this essay, and since a critical position toward Ogden is developed below, they can be ignored in the present context.

[3] Ogden, "Theology and Objectivity," pp. 74-76. While Ogden is extremely helpful in formulating this distinction and while he is generally accurate in describing its import, he makes a fatal error by oversimplifying the distinction as that between an "internal" awareness of ourselves as persons and an "external" awareness of the world or of ourselves as part of the world. By making the distinction this way, he falls into a basically Cartesian way of thinking and, therefore, overlooks that existential analysis first arose as an attempt to overcome such dualisms. He is correct that the existentialists distinguish between two different types of cognitive encounter with reality but wrong in describing this distinction as internal and external. Ogden's so-called "internal" awareness of ourselves as persons is itself constituted in and with an "external" disclosure of the world,

tential" and has to do with that original, pre-thematic[4] openness toward himself and his world in and through which man first constitutes himself as a person and comes to awareness of himself in a world. The encounter is called existential in order to indicate that it is not a mute presentation of an already given world to a passive and isolated ego but is rather an act of self-definition in which the self first constitutes itself by a disclosive openness to the world. The act is disclosive rather than isolating because the act of self-definition occurs in and through the various modalities of relation the self can take toward the world.[5] The encounter is immediate in a sense because the givenness of the world in the encounter cannot be detached from the existential act, but the encounter is not for that reason non-cognitive. It is not, that is, to be reduced to immediate feeling or unsynthesized perceptual intuition. It is cognitive because the self understands itself and its world according to various possibilities given with the existential actualization itself. But this understanding can not be separated from the existential act; the understanding *is* the existential act of self-constitution and disclosive openness. Hence, the existentialists use the concept "self-understanding" rather than a concept like Schleiermacher's *Gefühl*.

As a contrast to this, the second type of cognitive encounter is termed "objectifying" because it organizes and understands reality in abstraction from the existential immediacy of the original awareness. While it would be improper in the first instance to call all forms of this type of encounter scientific,[6] it is true that this form of awareness is the basis for system-

the latter of which, however, is not equivalent to the "external" awareness of the world given by scientific cognition. It is not too much to say that a proper understanding of how objectivity is a problem depends on *not* falling into a Cartesian dualism as Ogden does. The following discussion is more complex than Ogden's largely because this greater complexity is required if his oversimplification is to be avoided. For the attempt to avoid the internal/external trap, cf., Martin Heidegger, *Sein und Zeit* (Tübingen: Max Niemeyer Verlag, neunte unveränderte Auflage, 1960 (1927)), pp. 52-59, 63-113, 202-208; ET, *Being and Time*, trans. John Macquarrie and Edward Robinson (London: SCM *Sein und Zeit*, p. 363 (ET, pp. 414 f.).

[4] For Heidegger, to thematize something is to abstract it from its immediate context of worldly involvement and to examine it according to some methodological procedure. There is, thus, a direct relation between thematization and objectification. Cf., Heidegger, *Sein und Zeit*, p. 363 (ET, pp. 414 f.).

[5] This means that the act is not the constitution of a logical point of the self such as Kant's transcendental unity of apperception nor the constitution of an empty self which *then* can be filled with contents. Most existential philosophy relies on the transcendental move in some form, but it is distinguished by always trying to give an embodied interpretation to the transcendental self.

[6] It is important for the following discussion to see that various types of thinking and speaking which one would not want to call scientific might, nevertheless, represent forms

atization of knowledge under the canons of the special sciences. Indeed, objectivity and science are so often identified because in modernity a general consensus has arisen that (i) only through this kind of cognitive encounter is genuine knowledge available and (ii) only the canons of specification and adjudication in the special sciences are legitimate for organizing the encounter. Still, it is important to distinguish objectivity and scientific knowledge because the existentialists generally seem to want to say that objectivity in its broadest sense applies to a general "style" of approach to self and world and not merely to a specific kind of knowledge – even though it would also be admitted that this style is congenial to systematization under the canons of specifically scientific objectivity.

It is not necessary here to describe precisely the conditions which constitute something as an objectifying approach to reality since a great deal of the analysis of Buri will be devoted to this question. It simply needs to be noted that, in the general sense, objectivity seeks to detach all cognitive contents from the involvement of the existential act and to understand them on the model of objects of perceptual experience.[7] Systematically developed into scientific objectivity, it leads to impersonality, an abstraction from the richness of immediate experience and thereby the organization of this experience under generalizing categories of wide scope, a universalizing of descriptive application, and the possibility of meeting widely accepted canons of verification.[8]

Theologically, "non-objective" can have two meanings in relation to the distinction between these two types of cognitive encounter. Non-objective can be used, on the one hand, to designate the existential type of cognitive encounter as a way of emphasizing its irreducibility to the other type of encounter which defines the meanings of objectivity. On the other hand, it can mean that thinking and speaking in theology are not to be understood as the type of thinking and speaking found in objectifying knowledge. At this point, however, an ambiguity arises which is decisive both for the diversity and the unclarity in existentialist discussions of the problem of objectivity. In the first usage, non-objective designates *the nature of faith itself*. It is a way of saying that faith, the relationship of God and man, and the content of biblical and dogmatic

---

of this awareness and, thus, be objective — e.g., myth and metaphysics. Objectivity is a problem only if the conditions of objectivity are broader than the conditions of scientific knowledge.

[7] This applies also when objectifying reflection turns to examine persons or even the knower himself.

[8] Cf., Ogden, "Theology and Objectivity," pp. 74-76.

assertions are to be understood in terms of the structure of the existential encounter with reality. The second usage, in contrast, refers not to
the nature of faith but *to a particular type of thinking and speaking*. The
ambiguity of these usages is heightened by the further distinction that
must be made with the second type of cognitive encounter between objectivity in the general sense of a particular style of approaching reality
and scientific objectivity as the specification of this style under the canons of the special sciences.

If "non-objective thinking and speaking" has the purely negative
meaning of rejecting the exclusive rights of *scientific objectivity* to determine the canons of cognitivity, then this usage is not very illuminating
because there are many other historical options to modern science (e.g.,
speculation and mythology) not all of which would be acceptable to an
existentialist theology. Furthermore, on this usage of "non-objectifying
thinking and speaking," there is lack of clarity whether all the options to
scientific objectivity, insofar as they are forms of thinking and speaking,
could avoid falling under the broader meaning of objectivity in the general sense of a style for approaching reality. Should it be the case that
they could not, then there is little question that this locution ("non-objectifying thinking and speaking") so common in existentialist theology
today is more confusing than helpful. It might be replied that "non-objectifying thinking and speaking" refers to a type of theology that explicates the content of faith in a manner appropriate to the non-objective
character of faith itself. This is well and good so long as the distinction
between the act of faith and a thinking and speaking about that act are
not confused. But then one must ask again whether the theological articulation of the contents of this act can avoid falling under objectifying
thinking and speaking in the general sense. If they cannot, then surely
"non-objectifying thinking and speaking" is a misleading way to designate
what, nevertheless, may be a very important theological concern, namely, to take account of the non-objectivity of faith itself in constructing a
theological hermeneutics.

This confusion over the various meanings of "non-objective" is the
crucial ambiguity in existentialist theology today. It is obvious that
"non-objective" in the sense of the existential encounter with reality can
be given a clear meaning and analysis. Such an analysis is extremely
useful in helping to become sensitive to a whole range of experience
from which man has been alienated by the pervasiveness of scientific objectivity in the modern world. And as a way of understanding the content of faith, this meaning of "non-objective" offers great promise for

grounding a theological hermeneutics. But there is considerable ambiguity concerning how non-objectivity is to function in the language by means of which this hermeneutics can receive theological articulation. Do such phrases as "non-objectifying thinking and speaking" and "overcoming the subject-object dichotomy" mean that the non-objective act of faith requires a theological language which can interpret its non-objective content non-objectively? If so, what is such a non-objective language, and how can it be theological so that there can be some distinction between immediate experience and the interpretation of that experience?[9] The significance of these questions may be further clarified by taking up the second basic type within which objectivity and non-objectivity function, the subjective form of the encounter with reality.

(2) Under subjective form the twofold encounter with reality is distinguished by the one being "concerned" or "involved" and the other being "disinterested" or "detached."[10] As Schubert Ogden describes this distinction, "whereas existential thinking and speaking have to do quite directly with the gain or loss of our authentic existence as selves, our thought and speech about the objects of our external [sic] perception are only indirectly related to this paramount concern."[11] Objective thinking and speaking are "derived rather than original, peripheral rather than central, with respect to the real origin or center of human existence."[12]

Among some existentialist writers, notably Martin Heidegger in his early phase and those theologians dependent on that work, this distinction has led to a refinement of the understanding of objective thought that might initially seem to dispel much of the ambiguity noted above. They have seen that when the non-objectivity of the existential encounter with reality is connected with the non-objectivity of its subjective form (which latter is an essential constituent of the existential character of the encounter[13]), then the philosophical description of existentiality requires an

---

[9] It is important to distinguish between a language that *elicits* or *expresses* a non-objective act (e.g., the language of myth, dogma, proclamation, creed, or prayer) and that act itself. Even if one wants to call such a language non-objective (in the same sense that its true force is not to communicate a cognitive claim but to illicit or express the act — in the sense of Kierkegaard's indirect communication), it is difficult to see how a theological language that interprets either that language or the content of the existential act could itself be non-objective.

[10] Cf., Ogden, "Theology and Objectivity," p. 79.

[11] *Ibid.* Cf., *supra*, note 3.

[12] Ogden, "Theology and Objectivity," p. 79.

[13] Cf., Heidegger, *Sein und Zeit*, pp. 11-13, 41-43 (ET, pp. 32-33, 67-69) for the classical existentialist statement that an understanding of being is given in and with every moment of *Dasein's* existence because it is the kind of being for whom its own being is al-

objectifying, i.e., disinterested, form of thinking and speaking. That is, if the existential type of encounter is always "concerned" or "interested," and, thus, "non-objective" at the level of subjective form, then any attempt to describe the structure of this encounter philosophically will have to be objective in the sense of detached and disinterested. While such a description cannot capture the specific understanding uniquely actualized by each individual in his personal encounter with reality, it can describe the structures of personal existence involved in the individual actualizations. It will, thus, involve a type of objectivity appropriate to man's existential being yet not equivalent to scientific objectivity.[14]

A question arises at this point, however, that is decisive for Buri's position and for the import of the problem of objectivity for a radical theology in general. If one must assume that the non-objectivity of faith itself (subjective form) does not exclude a form of objective thinking and speaking which is appropriate to the personal character of existentiality, then *one must ask how this objectivity is related to objectivity in the general sense in the cognitive encounter with reality such that the former sense of objectivity permits a theory of theological language for which the problem of objectivity is of central importance.* As was noted above, it will not do to say that one is simply excluding scientific objectivity. This exclusion does not offer enough specificity for a positive theory of theological language on existentialist terms because presumably more than merely scientific objectivity is a problem. Furthermore, an uncritical affirmation of the objectivity of theological thinking and speaking in this context does not seriously enough consider how precisely the non-objectivity of faith itself must qualify the objective character of any theological language. In other words, in moving from a criticism of objectifying thinking and speaking to an affirmation of objectivity in the description of existentiality, the Heideggerian position is unclear concerning the general conditions of objectivity that make possible both the criticism and the affirmation. Is the problem a false objectivity, or is it objectivity as such? If this question cannot be answered clearly, then there is serious reason to think that the so-called "problem of objectivity" is a false problem for radical theology.[15]

---

ways at issue. Thus, while it is possible to distinguish the structural character of the existential type of encounter with reality from its subjective form for purposes of analysis, they are never separated in fact, and this subjective form is an essential ingredient in the nature of the existential encounter itself.

[14] Cf., Heidegger, *Sein und Zeit*, pp. 44 f. (ET, pp. 70 f.) for the distinction between "categories" and "existentials."

[15] Again, it is important to see that the issue is false in this case only at the level of a

Across the contemporary theological spectrum, three attempts to respond to this question may be isolated. In the middle an essentially unstable position is that of Rudolf Bultmann.[16] Verbally Bultmann has been ambivalent on the question of objective language, sometimes seeming to reject objectivity as such, sometimes seeming only to reject a type of objectivity that is theologically distorting. Still, Bultmann makes it clear through the full scope of his writings that his intention is to adopt the Heideggerian distinction, and his position shows the same ambiguity.[17] He becomes unclear, namely, over the range of the objectivity he is prepared to accept. He criticizes a type of thinking and speaking that falsely objectifies the being of man and God. He sees clearly, however, that theology requires an objectifying form of discourse, and he defends a type of theological objectivity appropriate to the existential structure of man's being. But he restricts an appropriate objectivity to man's being, denying that *the same type of objectivity* might be used to speak appropriately of the being of God. This is inconsistent because the conditions of objectivity that warrant an appropriate objectification of man's being are purely formal – that is, the conditions of this *type* of objectification do not themselves specify that they must be restricted to man's being – so that without additional reasons, which he never provides, the problem of objectivity alone is not sufficient warrant for Bultmann to deny the possibility of an appropriate objective discourse about the being of God. He seems to want to say, in other words, that objectivity *as such* both is and is not the problem. The instability derives, as above, from the uncertainty concerning the nature of objectivity in the general sense such that one can make a far-ranging criticism of objectifying theologies precisely because they are objectifying while also appropriating a legitimate form of objectification.

On the right, Schubert Ogden has met this difficulty in Bultmann

theory of theological language. No matter what hermeneutical model is adopted, the notion of the non-objectivity of existence or faith itself is an important and illuminating theological idea. But ultimately the non-objectivity of existence or faith is of little hermeneutical interest unless it directly influences a conception of the nature of theological language, and it is at this level that the confusion occurs over the status of objectivity and non-objectivity. Kierkegaard is of interest at this point largely because his idea of indirect communication represents an extreme but consistent proposal connecting the non-objectivity of existence and faith directly with a theory of theological language.

[16] When the notions of "right," "left," and "middle" are used below, it should be apparent that these designations characterize a spectrum of options within radical theology, i.e., positions that are all to the "left" of those who are unwilling to consider the hermeneutical problem radically.

[17] For the documentation of this point, cf., Ogden, "Theology and Objectivity," p. 78, note 8.

head-on by arguing that the only problem is a false objectivity, not objectivity as such, and that there is an appropriate way of speaking objectively about the being of both man and God.[18] Combining Bultmann's existentialism with process philosophy, he has proceeded to project a fully metaphysical theology which will use an appropriate objectification of the existential structures of man's being as the basis for metaphysical analogies that make direct and not merely symbolic cosmic reference. It may be, as will be suggested below, that the general direction of Ogden's approach has great merit for the foundations of a radical theology.[19] But at this stage of the analysis of the nature and limits of *the problem of objectivity* for such a theology, it is necessary to say that Ogden can establish his own position only by an oversimplification which ignores the full complexity objectivity and non-objectivity have had in existentialist literature.

Ogden can make an unproblematic transition to an appropriate metaphysical objectivity because he completely ignores the question of the conditions of objectivity in the general sense as a style of approach to reality and simply reduces the problem of objectivity to the problem of the canons of knowledge. This allows him to reject scientific objectivity as an adequate model for theological knowledge and, at the same time, to maintain that knowledge is not exhausted by the canons of assessment in the special sciences. Scientific objectivity is inadequate because its methods of verification are limited to actual or potential objects of perception; as a model for theology, it thus falsely construes both man's existential reality and the reality of God. In this way, Ogden's argument for the necessarily objective character of theological language becomes simply an argument for an *adequate* way of objectively conceiving man and God in contrast to traditional ways which are equally objective but which he judges to be conceptually inadequate to their "object." In other words, the question of objectivity and non-objectivity never really becomes a problematic hermeneutical question for Ogden, only, rather, the questions of the canons of knowledge and an adequate conceptuality for the realities of theology.

What Ogden fails to see by making this move is that the problem of objectivity is a problem for the existentialist interpretation of theological

---

[18] Cf., Ogden, "Theology and Objectivity," pp. 82-98. Cf., also, Ogden, "The Reality of God" and "What Sense Does It Make to Say, 'God Acts in History'?" in *The Reality of God*, pp. 1-70 and 164-187 respectively; *Idem, Christ without Myth*, pp. 147-153; and *Idem*, "The Understanding of Theology in Ott and Bultmann," in Robinson and Cobb (eds.), *The Later Heidegger and Theology*, pp. 157-173.

[19] Cf., *infra*, Chapter VII.

language only if the problem extends to the conditions of objectivity as such and is not merely a problem of alternative canons of knowledge, all equally objective in this more general sense. It may be, of course, that framed this way, the problem of objectivity admits of no solution and is ultimately a false issue resting on an equivocation. If this is the case, then Ogden's redefinition of the problem by simplification may be the only alternative. But as it stands now, his easy transition to metaphysical objectivity overlooks two aspects of the problem as it has been focused by existentialism: (i) that in some sense objectivity as such is a problem, and (ii) that it is the recognition of the non-objectivity of the existential act of faith itself, when taken as a hermeneutical foundation, which creates this problem and which therefore must have an integral effect not merely upon the way theology objectively looks at its "objects" but upon the formal nature of theological language itself.

Nevertheless, it is important to note that Ogden's failure here does not reduce to the ambiguity in Bultmann's use of Heidegger. Because he does not clarify the relationship among the non-objectivity of faith, the objectivity of theological language, and the conditions which permit *a theological criticism of the structure of objectivity in general*, Bultmann's refusal to accept the consequences his adoption of a form of objective thinking and speaking would seem to entail cannot be justified, and he becomes inconsistent. Ogden cuts through these ambiguities and overcomes Bultmann's inconsistency by denying that objectivity as such is a problem and thereby unequivocally affirming one horn of Bultmann's dilemma. If the result is essentially a denial of the existentialist problem, it is a position that is not hermeneutically confused.

The alternative on the left takes the other horn of Bultmann's dilemma and thus amounts to a diametrical reversal of Ogden's argument. Such thinkers as Heinrich Ott and the "new hermeneuticists" (e.g., Gerhard Ebeling and Ernst Fuchs) rely here on the later Heidegger's interpretation of objectivity. The later Heidegger locates the conditions of objectivity in general in a tendency toward the "forgetfulness of being" which has determined the Western mentality or "style" of approaching reality almost from the very beginning and which follows from a fundamental confusion of the "ontological difference" which always need to be made between being *(Sein)* and beings *(Seiende)*. With the rise of Cartesian dualism and science and technology in modernity, the ultimate logic of this tendency has become obvious. It results in the conquest, domination, and exploitation of reality by the projective imposition of human consciousness on being. The ironic but inexorable conclusion Heidegger draws is that objectivity in this sense is actually the height of subjectivity since the domination of being by human consciousness is a refusal to let being "be" or "appear" in its own right.[20] The result is a profound alienation of man from himself and from being, a pervasive sickness in the West that has grown ever greater as man has gained more and more mastery of the tools of material domination. Since it is human consciousness itself that is the model for this objectivizing (really subjectivizing) approach to reality, the only alternative is an approach which entirely frees itself from the centuries-laden self-evidence of the assumptions of thinking based on consciousness in order to regain a primordial "present-ness" of being in its own "letting be." In such a *Seinsdenken* (as opposed to *Bewusstseinsdenken*), the grasping, controlling attributes of consciousness are replaced by "thought" which is simply a "clearing" for the event (much in the sense of "advent") of being, and man recovers his wholeness by becoming the locus for this event.[21]

On the basis of Heidegger's analysis, Ott, Ebeling, and Fuchs are successful in specifying the conditions which make objectivity as such theologically suspect and consistent in trying to understand theology as a form of non-objectifying thinking and speaking on Heidegger's model of "thought." Ott rejects any kind of metaphysics as "subjectivistic-objectivistic thinking" in the sense of Heidegger's criticism and affirms that theology is "a movement of faith itself" in which "it is not permissible in the sphere of believing to distinguish strictly and in principle between believing as existential actuality and theology as thinking" because "essential thinking has experiential character."[22] In much the same vein, Ebeling says that "the primary phenomenon in the realm of understand-

---

[20] Cf., Martin Heidegger, "Brief über den 'Humanismus'," in *Platons Lehre von der Wahrheit* (Bern: Francke, 1947), pp. 53-57 *et passim*.

[21] These themes are pervasive in Heidegger's later work after about 1935. For a summary discussion, cf., Robinson, "The German Discussion of the Later Heidegger," in Robinson and Cobb, eds., *The Later Heidegger . . .*, pp. 25-30, 43-45, and Robinson, "Hermeneutic since Barth," in Robinson and Cobb, eds., *The New Hermeneutic*, pp. 27 f. It is important to note that a theology which takes this later-Heideggerian approach to the problem of objectivity (as e.g., Heinrich Ott and the new hermeneuticists) probably should no longer be called existentialist since it has effectively severed the existential focus on human subjectivity.

[22] Heinrich Ott, "What is Systematic Theology," in Robinson and Cobb, eds., *The Later Heidegger . . .*, pp. 92, 109. It must be admitted that these quotations somewhat distort Ott's position by being taken out of their total context. In particular, Ott attempts to avoid the consequence which seems to follow that only a believer can understand theological writing (cf., *Ibid.*), but he never convincingly shows how this can be so given the documented assertions. Cf., Ogden, "The Understanding of Theology in Ott and Bultmann," in Robinson and Cobb, eds., *The Later Heidegger . . .*, pp. 161-166.

ing is not understanding *of* language, but understanding *through* language"
so that the "word itself has a hermeneutical function."[23] Ebeling, thus,
transforms theology as such into "hermeneutic" and understands hermeneutic as the "letting be" of the "language event" (*Sprachereignis*) in
language itself, in this instance the traditional language of witness and
theology.[24]

These positions are the opposite of Ogden because they reject objectivity as such and seek a truly non-objectifying thinking and speaking for
theology in which theology is understood as an event and thus becomes
the reality of faith itself. The obvious difficulty is that a non-objectifying
theological language in this sense makes it difficult, if not impossible, to
distinguish theology from faith. At this point, Buri has made the definitive criticism of these attempts to found theology on a non-objectifying
thinking and speaking. In the first place, Buri repeatedly points out that
the subjective genitive in *Seinsdenken* tempts the theologian to forget
that it is not being, or God, or the Word of God itself that speaks in
theology but simply a man, a man who does not and cannot possess either God or God's revelation but who can only seek to understand them
and witness to them.[25] That this temptation should arise follows directly
from the tendency in these theologies to collapse theology into faith. In
the second place, the very idea of a non-objectifying thinking and speaking is self-contradictory because the language in which it comes to expression – even if the new hermeneuticist allows himself to lapse entirely into poetry or proclamation – must still involve concepts and distinctions and, thus, objectification. Yet the attempt somehow to maintain
this contradiction by continuing to speak of a non-objectifying thinking
and speaking makes it impossible for the theologian to attain a critical
posture toward his own assertions. How, for instance, is it possible to
distinguish in the theologian's own "thinking of being" between the occurrence of an objective or a subjective genitive?[26] The arbitrariness and
personal whim to which this loss of a critical posture exposes theology is

---

[23] Gerhard Ebeling, "Word of God and Hermeneutic," in Robinson and Cobb, eds., *The New Hermeneutic*, pp. 93 f.

[24] Cf., Robinson, "Hermeneutic since Barth," in *Ibid.*, pp. 45-68. For Fuchs's similar position, cf., Ernst Fuchs, "The New Testament and the Hermeneutical Problem," in *Ibid.*,
pp. 111-145, esp., pp. 140 ff.

[25] Cf., PuDR, p. 361 (ET, p. 143); Buri, "How Can We Still Speak Responsibly of
God?" trans. Charley D. Harwick in *How Can We Still Speak Responsibly of God?*
(Philadelphia: Fortress Press, 1968), pp. 18 f. (Hereinafter abbreviated as HSRG); and
Buri, "Zehn Thesen zum Thema Gotteswort und Menschenwort," in *Kirchenblatt für die
reformierte Schweiz*, 122. Jahrgang, Nr. 12 (9 Juni 1966), pp. 178-179.

[26] Cf., PuDR, p. 361 (ET, p. 143).

dangerous because "this so-called thinking is handed over to every power and buffeting of the time and allows itself to become their seductive advocate and dangerous tool."[27]

A further problem for the particular task of founding a radical theology is that Ott, Ebeling, and Fuchs, despite their disclaimers to the contrary, undercut the radical hermeneutical problem as Bultmann initially conceived it. Bultmann clearly saw that the program of a radical theology based on demythologizing must assume a distinction between language and "the understanding prior to, and more authentic than, the language."[28] When this distinction is rejected in the effort to recapture the event of the primal language, when, that is, language itself becomes the understanding, the original linguistic forms (mythological, dogmatic, theological) inevitably remain hermeneutically unreconstructed and opaque (since to reconstruct them critically requires precisely the above distinction between language and understanding). Consequently, all kinds of assumptions must be made not only about the authenticity of any original language but also about the nature of the reality it mediates.[29] Yet precisely these are what are at stake in a radical theology, and they can be addressed only if Bultmann's distinction is maintained.

In sum, it is difficult to avoid the conclusion that the question of the hermeneutical relevance of the problem of objectivity requires further analysis of the precise issue objectivity and non-objectivity pose for theology. One cannot offer a solution to an unclearly formulated problem. Ogden achieves an unambiguous theory of language but at the cost of ignoring certain themes which seem central to existentialist interpretation. In effect, he denies the problem by redefining it. The new hermeneuticists take the problem seriously by incorporating non-objectivity directly into a theory of language but at the cost of sacrificing theology. And

---

[27] *Ibid.* (My translation.) It should be noticed that even Kierkegaard's theory of indirect communication avoids this danger because he never claimed actually to embody the event of revelation in his theological reflection but only by indirection to seduce the reader into standing before the revelation for or against which he must then decide.

[28] Robinson, "Hermeneutic since Barth," in Robinson and Cobb, eds., *The New Hermeneutic*, p. 38. This is nothing more than the above distinction between the reality of faith and theological language which is the interpretation of faith.

[29] Interestingly enough, at certain points (as with the language of the Christian tradition), the new hermeneutics seems to assume the same kind of "Burkeian" view of language that one often seems to find in contemporary Anglo-Saxon ordinary language philosophy, namely, the assumption that any language in use is always "in order." The result is to exclude the legitimacy of asking theoretical questions that might call into question the cognitive efficacy of the language itself or of its content. Cf., W. H. Walsh, *Metaphysics* (London: Hutchinson University Library, 1963), pp. 130-132.

Bultmann's position is shot through with an instability that allows it to be taken in either direction.

Against this background, Buri offers a position both distinctive and clarifying. While Ogden adopts an undialectical metaphysical objectivity and the new hermeneuticists an undialectical and contradictory non-objectifying language, Buri's position is a *dialectic between objectivity and non-objectivity*. Like Ogden, Buri is clear that theological language cannot avoid being objective, but like the new hermeneuticists, he is also clear that the non-objectivity of faith requires a critical posture toward the conditions of objectification in general (and not merely toward a specific form of objectivity such as scientific knowledge) which must directly qualify the formal character of theological objectivity. Consequently, unlike Ogden, Buri disallows any easy transition to metaphysical objectivity. And he does this not in the first instance because metaphysics is questionable as knowledge but because the formal character of its objectivity is questionable religiously. But he remains clear, unlike the new hermeneuticists, that the manner in which theology must take non-objectivity into account cannot be allowed to abrogate the necessarily objective character of its language, for in that case, theology becomes impossible. A genuine theological hermeneutic must, therefore, involve a dialectic between objectivity and non-objectivity.[30]

If Buri's answer to the problem of objectivity is to be viable, his dialectic of objectivity and non-objectivity must avoid the confusions over the definition of the problem which have been analyzed above. These confusions can be summarized under two headings, and from each of them a criterion can be developed for assessing Buri's analysis of the problem. One source of confusion in some positions is a tendency to switch back and forth between meanings of objectivity and non-objectivity when they apply to the reality of faith itself and meanings when they ought only apply to the nature of theological language. Consequently, one criterion for the successful clarification of the problem will be clear-

---

[30]These remarks are in part an attempt to respond to a quite legitimate criticism Buri has made of an earlier version of this study. (Cf., Buri, *Gott in Amerika*, pp. 244-253, and Charley D. Hardwick, "The Problem of Objectivity in Existentialist Theology as Illustrated by the Thought of Fritz Buri." Unpublished dissertation. Departement of Religious Studies, Yale University, 1967.) Buri objects that the criticism made of him does not take into account his explicit statements that theological language must be objective. It must be admitted that this point was not sufficiently emphasized in the earlier version, though it was not omitted entirely. However, to the contrary of Buri's response and despite the need for the change of emphasis reflected above, it must also be said that this point does not alter the accuracy of the criticism made of Buri either in the earlier version or below.

ly and self-consciously keeping these levels of meaning separated. It will be particularly important to resist any temptation to say that theological language is or can be non-objective since attempts to assert this are one of he primary causes of befuddlement. (Quite another question not touched here, of course, is how the non-objectivity of faith is related to the admitted objectivity of theological language.)

A second source of confusion arises at the point where the above distinction is clearly maintained, for the non-objectivity of faith seems to require a criticism of objectivity in general even though there is no escaping the objectivity of theological language. A proper theological language must therefore be able to attain a critical distance over against its own objective form, incorporating at one and the same time both the non-objectivity of faith and a criticism of objectivity in general. On the surface, this seems to be contradictory: a criticism of objectivity *as such* combined with the legitimacy of one's own objective thinking and speaking. A potentially attractive way out, as in the case of Ogden, is to distinguish between legitimate and illegitimate forms of objectivity, illegitimate forms being, for instance, mythological and scientific objectivity. The difficulty with this approach, however, is that it is really no longer the problem of *objectivity* which is at issue but only various kinds of knowledge claims. Objectivity no longer applies to the conditions of thinking and speaking as such but is redefined to refer only to particular kinds of knowledge which are then judged inadequate as models for assessing the subject matter of theology. But since the "problem of objectivity" is in some sense coterminous with the way the non-objectivity of faith qualifies *any* theological language, the hermeneutical usefulness of the problem requires a critical posture toward objectifying modes of discourse as such. When this posture is reduced merely to a criticism of distinctive types of knowledge claims, the result is an equivocation on the "problem of objectivity." The reason is simple. While one canon of knowledge may be defended as appropriate for theology in contrast to others, the purely formal mode of theological discourse (i.e., the mode of discourse in distinction from the canons for assessing knowledge) will be identical with the formal character of discourse in the rejected types of knowledge.[31] In that case, the problem that leads to the acceptance of one and

---

[31]Ogden, for instance, rejects the theological adequacy of scientific objectivity and elaborates a legitimate alternative for theology. But once this is granted, why should not Hegel, Barth, or Aquinas also be accepted as adequate alternatives — since their understandings of theological knowledge each involves a rejection of the theological adequacy of scientific objectivity (or what Tillich calls "technical reason"). At this point, they can be criticized (as Ogden does) only from the perspective of some material mode of know-

the rejection of others will not be objectivity but something else. It is important to acknowledge, of course, that there is an intimate relationship between the problem of objectivity and various types of knowledge claims with their respective canons of assessment, but there is an equivocation in reducing the "problem" to one or more rejected types of knowledge while continuing to assert that theological language is objective. Then "objective" is being used in a narrow sense to designate an illegitimate form of knowledge (which could almost always be described more accurately by some other term than "objectifying") and in a broad sense to designate the general mode of theological language, which must also be distinguished from the existentiality of faith itself, without separating out the various meanings that allow the apparently equivocal usages. If objectivity is a theological problem, it must be an attribute of thinking and speaking that cuts across the different types of knowledge claims. If the only theological problem is to isolate a canon of knowledge appropriate to the subject matter of theology, it would be better to cease speaking of a problem of objectivity.

Since, however, it is assumed here that objectivity is a problem and since it cannot be reduced entirely to the problem of material modes of knowledge, a further criterion of the hermeneutical usefulness of the problem will be the adequacy with which the general conditions of objectivity as such are clarified. Only this clarification can account for the formal objectivity of theological language and at the same time make it possible to understand the relationship of theological objectivity both to different types of knowledge and to the non-objectivity of faith. And only on the basis of clarity about these relationships will it then be possible to assess the hermeneutical scope of the problem. Buri's analysis of objectivity and non-objectivity has the great merit of avoiding each of these sources of confusion and thereby meeting each of these criteria. Whether his solution to the problem thus clarified is adequate is quite another question indeed.

B. KNOWLEDGE AND THE MEANINGS OF OBJECTIVITY

The problem of objectivity emerges at the center of Buri's theology

edge taken to be more adequate (in Ogden's case, the material claims of process philosophy correlated with the assertions of the Christian tradition). But at a purely formal level, each of these options, including Ogden, represents an equally objective conception of theological discourse. Therefore, objectivity cannot be the *differentia* of adequacy and inadequacy, and indeed, the problem of objectivity ceases to be relevant at all for the debate among these proponents of differing conceptions of theological knowledge.

from that characteristic concern of his career to construct a theology
which does not depend at crucial points on special pleading. This concern may indeed be taken as the hallmark of radical theology. Despite
its peculiar subject matter – revelatory acts of God and the historical
witness to them – and however much it is a function of the faith of a
particular historical community, Buri insists that theology must attempt
to be a scientific undertaking. It must speak, that is, in none of the
forms of prophecy, poetry, proclamation, or mythology, nor must it confuse its language with the Word of God itself. Its task is to give an adequate conceptual and systematic articulation to the "content of the
Christian tradition" and to the "assertions of faith based on it" in a
manner that is publicly comprehensible and subject to all the canons of
rationality. (I, p. 85.)[32] It, therefore, becomes important at the outset for
Buri to clarify the nature of knowledge and to specify its relation to
theological concerns. He does this by breaking knowledge down into four
constituent features. The first of these specifies the conditions of objectivity as such, the three others specify the conditions of knowledge and
represent a special refinement of objectivity in general in the direction of
knowledge claims admitting of criteria of public assessment. Objectivity
in general is, thus, a necessary but not sufficient condition of knowledge
or "scientific objectivity" while, on the other hand, scientific objectivity
does not exhaust that class of encounters with the world that may legitimately be called objective.[33]

1. The Conditions of Objectivity in General

For Buri objectivity is the structure of consciousness, and as such, it

---

[32]Cf., I, p. 45.

[33]In his *Dogmatik*, Buri is less than clear concerning the distinction between the conditions of objectivity as such and the features of knowledge which arise from the former
conditions. There he discusses the conditions of objectivity as such simply as the first among
the four features of knowledge without indicating that this first feature has a logically
different status from the three features of knowledge themselves. It has a different status because it defines the structure of consciousness, of all presence to the world, and
not just scientific knowledge. This confusion in the *Dogmatik* makes it more difficult
than it should be to understand Buri's conception of the problem of objectivity. The author pointed out this confusion to Buri in several conversations and in an unpublished pa-
per, and he has acknowledged the unclarity and corrected it in a later article. (Cf., Fritz
Buri, "The Reality of Faith," in *How Can We Still Speak Responsibly of God?*, pp. 52
f. Hereinafter abbreviated as RF.) As a consequence, Buri's corrected position can be assumed and read back into the *Dogmatik*, and it will not be necessary to go into any
further detail concerning the unclarity in the *Dogmatik*.

is the structure of all presence to the world. In his most explicit description of this structure, Buri writes that objectivity is

the moment... in conceptual-logical thought which, not *quoad se* but indeed *quoad nos*, stands at the beginning because everything which we cognize necessarily becomes object for us. Without objectivity there is no cognition. All thinking is thinking of something. At the same time, however, a thought or cognized object is always object for a subject by which it is thought or cognized. As there is no object without a subject, so too, no subject without an object. Whatever is thought or cognized by us stands in the dichotomy of subject and object. By no means is that true merely of the so called outer world but as well of the I and of cognition itself. The I and cognition also become objects when cognition directs itself to them. (I, pp. 77 f.)

Buri speaks here of "conceptual-logical thought" and "cognition," but the reason for this is that in this context he is specifically concerned to define the character of knowledge. In other contexts, however, he makes it clear that this subject-object structure is definitive of all consciousness.[34] "Even the unconscious, the dream, ecstasy, vision and audition contain objects."[35] It is necessary, therefore, for Buri to assume (and sometimes to make explicit) a distinction between forms of "consciousness," "thinking," "thinking consciousness," even "cognition" which are objective but not scientific and scientific objectivity itself.[36]

The subject-object structure functions, therefore, not as one feature of thinking or knowledge among others but as the encompassing medium of all thinking and speaking in the sense of a transcendental condition. "It is not the result of an act of thinking; rather, every act of thinking presupposes this schema as the basic structure in which it occurs."[37] Because it functions as the transcendental condition of all presence to the world, this structure, when it is acknowledged as a basic condition, effects the evaluation of various forms of thinking and speaking that occur within it. Specifically, it means that any assessment must include the conditioning factor of subject-object relatedness. Hence, the world is never given to consciousness as "being-in-itself" but always in the form of intentional objects for a conscious subject, and putative claims about "being-in-itself" or "the world as a whole" must have this taken into account when they are assessed. The subject-object structure means there is no *tran-*

---

[34]Cf., I, p. 78; PuDR, pp. 353 f.; RF, pp. 49-53; and Buri, "Über Orthodoxie und Liberalismus hinaus," in *Theologische Zeitschrift*, 16 (1960), pp. 36-39.

[35]PuDR, p. 353.

[36]Cf., I, pp. 75 f.; PuDR, pp. 353 f.; RF, pp. 50 f.

[37]RF, p. 51.

scendent viewpoint for consciousness by means of which the world as a whole as it is in itself can be seen; consciousness is always objective consciousness *immanent* to the world, immanent to the intentional determinations of a relation.[38]

By thus making the conditions of objectivity as such a transcendental condition of all presence to the world, Buri goes far toward meeting one of the criteria for an adequate clarification of the hermeneutical scope of the problem of objectivity. He lays the groundwork for showing the senses in which theological thinking and speaking are objective while at the same time making it possible to separate various kinds of objective consciousness depending on the configurations they assume in the subject-object structure. It thereby also becomes possible to specify how the concept of the non-objective functions in relations to various senses of objectivity.

Despite this wide generality of the subject-object structure, however, it is important to note that in one sense it bears a particularly intimate relation to scientific objectivity. While there are various kinds of non-scientific, objective consciousness, such as myth, which are conditioned by the subject-object structure, the reflexive acknowledgement and distinguishing of these various forms as well as the recognition of the subject-object structure itself depends on the development of a strict scientific objectivity. "We become aware of the structure of our conscious world only in a logical conceptuality. Without judgments and definitions we have only an intimation but no clear consciousness of this fundamental structure of all thinking and knowing." (I, p. 78.)

The distinction between pre-scientific and scientific thinking consists in this regard only in the fact that the pre-scientific is not aware of. . . logico-conceptual objectification whereas it has become conscious for scientific cognition. The latter is therefore able to draw out the consequences from this which in the long run allow it to go in different directions from mythical thinking. When they are consciously recognized for what they are, myth and logos, which originally form a unity, go their separate ways. (I, p. 76.)

[38]For the philosophical foundations of this viewpoint, cf., Karl Jaspers, *Psychologie der Weltanschauungen* (Berlin: J. Springer Verlag, 1919), pp. 20 ff.; Jaspers, *Von der Wahrheit* (München: R. Piper und Co. Verlag, 1947), pp. 231-233; Bernard Welte, *Der philosophische Glaube bei Karl Jaspers und die Möglichkeit seiner Deutung durch die thomistische Philosophie* in *Symposion: Jahrbuch für Philosophie, II* (Freiburg: Verlag Karl Alber, 1949), pp. 18, 32 f.; Ulrich Schmidhäuser, *Allgemeine Wahrheit und existentielle Wahrheit bei Karl Jaspers* (Bonn: Dissertation der rheinischen Friedrich Wilhelms-Universität philosophische Fakultä, 1953), pp. 14 f.

If the conditions of objectivity as such are not a function of scientific objectivity alone, nevertheless, the *recognition* of these conditions is such a function, and furthermore, the critical consciousness on which this recognition depends will thereafter determine the assessment of the various forms of objective thinking and speaking. This means that while all thinking and speaking have objective *form* for Buri, he limits knowledge to the canons of scientific objectivity. This factor, as its implications will be drawn out below, explains why it is impossible for Buri to move in Ogden's direction, and it makes it necessary for him to develop an entirely different understanding of theological language.[39]

2. The Conditions of Scientific Objectivity

The three characteristics of that scientific objectivity which occurs within and presupposes the subject-object structure are: (a) general demonstrability (*allgemeine Ausweisbarkeit*), (b) methodical (*methodisch*) appropriateness in both an objective and a subjective sense, and (c) relativity and open-endedness.

(a) By *allgemeine Ausweisbarkeit* Buri simply means that scientific knowledge must be publicly verifiable. Verification for him does, however, signify something looser than the "verification principle" of logical positivism. The methods of verification are those appropriate to any particular discipline. As the word *allgemein* indicates, Buri places emphasis on the fact that such demonstrable knowledge is (i) universal, (ii) abstract, and (iii) detached. As a result of these characteristics, such knowledge can be checked repeatedly by anyone who will submit himself to the proper methods and controls. Buri assumes that such knowledge is made possible by conceptual schemes which are wider than any specific results. These schemes are universal and abstract in that, while they have no independent metaphysical status in themselves, they provide a grid which can be imposed on the immediacy of experience to organize it and make it intelligible. The results of such objectivity are purchased at the price of sacrificing much of the immediacy and richness of the concrete *Lebenswelt* of experience. What is gained is the inclusion of wider and wider ranges of diverse forms of experience in conceptual schemes which order them, make them comprehensible in terms of overarching unities

---

[39]Cf., HSRG, pp. 34-39. It is self-evident and needs no further comment that the non-objective thinking and speaking of the new hermeneutics can in no way be an option for Buri.

and laws, and open up new, unexpected ranges of experience for investigation and inclusion.[40] In this context, Buri introduces a somewhat artificial distinction between *Richtigkeit* and *Wahrheit,* correctness and truth, which it is, nevertheless, necessary to use because they have some importance as *termini technici* in his system. He asserts that the *Richtigkeit* of scientific knowledge is established functionally. It proves itself beyond the need of any further justification because the possibilities of "repeatability (*Nachvollziehbarkeit*) and verifiability (*Nachprüfbarkeit*) on the basis of the principles of logic as these are used in reference to empirical reality" demonstrate themselves through their fruitfulness. (I, p. 80.) *Richtigkeit* is used to designate the results of scientific knowledge because Buri wants "to reserve the concept of truth for a situation which is, at once, entirely of this world (*ganz irdisch*), historistic (*geschichtlich*), individual and, at the same time, also an immediate relation to the eternal. Both these peculiarities are denied to scientific judgments." (I, p. 80.)

(b) By objective and subjective methodical appropriateness, Buri means that the universality and detachment of scientific knowledge are limited in two directions. Scientific knowledge must be objectively appropriate in that the concepts it uses must be appropriate to the data and to the particular kind of information sought. Results from one discipline or one line of enquiry cannot be indiscriminately applied to another, nor can the results of several be added up to a single sum. The generality of scientific knowledge does not imply universality of method.[41]

Subjective appropriateness means the readiness on the part of the knower to submit himself to the data. In this sense, the subjectivity of the knower must intrude because the ideal of scientific knowledge (no matter how detached) involves what Van A. Harvey has recently called a "morality of knowledge."[42] Buri makes the same point when he says that

appropriateness signifies, in this regard, that I desire to know no matter what – whether under the greatest possible exclusion of my subjectivity or its necessary intrusion depending on the nature of the cognitive object. That means that what is at stake for me may not be the defense of a standpoint taken in advance or the attainment under any circumstances of certain results. Instead, I must be prepared to place in question and to allow to be placed in question every starting point and every result. (I, p. 82.)

---

[40]Cf., I, pp. 78-80.
[41]Cf., *Ibid.,* pp. 80 f.
[42]Van A. Harvey, *The Historian and the Believer* (New York: The Macmillan Co., 1966), pp. 102 ff.

(c) The universality of scientific knowledge is limited in still another direction by its relativity and open-endedness. Whatever is known by scientific knowledge within a system of concepts is known absolutely. That is, the results of any enquiry are valid for everyone, and they can be checked again and again by anyone who follows the procedures which led to them. But these results are still relative to the particular sphere of objects, the methods, and the system of concepts by which they are attained. While he in no way wants to deny the validity of such knowledge within its limits, Buri does argue that ignoring its relativity leads to the absolutization of particular standpoints and spheres of objects. This, in turn, makes impossible the clear specification of its objects which is the goal of scientific knowledge. He notes that such absolutizations have always been called into question by the history of science itself.[43]

One of the main conclusions Buri draws from this sense of relativity is that none of the objects of scientific knowledge nor their totality is a presentation of the "objectivity of being as a whole." (I, p. 83.) Being as a whole is inaccessible to scientific knowledge. Such knowledge is limited to the determination of specific objects or ranges of objects immanent to the encompassing structures of being as a whole – which is to say that for Buri, rigorous knowledge for which it is possible to provide justifying reasons is limited to formal logic and empirical reality accessible through the various special sciences. Metaphysics, ontology, and cosmology are ruled out as providing any knowledge. If there is an approach to such realities (i.e., to "being as a whole"), it is not a cognitive one as this is defined under the ideal of scientific knowledge.

Correlative with its relativity is the open-endedness of scientific knowledge. Scientific knowledge is by nature progressive. New discoveries and new results always lead beyond themselves. "But an end result cannot be envisioned; rather, all results are only partial in a process whose beginning we do not know and whose completion we cannot anticipate." (I, pp. 83-84.) Consequently, the defense of any result as final and absolute would mean a retreat from scientific knowledge and would imply a new kind of absolutization which the continuing development of knowledge would dispel.

[43]I, p. 83.

C. THE PROBLEM OF OBJECTIVITY AND THEOLOGICAL LANGUAGE

Objectivity has two clearly distinguishable though closely related meanings for Buri. One is objective consciousness in the subject-object structure as the condition of all presence to the world, and, thus, of all thinking and speaking; the other is scientific objectivity as the specification of objective consciousness by the conditions of knowledge. (Because the English language has only one word for objectivity, these different meanings will henceforth be abbreviated respectively as "obj-A" and "obj-B.") Objectivity is hermeneutically relevant because objectivity in each of these senses poses problems for theological thinking and speaking. At the same time, an awareness of these problems forms the necessary context within which the foundations for an adequate, i.e., radical, theology can be constructed.

(1) The first and most serious problem occurs with the structure of consciousness itself (obj-A). It cannot be denied, to be sure, that much of the actual subject matter of theology has to do with determinate objects of faith and history that fall quite legitimately within the purview of the ordinary structure of consciousness: the *assertions* of the Christian faith and its tradition which are dependent on the *message* of God's revelation in Jesus Christ.[44] A major part of its work can, thus, take place at the same level as any other cognitive undertaking that presupposes the structure of consciousness. This is especially true for the historical-critical work of the theologian in which the attempt is made to provide the most accurate possible reconstruction of the literary and historical sources of the tradition and to clarify in their historical setting the nature of the theological claims which have been made on the basis of those sources.

But at two points, Buri says, the subject matter of theology is "completely non-objective and non-objectifiable" in the sense that it can in no way be brought under the conditions of consciousness without becoming entirely different from what it is. (I, p. 85.) These two points are the act of faith (*Glaubensvollzug*) and Transcendence[45] to which faith is related.

---

[44]Cf., *Ibid.*, pp. 84 f. Notice that the assertions of the tradition and the message witnessing to revelation are objective even though the content of revelation and of faith may not be.

[45]"Transcendence" is, for Buri, a philosophical *terminus technicus* which indicates the unconditioned pole of every self-understanding. It cannot immediately be identified with God because "God" is a mythological concept (i.e., is immanent to the subject-object structure) for referring to Transcendence and as such is only one among many different ways in which Transcendence may be expressed. Because Buri's philosophical theology is

The act of faith is non-objective because it is an existential act in which
the self is not related to itself as to a self-objectification but understands
who it is in the *actual* process of self-definition (or *self-understanding*, to
use Buri's technical language.) The act of faith "is not a something at all"
which can be objectified "but pure actuality." (I, p. 86.) In it "the believer cannot once more turn around and observe himself. He himself is the
one who believes." (I, p. 85) This existential reality is, thus, transcendent
to the conditions of objective consciousness. An objective presentation of
faith within the subject-object structure cannot catch this act in the reality appropriate to it but only its "precipitates," the externalized "forms it
takes," or "possibilities" offered for new acts of faith. (I, p. 22.)

Despite its transcendence of the subject-object structure, the act of
faith is not its own ground; but it is grounded relationally only in the
non-objective act. This ground, what Buri terms Transcendence, also
falls outside the conditions of objective consciousness. Speculative and
mythological forms of speaking which objectify Transcendence as "God"
relativize Him by bringing Him into the immanent relations of worldly
consciousness. Brought under these general conditions, God can only be
represented by images modeled on phenomenal objects which are themselves transcendentally grounded in the structure of consciousness. The
problem for Buri here is not so much the traditional problem of drawing
analogies from phenomenal images but the more radical problem of the
transcendental ground of both images and analogies, i.e., the subject-object structure itself. Everything that falls within it is conditioned by its
relational structure. This is the real reason why objective analogies are
problematic for Buri, for whatever else God is, He is unconditioned.
From an epistemological point of view, His unconditionedness (*Unbedingtheit*) must be His transcendence of the conditions of consciousness.
In this sense speculative and mythological references to "God," to that
which is unconditioned, are references to Transcendence. While faith
means a relationship to this ground, neither faith nor Transcendence can
be brought into the subject-object structure.[46]

(2) The problem of objectivity receives its distinctive shape in Buri's
theology from this problem at the level of obj-A, for however much the
subject matter of theology is non-objective in principle, theological thinking and speaking necessarily fall within the subject-object structure. But

itself limited by the subject-object structure, it is extremely difficult for him to give an
analysis of Transcendence, and it remains one of the crucial unclarified concepts of his
system. Its various possible interpretations will receive considerable attention below.

[46]Cf., I, pp. 85 f.

in addition to having an objective structure (obj-A), theological language also must meet the conditions of scientific objectivity (obj-B), and here the problem of theological language (obj-A) is further qualified by these specific conditions.

(a) The first of these concerns the distinction Buri makes between *Richtigkeit* and *Wahrheit*. In so far as theology makes systematic, conceptual assertions, it must expose itself to the appropriate criteria which lead to generally demonstrable *Richtigkeit*. This generality will include universality, detachment, and abstractness leading to verifiable conclusions in the context of the relevant conceptual schemes and will be particularly applicable to that range of theological subject matter which falls intrinsically under the subject-object structure. But the "truth" of which theology speaks is not general nor can it be abstracted from the existential reality in which it occurs. "Unlike conceptual-logical thinking, there is, in the truth, no abstraction from the subjectivity of the thinker and from the concreteness of the content of thought; to the contrary, as just this single one *(als je einzelner)*, the thinker identifies himself with the total concreteness of his situation in order thus in the midst of its contingency to hear the claim of eternity." (I, p. 87.) Furthermore, this applies not merely to the act of faith but also to the "truth" of revelation and to the "truth" claimed by proclamation.[47] At each of these points, the clarity of theological assertions will depend on a "preceding rational clarification" and "a subsequent critical examination;"[48] but their "origin" (*Ursprung*), their "mode of certainty," and their "power of conviction lie outside the *Richtigkeit* of conceptual logical proof." (I, pp. 87 f.)

(b) With subjective methodical appropriateness, one of the most important consequences of the "will to know" is that the knower will try to free himself from attitudes and assumptions about his material held in advance. But the decisive "presupposition" which theology cannot surrender without surrendering itself is precisely that of faith. Behind the objectively articulated message stands the act of faith and its claim to "truth," and it is just these that theology must presuppose. Objective appropriateness assumes "some measure of comparability, similarity, analogy, or, in psychological terms, congeniality" between concept and object, and scientific knowledge develops methods by means of which this ap-

---

47 *Ibid.*, p. 87.
48 This formula of a "voraufgehenden und nachfolgenden Klärung und Erhellung" (*ibid.*, pp. 23 f.) is often repeated by Buri to emphasize that even a theology oriented ultimately to the non-objectivity of faith and its content must adhere to the canons of rationality. (Cf., e.g., *ibid.*, pp. 141-143, 198-206.)

propriateness can be continually re-examined and refined. (I, p. 89.) The problem is that theology speaks of revelations, self-attestations, acts of *God*. How is "similarity," "analogy," or "congeniality" possible here? The historical sciences can establish what a tradition has claimed the revelation to be, and it can investigate the historical origins of such a tradition and the ways in which its beliefs have influenced human behavior. But it has no way to take account methodologically of acts of God in explaining historical events.[49]

(c) Finally, the most basic assertions of theology admit of neither relativity nor open-endedness. No matter what conceptual considerations may enter into the act of faith or may follow from it, the act itself and its claim to an unconditioned relation to God dissolve the preliminary, tentative, and relative nature of scientific thought. "Faith dares to know itself related to Transcendence in a moment which interrupts" (I, p. 90) the "infinite approximation process" involved in all rationality.[50] This is not to deny that the believer still thinks conceptually, that he may be aware of the subject-object structure of consciousness and, thus, of the inappropriateness of his discourse about God, nor that he may be aware of the conditionedness of his standpoint. But precisely here "in the midst of the provisionality (*Vorläufigkeit*) of time, faith is aware of a now-of-revelation and of a once-for-allness of decision." (I, p. 90.) While relativity and open-endedness may prevent science from absolutizing its own position by rejecting unconditioned claims out of hand, this openness and caution is not a preparation for faith, for the decision of faith does not and cannot await the judgment of the knower that it is adequately grounded. Historical science may register that unconditioned claims are made, but in doing so, it relativizes their undconditionedness. Between the conceptual consideration of the nature and warrants for faith and the decision to become a man of faith there is a logical break in kind.

At each of these points of tension in obj-B, the problem is occasioned by the way faith and its content are transcendent to the structure of objective consciousness (obj-A). These problems do not arise for scientific thinking because its subject matter is appropriately given in the subject-object structure. But theology must attempt to speak scientifically about that which is given only in the act of transcending the subject-object structure, and this act can occur only existentially, not cognitively (in the sense of scientific cognition). Methodological questions in theology will tend to concentrate on issues at the level of obj-B because theology must

---

[49]*Ibid.*, pp. 89 f.
[50]Cf., Kierkegaard, *Concluding* . . ., pp. 42, 173, 178 f., 182.

be rigorously self-conscious about the nature of the language it must in any case use, but even at the level of obj-B, the questions about how to construe this language will always be occasioned by the unique theological problem of obj-A. In Buri's view, the shortcomings of traditional theological language, the problem his theology is designed to solve, all grow out of an insufficiently critical awareness of how obj-A problematically qualifies actual theological usage (obj-B). This then makes it impossible to deal adequately with the intrinsic tensions at the level of obj-B, and they are either ignored or recourse is taken to various kinds of special pleading.

This lack of critical self-consciousness crystallizes in traditional theology into a back and forth movement between two forms of obj-B which are equally inadequate for theological formulation, between what Buri calls subjectivism (*Subjektivismus*) and objectivism (*Objektivismus*). Within obj-B, "objective" and "subjective" can each have two further meanings which cut across each of the specific characteristics of scientific objectivity. First, "objectivism" means a set of judgments about what is other than the self whereas "subjectivism" means a set about the self. But second, "subjective" can also mean subjective opinion or bias whereas "objective" refers to the neutrality and public nature of a judgment that meets the conditions of scientific objectivity. In this latter sense, a scientific judgment is made when the attempt is to be as objective as possible whether the judgment is about the subject (subjectivistic) or the object (objectivistic). Thus, when Buri discusses objectivism and subjectivism as the two basic types of traditional theology, taking Barth and Schleiermacher as his examples, he assumes that, despite the different references of their categories, the formal character of their language is equally objective in the sense of obj-B.[51]

When the theologian is insufficiently self-conscious of the transcendental structure (obj-A) within which his theological references (obj-B) are made, he unavoidably assumes that the *An-sich* subject matter of theology can be referred to directly in the objective form (obj-B) of his theological language. This gives rise to the fruitless debate in history of theology over whether the basic subject matter which defines theological method is "objective" (objectivistic), given in objective realities independent of faith or "subjective" (subjectivistic), confined to modalities of the self in the disposition of faith.[52] In either case, however, the objective

---

[51]Cf., II, pp. 309-317, esp. p. 315.
[52]Classic instances of this debate in the history of theology are Anselm and Abelard on

form of theological language itself (obj-B) does not come into question with the result that faith and its content are ossified into objectivistic or subjectivistic states of affairs accessible unproblematically to objective description.[53] Then with refinement of the canons of objective knowledge in modern science, the objectivity (obj-B) of each of these forms of theology falls prey to the inherent tensions at the level of obj-B.

A critical awareness of the transcendental structure of all theological language (obj-A) makes this procedure impossible, for the putative *An-sich* references of both objectivistic and subjectivistic theologies are made problematic and relativized by being conceived within the subject-object structure. When objective language (obj-B) is viewed from the perspective of the structure of consciousness (obj-A), it is apparent that the world never appears as it is in itself but always as it is for us. This defines the world as a phenomenal object for consciousness. Because of the phenomenal structure of consciousness (obj-A), there can be no objective (obj-B) transcendence of the relational structure of the world. The object is never given *An-sich* because it is never given without being an object for a particular subject. And the subject is never given *An-sich* for consciousness because in reflecting upon itself the subject only grasps an objectification of itself which presupposes the subject pole in such an enactment.[54] This involves no problem for modern, scientific thinking in that the sciences "dispense with the question of the *An-sich* character of reality and content themselves with the verifiability of their statements within the context of their [the sciences] possibilities of knowledge."[55] But theology deals with an *An-sich* reality both in relation to the "subject" and the "object" of faith. The content of faith is given to faith in such a way that theological statements must somehow attempt to focus at one and the same time on the existential reality of faith and on the reference of faith (its "object"). But the nature of cognitive judgments (obj-B as it presupposes obj-A) is such that statements of this sort continually tend to fall off into an objectively falsifying isolation of either the subjective or the objective. The nature of consciousness cannot encompass the totality which is the "reality of faith."[56]

---

the atonement, Calvin and Luther on the person and work of Christ, and Barth and Schleiermacher on revelation versus religion.

[53]Cf., II, pp. 28-34, 304-317, 379-386.

[54]Cf., RF, pp. 50-53.

[55]*Ibid.*, p. 49.

[56]For the philosophical basis of this view, cf., Jaspers, *Von der Wahrheit*, pp. 1022-1054. That Buri's somewhat idiosyncratic analysis of this problem is not unique but re-

The obj-B statements of theology will, of course, inevitably be either "objectivistic" or "subjectivistic" or some combination of the two. But the dependence of consciousness on the subject-object structure means that the intention of theological language to speak of *An-sich* realities cannot succeed if its language is taken literally. Unless its subjectivistic and objectivistic statements are seen in their relation both to the structure of consciousness, and to the non-objectivity of the subject matter of theology, such statements will be given a status in themselves which makes an adequate hermeneutics impossible. By elucidating the non-objectivity of the content of theological statements, Buri hopes to establish a dialectic in which he can play off subjectivistic and objectivistic traditional theological positions in order to allow their non-objective content to "show" through without his own obj-B statements falling into either the objectivistic or the subjectivistic fallacy. He can achieve this, however, only provided that the conditions of objectivity (obj-A and obj-B) do not so circumscribe the possibilities of linguistic usage as to make it impossible. At the purely formal, epistemological level of theological hermeneutics (i.e., prior to the actual interpretation of traditional doctrines), his most pressing concern is, therefore, to show that there are limits to the conditions of objectivity which can be adduced within the confines of objective linguistic usage.

D. THE LIMITS OF OBJECTIVITY

Buri's concern with the "limits of knowledge" is to show that at certain points the conditions of objectivity (obj-A and obj-B) become anomalous with regard to the actual contents of objective thought.[57] These limits occur at points where the conditions that found objective consciousness seem to turn back on themselves because they cannot provide their own ground. They are, thus, points at which the conditions of objectivity seem to touch something non-objective even though how this is so cannot be objectively conceived. These limits are theologically relevant because each of them occurs at a point analogous to those places where the non-objectivity of faith and its content seem to "spring" the possibili-

---

states a perennial theological issue is made apparent by a similar discussion in Victor Preller's brilliant analysis of the problem of "reference" in Aquinas. Preller, *Divine Science and the Science of God: A Reformulation of Thomas Aquinas* (Princeton: Princeton University Press, 1967).

[57]Cf., I, pp. 103-105.

ty of meeting the conditions of objective articulation. This is not to say that Buri's consideration of the limits of knowledge serves an apologetic function as though he were trying to argue that knowledge itself is already shot through with faith. Nor is his goal to give the theologian license to say anything he pleases. Buri remains clear that there is no exempting theology from the conditions or the canons of critical rationality. But to the extent that the conditions of objective thinking and speaking are themselves "fissured" by a relationship to the non-objective, it may be possible for theological language (obj-B) to take account of its non-objective content without relinquishing critical rationality. In other words, an adequate theological hermeneutics may still be possible.

A discussion of the limits of knowledge is strange because the assertions pointing out the anomalous character of the conditions of thinking will be anomalous in relation to those conditions. The reason is that every attempt to think the limits must already presuppose precisely those characteristics the limits of which it defines. For instance, a consideration of the limits of logic must make use of precisely those logical axioms it is questioning; or a definition of the subject-object structure conditioning consciousness must itself already be in the subject-object structure.[58] Consequently, while such a discussion must be objective in form, its results are, strictly speaking, non-objective. It will be a meta-level discussion which does not produce any "new, generally demonstrable objectivity of conceptual-logical cognition" but, viewed from the standpoint of such cognition, is merely circular and empty. (I, p. 105.) In effect, a definition of the limits of knowledge will not itself be knowledge. Its intention will be entirely different from one seeking positive, objective results. Despite the fact that such reflection must be objective in form, "it might," Buri says, describing this intention, "lead to a different basic attitude toward this objectivity, a new stance expressing an inner awareness which is no longer susceptible to objective knowledge. Out of this awareness, then, a new attitude regarding the scientific nature of dogmatics might result." (I, p. 105.) Appealing directly to Jaspers' method of philosophical transcending, which he follows in these remarks, he says that such an approach to the limits of knowledge is a philosophical movement of thought "which leads to no new knowledge but, for all that, as a transforming act of inwardness, results in a new attitude toward knowledge." (I, p. 105.)

---

[58]The first example is Buri's (I, p. 104), the second Jaspers' in *Einführung in die Philosophie* (München: R. Piper und Co. Verlag, 1953), p. 32.

Although Buri speaks here of an attitude as the goal of this transcending movement of thought, it is important to recognize that the process by which this attitude is achieved is a *movement of thought.* The process itself is not merely dispositional or attitudinal. For all its emptiness, it is a genuine thought movement something like a limiting concept between knowing a specific, determinate state of affairs and the non-objective movement by which the knower constitutes himself as knower. The idea of such a movement of thought is difficult to grasp, Buri would say, precisely because ordinary movements of thought are defined by specific, objective content. Such an undertaking seems strange because, having nothing other than the ordinary structure of consciousness, it attempts to transcend to the frame or encompassing medium within which that structure legitimately operates to arrive at determinate results of knowledge.

1. The Transparency of the Subject-Object Structure

The subject-object structure is, Buri says, the "contingent structure of all cognition." (I, p. 106.) By contingent he means that it is *quoad nos* but not *quoad se.*[59] It is the necessary grid through which all experience is filtered, but there is no way to establish its ontological equivalence with being-in-itself. It is epistemologically necessary but ontologically contingent. Yet there is no way to escape it in order to establish its ontological status *quoad se.* Even the attempt to define it as an encompassing structure must presuppose it. Even if it is epistemologically necessary, however, it is also the limiting factor on knowledge because, while there is no escaping it, an awareness of its structural features and of its contingency produces the realization that it does not enclose all being but is grounded in that which it can never define. To define what encloses the subject-object structure would be to make this encompassing reality into another object. Consequently, the present type of reflection is finally empty and circular. When consciousness is directed to the determination of objects within the structure, it is at home, and the extension of knowledge becomes richer and more multifarious; but when it turns itself on itself, it no longer determines an object but that which is the transcendental condition of all objects; it determines as an object that which can never be one. This empty movement makes the difference, however, of shocking out of the easy complacency (or dogmatism) that what is acces-

[59] I, p. 77.

sible in consciousness is exhaustive of reality. But nothing new is added
to what is known because what encompasses the structure cannot itself
become an object. Instead, it brings about a transformation in the manner in which the known is known. That is what Buri means by a transformation of attitude.[60] Buri sums up the importance of this transformation in the following crucial statement:

> The contingent character of objectivity and subject-object splittedness (*Subjekt-
> Objektgespaltenheit*) in the known is not itself in turn something objective in the
> subject-object structure of the knowable. It is empty and says nothing in such cir-
> cular reasoning. But as the structure of all knowing in objectivity and in the sub-
> ject-object relation – the structure which may not itself be objectified – the non-ob-
> jective which lies entirely prior to the subject-object split appears in it. This non-
> objectifiable reality *(das Ungegenständliche)* shines through *(aufleuchtet in)* all the
> splits of objectivity into subjectivity and objectivity as their incomprehensible *(un-
> fassbarer)* yet continually present origin *(Ursprung)*. (I, p. 108.)

In other words, Buri claims that a sensitivity to the structure of consciousness and to its *Begrenztheit* can effect and awareness of the encompassing ground of that structure in and through the mundane consciousness of objects even though it never itself becomes an object.

This elucidation of the non-objective that surrounds, grounds, and sustains the ordinary determinations of objects within consciousness has
particularly important implications for "world-views." In Buri's thought,
a world view – inclusive of metaphysics, cosmology and ontology – is
an attempt to extend conceptions of objects immanent to the subject-object structure to a vision of things entire. It is an attempt to gain knowledge of the non-objective reality grounding the contingent structure of
consciousness on the basis of structures immanent to consciousness. The
transcending movement of thought makes evident that these attempts,
i.e., all metaphysical world views, in so far as they make a cognitive
claim, are doomed to failure. But no less than the old metaphysics, the
modern conception of science based on the special sciences also seeks to
attain a picture of the world. In both of the directions it faces – in the
striving for "the widest possible interconnection as well as the most
exact investigation of particulars" – it seeks to extend knowledge to an
inclusive picture of the world. (I, p. 108.) The difference between the
pictures of the world projected by the special sciences and the old metaphysical ones is that the modern knower "is aware of the conditionedness and particularity of his world-pictures;" he has a critical conscious-

---

[60] Cf.,*Ibid.*, pp. 106 f., 111.

ness of the "limitation on their universality, absoluteness, and unalterability." (I, p. 109) Unlike the old attempts to gain a single, unitary *Weltbild,* the pluralism of methods in modern *Wissenschaftlichkeit* has produced "a series of different, scientific *Weltaspekte*" – a physicist's, a biologist's, an historian's. The danger with such limited pictures is that there is always the temptation to extend them to a claim to exhaust reality by comprehending it as it is in itself. Because then the claims of particular areas of research become no less absolute than the less critical metaphysical claims, there is always the temptation to "replace the lost myth and the surrendered dogma" by a new scientific myth or dogma. (I, p. 110.)[61] Even when scientific knowledge remains conscious of its relativity it "knows no limits" because then relativism itself "becomes the absolute world-picture." (I, p. 110.)

It is in this situation – both in relation to the old attempts to determine the non-objectivity of being in itself and to the temptations at claiming exhaustive knowledge in modern scientism – that the significance of the transcending movement of thought described above becomes apparent. It is a movement of thought which results in a new attitude toward what is known and, consequently, requires no limitation on the extension of knowledge in specific spheres. Instead, this new attitude effects a sensitivity to and an awareness of the encompassing yet non-objective ground (*Ursprung*) which sustains all particular objectifications. As such, it effects a relativization of knowledge appropriate to knowledge. Relativism itself does not become a new world-picture because the qualified relativity of scientific knowledge is maintained in the consciousness of the Absolute which conditions it. As Buri says, this limit is not one that "stands at the outermost rim of everything relative and open-ended but perpendicular to it as the mystery in every moment of everything objective we know." (I, p. 110.) The result of this new attitude toward normal objects of consciousness is that they can become "transparent" to their non-objective ground:

This non-objectivity subsists in the *transparency* of the objective for the non-objective. Because it [*das Ungegenständliche*] is the transparency, it is not itself an object *(ist es selber nicht mehr Gegenständlichkeit).* The non-objective becomes ac-

---

[61]Buri consequently grants speculative claims no higher cognitive status than mythological ones. Traditionally speculative theories have sought to commend themselves as "scientific," but Buri, on the basis of his understanding of scientific knowledge, denigrates this attempt as no more than *Wissenschaftsmythos.* Below it will become apparent that this "mythological form" of both speculative and mythological objectivity plays an important role in his theory of symbol and myth. It obviously has important ramifications for the dialectic of objectivity and non-objectivity. Cf., *ibid.,* pp. 178-181, 201-204.

tual in the possibility in all pictures of the world for becoming transparent for that which can no longer become a picture of the world. (I, p. 110. My italics.)

It is not entirely clear how this transparency can manifest itself since the moment the non-objective enters consciousness it becomes an object. The last sentence in the quotation gives a hint at Buri's meaning, however, and it becomes clearer in the approach he takes to the interpretation of objectively (obj-B) stated theological doctrines. While he has rejected the *cognitive* or *scientific* fruitfulness of metaphysical attempts to define ultimate reality, his theory of world-pictures still makes it possible for him to interpret speculative, mythological, and doctrinal assertions as *symbolic indicators* pointing toward this reality. The crucial question is how such symbolic assertions point so that they can be interpreted in the objective form of language. While the non-objective cannot be determined objectively, it does become an actuality, Buri will argue, in the existential inwardness of acts of freedom and responsibility. To the extent, then, that objective language can be transparent to it at all, this will occur when such language either elicits the non-objective relation or can be interpreted symbolically as *re-presenting* the structure of the existential act. Having rejected the cognitive adequacy of metaphysical claims, Buri can, thus, reappropriate them once the limits of objectivity have been clarified. That is, he can propose to interpret them existentially. In fact, on the far side of this transcending movement of thought, Buri finds that speculative, mythological, and doctrinal world-pictures provide a world of imagery far richer in possibilities for becoming transparent to the non-objective in this sense than the rather sterile and spare *Weltaspekte* of modern scientism. This enables him to argue later that, although the objective forms of mythology and speculation cannot stand up under the criticism of scientific rationality, they, nevertheless, cannot be reduced to nothing by scientific criticism. When properly interpreted, they give indirect expression to the non-objective. This status of mythological and speculative forms of discourse is what allows him to make the Christian self-understanding the material principle of his system.

2. The Limits of Scientific Objectivity

a. Richtigkeit as Medium for Wahrheit

According to Buri, *Richtigkeit* is a quality of judgments, and it endows them with their scientific character; *Wahrheit* or truth, in contrast, is a quality of existential decision and existential self-constitution. Despite the artificiality of this distinction – as though "truth" where not an appropriate designation for the deliverances of the special sciences – it serves an appropriate purpose for Buri as a recommendation for linguistic usage by indicating the incommensurability between the canons of objective verification and the existential reality of faith. When faith is understood to be an existential self-understanding, it is inappropriate to speak of a rational justification of faith since the "that" of becoming a faithful man cannot be reduced to the rational canons of evaluating arguments. And when the "that" of the existential act of faith is taken as the model for interpreting the very content of objectively expressed theological doctrines, the gulf between *Richtigkeit* and *Wahrheit* becomes wide indeed. Yet if theology is possible at all, there must be some point of contact between *Richtigkeit* and *Wahrheit,* for otherwise there is no way to distinguish between adequacy and inadequacy among theological assertions, no way, in fact, to distinguish theology from mindless raving. The theologian must speak in a fashion that meets the canons of critical rationality.

This point of contact may be established by another transcending yet empty movement of thought in which Buri shows that intrinsic to knowledge which is generally demonstrable is a *Gehalt* or content which is the ground of specific results in cognition but which can never itself be demonstrated generally. It is that which makes knowledge possible and gives it substance and actuality,[62] but never becomes a particular, objective *Inhalt* (or "content" in the sense of particular intentionality in the subject-object structure).[63] Since scientific objectivity assumes that the potentiality for *allgemeine Ausweisbarkeit* is exhaustive, it will be particularly important if this potentiality is *intrinsically* limited – not in the sense that scientific knowledge is prohibited from investigating certain domains of experience but in the sense that demonstrability itself rests on certain assumptions which are indemonstrable.

Buri claims that general demonstrability is conditioned by such a *Gehalt* at three points. (i) The first concerns the logical axioms of thought.[64] These are the principles of all thinking; any act of thought depends on them either implicitly or explicitly, but they cannot themselves be logically demonstrated since their demonstration (or the reduction of others

---

[62]Cf., *ibid.,* pp. 115 ff.

[63]Cf., *ibid.,* pp. 114 f.

[64]According to Buri, these axioms are the principles of identity, contradiction, excluded middle, and sufficient reason. Cf., *ibid.,* p. 113.

back to one or another taken to be primitive) must already presuppose and make use of the principles which are to be demonstrated.[65] (ii) Next, there is always a "given" for thought which is not produced by thought but which must be assumed before the canons of verification can come into play. Even the circular movement of thinking about thought pre-supposes a given element in that, in making itself an object, "thinking does not produce itself, but only, through [turning back on itself], achieves a consciousness of itself." (I, p. 114.) Knowledge of this "given" is always interpretive, however, and never a knowledge of the given as it is in itself; it is a knowledge of the given simply as it is for the knower who must assume that something in itself is given. He can, nevertheless, expect a certain assurance of the warrantability of his interpretive schemes because of a "concomitant variation"[66] between his images and con-cepts and the reality given to thought which can be "checked, widened, and corrected through experiment and understanding." (I, p. 115.) (iii) There is, finally, the unity of self-consciousness, the transcendental iden-tity accompanying and conditioning the actualization of specific acts of knowing but never itself becoming the object of one of them. The self that knows cannot unconditionally know itself. "The one who enacts the act of cognition is not exhausted in it." (I, p. 116.) What it knows of it-self is always an object and never itself in the immediacy of its self-ac-tualization. Yet, this transcendental given, which is the condition of all specific cognitive acts, is nothing other than the self, and the self has no other avenue by means of which to come to awareness of itself than through the vehicle of ordinary cognitive acts even though it never di-rectly becomes an object of one of them.[67]

From these remarks on the given element in knowledge, Buri draws the following cryptic conclusion:

This content of the generally demonstrable *Richtige* which is itself no longer gen-erally demonstrable and which first makes cognition possible we designate . . . . as the sphere of truth for faith and consequently as the sphere of truth which is re-lated to revelation. (I, p. 116.)

---

[65]*Ibid.*, pp. 13 f.

[66]This is not Buri's phrase but Dorothy Emmet's. (*The Nature of Metaphysical Thinking* (London: Macmillan and Co., 1945), p. 87.) It does, however, nicely catch the basic thrust of Buri's difficult argument. Significantly enough, Emmet's argument, which has certain similarities to Buri at this point, is based on an epistemological phenomenalism even though she is more optimistic about cognitive access to the non-objective than is Buri.

[67]I, pp. 115 f.

This statement is introduced so abruptly and with so little preparation that it requires some explanation. Surely Buri is not saying that theological truth is to be *identified* with the specific features of *Gehalt* and they structure the possibility of knowledge. That is, he could not mean that theological truth is the set of logical axioms presupposed in all logical thought, the reality given to be thought but not produced by the act of its being thought, or the transcendental condition of the act of knowledge. His point is obviously more indirect. The key is the word "sphere" used above. The points at which the limits of demonstrability appear are analogous to those points in theology in which the content of theology seems to break out of the possibility of formulation under the canons of scientific rationality. The possibility of theological language will, therefore, depend to a large extent on the formal possibility within scientific objectivity of a relationship between its *Gehalt*, the sphere analogous to *Wahrheit* in theology, and general demonstrability.

The question of a relationship between *Gehalt* and the specific results of objective cognition is not an indifferent question for scientific objectivity, for if there is no cognitive relation, then all forms of objective articulation become problematic. There could be no assurance that they are grounded in any reality, and even the results of the special sciences would be threatened by a kind of solipsistic void.[68] Buri claims that the actual success of demonstrability in the special sciences amounts to a pragmatic solution to this problem:

> The content *(Gehalt)* of knowledge as it has previously encountered us in the pre-givenness *(Vorgegebenheit)* of the logical, in the reality intended by

---

[68]Given the Kantian epistemological framework of Buri's theology, it is worth noting here that it was just this problem in relation to the *Ding-an-sich* that forced Kant to posit the notion of a *Bewusstsein überhaupt*. Yet, Kant could, on his own terms, only posit but not justify such a consciousness, and even its meaning remains questionable in his system. It certainly does not mean an ontological, supra-personal reality. But if it is not such a reality, then probably its only meaning is a pragmatic one, and that still leaves its ultimate basis in relation to the *Ding-an-sich* open to question. Just because Kant could only posit such a consciousness, it would probably be possible to interpret the move from Kant to idealism in terms of this problem. That is, it was the attempt to justify some intrinsic relation between intersubjective consciousness *(Bewusstsein überhaupt)* and its content (the *Ding-an-sich*) through the only medium left to a genuinely post-critical philosophy, namely, through thought or subjectivity alone. It is doubtful that any thinker who stands in the lineage of Kant and yet who has attempted to avoid the idealist move has been able to avoid this problem. Certainly Jaspers' concept of *Bewusstsein überhaupt* and Heidegger's notion of the pre-thetic givenness of a common *Lebenswelt* do not move beyond it. And Buri's answer (given below) is nothing more than a falling back on a quasi-pragmatic answer in view of the irresolvable dilemma presented by the subject-object structure of consciousness.

cognition, and in the unity of consciousness which enacts cognition raises a claim to be recognized. Recognition (*Anerkennung*), however, is only possible on the basis of cognition (*Erkennen*). What cannot be cognized cannot legitimately be recognized, for before I have cognized something, I do not know what I have recognized. But now, this content of knowledge, that which gives to knowledge possibility, substance, and reality, is such that it cannot be encapsulated in the generally demonstrable which belongs to the essence of scientific cognition . . . The possibility, substance, and reality of cognition are different from that which in cognition is knowable as generally demonstrable *Richtigkeit*. There is no identity between the two spheres; *but there is a correspondence (Korrespondenz) which we can comprehend, verify, and confirm.* And that which can be an object of generally demonstrable knowledge is nothing other than this correspondence of the two realms – the realm of the *Richtigen* which can be verified and the realm of that which we have provisionally designated as the claim to truth of faith relating itself to revelation. As a correspondence which is generally demonstrable, however, it must also be a cognitive object. This correspondence is generally demonstrable because what is at stake both for the objects of the natural sciences as well as for those of the historical and social sciences are logico-conceptually definable givens (*Grössen*). With the methods and the criteria of scientific cognition, the correspondencies (*Entsprechungen*) as well as the divergencies between conceptual operations and the therein intended states of affairs can be made comprehensible in their *Richtigkeit* – never conclusively and absolutely, but still as generally verifiable. This is the case necessarily, however, because only in this way can our engagement with the reality that announces itself to us, and which takes place in any case, be adequate. (I, pp. 116 f. My italics.)

In this way, through the specific results of knowing, the logical axioms of thought are operationally effective, the "given" of reality is structured so that it meets expectations, and the transcendental self is confirmed in its cognitive enactments. Whether logically or illogically, grounded or ungrounded, the conscious subject always does relate in some way to the reality which announces itself to him. Yet, it is never "that which it is for us apart from the hold we take on it," and this hold is always defined by the concepts and images in terms of which it is structured. "Without having to claim that we produce that which is reality for us, we can still say that by means of our standpoint in relation to it is decided whether we therein have to do with pure fantasy, with adequacy, or some mixture of the two." (I, p. 117.)

In an analogous manner, Buri now believes it is possible to say that the canons of scientific objectivity can serve as the *medium* for articulating theological truth. Just as the knower has no direct access to being-in-itself but can define the relation to it which conditions all his thinking only through the patient use of the conceptual tools he has, ever sensitive to their limits and to the encompassing ground which is always more than can be known directly, so the subject matter of theology gives the theologian no license to say anything he pleases but requires of him the same conceptual rigor. It is especially important to emphasize here that the canons of rationality and intelligibility are the *medium* of theological truth. They must not be *identified* with the truth the theologian seeks to elucidate. But given the dialectic that already obtains between the specific results of scientific knowing and the *Gehalt* which conditions this knowing, Buri believes an appropriately rigorous form of theological language is possible. An analogous dialectic between its non-objective *Gehalt* (its *Wahrheit*) and its objective form makes possible a critical stance toward the uncritical objective assertions of the theological tradition. At the same time, a critical self-consciousness about his own use of objective language (obj-B) allows the theologian to play off the objectivistic and subjectivistic forms of the traditional assertions against one another so that the "truth" they portray together for the existential enactment of faith can "show" through. His critical, reflexive awareness of his own language will prevent him, however, from confusing the medium through which the elucidation occurs and *what* is elucidated. "For all the difference between what is correct (*richtig*) and what is true, between logical clarity (*Einsichtigkeit*) and faith in revelation, the claim on truth of a faith which appeals to revelation can only be preserved from phantasy and mere assertion through the medium of generally demonstrable knowledge based on *Richtigkeit*." (I, p. 117.)

b. *The Self as Final Analogy for Conceptual Appropriateness*

The drive toward both sides of methodical appropriateness in scientific knowledge – the attempt to be free from all subjective presuppositions and the attempt to find categories appropriate to different states of affairs – is limited by the third "given" of general demonstrability, the transcendental self which is presupposed in all cognition but which never becomes a cognitive object.[69] Buri's notion here obviously traces back to Kant's idea of the transcendental unity of apperception. In Kant's theoretical philosophy, this transcendental ego tends to become a merely logical point necessitated by the transcendental method and presupposed in all acts of cognition. In opposition to this empty logical

---

[69]Cf., I, pp. 120 f.

point, Buri tries to interpret the transcendental ego in terms of the existential self embodied directly in all its concrete acts yet never reducible to them.[70] It is not a logical point because the unity it gives to concrete experience is not merely formal. It is the unity of just this (*je bestimmt*) historically situated self.[71] Buri tries to make this re-interpretation of Kant's notion because it is important for his concept of an existential self-understanding embodied in a concrete historicity. He wants to say that the intrinsic self can never be reduced to any series of objectively determined states. At the same time, the self is constituted by its embodiments; it *appears* in its concrete *Anschaulichkeiten*.[72] A self-understanding is not some esoteric, free-floating spiritual substance but the concrete embodiment of a man's historicity. Buri articulates this dialectic of "appearance in" yet "transcendence of" through the concepts of freedom and responsibility. Freedom and responsibility are non-objective because they can never be reduced to objective processes in the world (though such processes may be relevant to *how* a man decides freely and responsibly). Who the self is is constituted by the way it freely and responsibly understands itself in its historical situation, and its experience is organized by this non-objectifiable self-understanding. As Buri says, "what we term personality is the whole of such a nexus of meanings (*Bedeutungszusammenhangs*) organized around (*ausgerichtet auf*) a non-observable

---

[70]Buri tries to articulate this concept of the transcendental self through a play on the word *Anschauung* which is impossible to render in translation. He writes: "Seiner selbst inne wird das Ich aber nicht als eine bloss unanschauliche Abstraktheit, sondern als der Beziehungspunkt aller konkreten Anschaulichkeiten, in und mit denen es sich seiner selbst bewusst wird." He is clearly alluding here to the Kantian notion of intuition although the more ordinary meaning of *anschauen*, "to look at," should not be overlooked in view of the meaning he wants to attribute to *Anschaulichkeiten*. To the Kantian notion of possible experience originating in sensible intuition and structured by a formalized schema of concepts and a logical point in the ego, he wants to contrast a self embodied directly in its concrete experience but never reducible without remainder to it. He needs the Kantian idea of a transcendental self, but he wants to give an existential interpretation to it. Consequently, he plays on the word *Anschaulichkeit* which ordinarily means "vividness" or "perspicuity." He continues in this passage: "Diese Anschaulichkeiten gehören mit zum Ich, wenn sie auch nicht das Ich selber sind. Dadurch, dass sie in je bestimmter, geschichtlicher Situation zu einem Ich gehören, werden sie zu einem von einem Zentrum aus strukturierten Ganzen, und bekommen sie in diesem Ganzen ihre spezifische Bedeutung. Unser Denken und Erkennen mögen noch so abstrakt sein — stets ist es doch ein Denken von etwas und ein Erkennen als etwas, und deshalb erscheint das Ich stets in einer solchen konkreten Anschaulichkeit, die zu ihm gehört, und in der es doch nicht aufgeht." (I, pp. 121 f.)

[71]Cf., *ibid.*, p. 121.

[72]*Ibid.*, p. 122.

center and enacted in the consciousness of freedom and responsibility."
(I, p. 122.)[73]

This concrete yet transcendent center of personhood is the limiting
factor on methodical appropriateness. While methodical appropriateness
can be objectively determined up to a point, it is always determined finally by the centered self which actualizes the cognitive act yet never becomes an object of such appropriateness. In Buri's words:

> Without the presupposition of such personhood, cognitive appropriateness would
> be entirely impossible. For it is this personhood alone that can desire appropriate-
> ness. The self can desire it, however, only as that which the self itself is. There-
> fore, no matter what categories are used to carry it through, appropriateness is de-
> termined at the same time also by the personal center that is concerned with it.
> That means, however, that a judgment of appropriateness is always co-determined
> by the self-understanding of the knower. There is no merely objective knowledge.
> Were there, then it would mean it is possible to objectify this personal center. (I,
> p. 122.)

Buri insists that this does not mean that all knowledge is irretrievably
subjective.[74] There is no limitation on the objective determination of the
adequacy of concepts to subject matter. It does mean, however, that
knowledge is misunderstood if the will to truth (subjective appropriateness) or the engagement of the knower with his subject matter in the responsibility for appropriateness (objective appropriateness) is abstracted
from the act of knowing. In this sense, there is no *pure* objectivity as
though what is known has no relation to its being known. "In order to
be appropriate, it is not enough to explain the spatio-temporally measur-

---

[73]Aside from the concretely existential interpretation he gives the existential self, the
important point to note here is that Buri sees this self as "appearing" in and through its
concrete experience. He would insist that the transcendent dimension of the self not be
read as a "ghost in the machine". This would be a misreading resulting from a false
objectification of what he is here attempting to elucidate. He is not trying to separate
the self from its embodiments. But he is saying that who a self is is not reducible to
any series of external manifestations. The self always transcends any such series because
its embodiment is a manifestation of how it freely and responsibly decides to understand
itself, and this decision is not reducible to any series of conditions in the world. To say
he is separating the self into a kind of spiritual substance distinguished from its material
manifestations would be to objectify just the non-objectifiable center he is trying to elucidate. To avoid such a reading is the point of his argument that this elucidation of the
limits of knowledge results in no new objective knowledge but can effect a transformation of consciousness. At the point of such a misreading, Buri's argument is that the
self *is* its embodiment; who the self is is not separable from what the self becomes. But
its embodiment is the expression of a self-understanding which is non-objectifiably transcendent to any series of objectively specified terms or conditions.

[74]I, p. 123.

able with quantitative categories and to understand the spiritually understandable with qualitative categories. More than that, explanation and understanding must, rather, derive from, be accompanied and be carried by that insertion of personal responsibility without which the most exact explanation and the most congenial understanding can be deaf and blind to the content of an appearance in just this specific hour." (I, pp. 123 f.)

From this Buri draws the conclusion that this non-objective center of personhood is the basis of all analogies between concept and subject matter. "Behind all analogies erected by thought and elaborated cognitively is the analogy of personal consciousness which is the ground (*Ursprung*) for all analogy. That is the genuine *analogia entis*." (I, p. 122.)[75] Again, Buri's meaning is not entirely clear. His choice of terms is somewhat unfortunate because a single thing can never be an analogy. Obviously, he means that the non-objective, centered self is the basis upon which all analogies are erected. All objective analogies, no matter what cognitive independence they may claim, finally rest on the self-understanding of the knower. Unless this is taken into account and related to the limits of knowledge, then the putatively objective knowledge claimed by a use of analogy hangs in the air. It either becomes mythological or itself requires interpretation in terms of the non-objective act of the knower.

However questionable and unclear Buri's brief remarks about analogy may be as an exhaustive account of conceptual thinking, his remarks here are directly applicable to an existentialist theological hermeneutic. The problem with traditional uses of analogy in theology, according to Buri, is that they have attempted to make theological statements objectively independent, on the basis of either a purely rational analogy of being in speculative idealism, or an analogy of being between the natural and the supernatural (and thus ultimately based on the teaching office of the church) in Catholic theology, or an analogy of faith based on the objective, once-for-allness of the incarnation and the testimony of the Holy Spirit in neo-orthodoxy.[76] They are thereby exposed to the criticism by scientific thinking of subjective bias and objective question-begging. Even traditional protestantism's strong emphasis on "the experiential and personal character of faith as the presupposition of dogmatics" is open to the objection of confusing 'the unobservability (*Unanschaulichkeit*) of the personal with its observable (*anschaulichen*) appearances." (I, p. 125.) The only way out of these difficulties is to see that all objective

[75]Cf., also, *ibid*., pp. 124-126.
[76]Cf., *Ibid*.

claims and assertions in theology have the ground of their methodical appropriateness solely in the fully non-objective act of personal existence. In this way, the limit of the transcendental self on subjective and objective appropriateness provides Buri with his fundamental hermeneutical category of "self-understanding." The non-objective act of the existential self, which is totally *unanschauliche*, is the analogical basis for theological language in the sense that all objectively articulated assertions in theology have no independent status in themselves but become hermeneutically significant only to the extent that they can be interpreted as expressive of the structure of the self's existentiality.

Here Buri builds into the foundations of his mature theology the same reversal he earlier suggested in his dekerygmatizing essay: nothing objective, be it a belief, a doctrinal or metaphysical claim, or an event, is the basis for faith; rather the reality of faith which is a non-objective self-understanding is the basis and the only reference for all theological objectivity, either events or ideas.[77] The radical implications this has for a theological hermeneutic become evident when one realizes that it extends even to the once-for-all event of Jesus Christ or the incarnation which Christian theology has traditionally taken to be the objective foundation of faith. Many so-called radical theologies have equivocated at this point by saying that the objective event of Jesus Christ (or an objective metaphysical interpretation of it) cannot be *understood* unless related to the existential character of faith but that in some sense such an event is still the *basis* of faith.[78] This is an equivocation, Buri sees, because it is impossible to maintain this kind of basis for faith without at some point refusing to relinquish an objective ground outside of the existentiality of faith. And such an objective ground will always be hermeneutically opaque, the hanging on to some hermeneutically unreconstructed core which is then inconsistenty taken as the basis for other hermeneutical reconstructions. It will always, that is, involve a radical theology in some form of special pleading. Buri, therefore, intends the reversal in a fully consistent way: nothing objective provides the basis of faith; rather, the non-objectivity of faith is the basis for interpreting everything objective

[77]Cf., EoE, p. 97 and *supra,* pp. 11 f.

[78]This equivocation occurs in Bultmann, Gogarten, Ebeling, Ott, and throughout the "new quest for the historical Jesus."

[79]To say that the non-objectivity of faith must be the basis for interpreting everything objective in theology does not entail that faith is its own basis, i.e., Feuerbach's position. It simply means that the basis for faith cannot be located outside the non-objectivity of its enactment.

in theology, and the basis of faith must be understood in an entirely different fashion.[79]

Only if there is absolute clarity over Buri's meaning at this point is it
possible to appreciate the full radically of his proposal to interpret all
theological doctrines as expressions of the Christian self-understanding.
While it does not fully explicate how this proposal can be carried
through, his understanding of the foundation of theological analogy in
the transcendental limit imposed on subjective and objective appropriateness is the basis for the theological importance he gives to the concept
of self-understanding.

c. Historicity as the Unconditioned Point in Relativism

Buri finds the limit intrinsic to relativity and open-endedness in the
historicity of the knower. Relativity and open-endedness as operational
principles in any particular area of knowledge define not so much a self-
conscious method the knower follows as the nature of such knowledge itself. They reflect the unending desire to extend knowledge and to attain
exact results through appropriate methodologies. Taken as descriptive
norms, however, they become empty and Pickwickian. The most obvious
example is historicism which elevates relativity as an operational principle into a description of knowledge *per se*. The statement, "all knowledge is historically conditioned," is apparently a knowledge claim which
is not historically conditioned.

While the principle of historical relativity may be objectively untenable for this reason, Buri argues that the movement of thought leading
to it can effect a transcending consciousness of the historicity of the
knower, of "the historicity within history." Intended as an elucidation of
the "inwardness of knowledge" this movement of thought at the limits of
knowledge is not merely empty and paradoxical. (I, p. 128.) Rather, Buri says, "in this dissolution of every demonstrable (*begründbar*) standpoint, it can make us aware of that position (*Ort*) we have always already
assumed (*den wir ... bezogen haben*) when in thought we become
conscious of ourselves and proceed to know, namely, the position of our
historicity." (I, p. 128.) He goes on to explain that

before we can call everything into question, we have always already taken (*bezogen*) a position from the point of which everything, including this position, can first
be called into question .... For all the relativity and open-endedness of knowledge
... there always remains the point to which these principles are related and on
which their self-dissolution is enacted. My real situation first comes to conscious-

ness in these principles and through these movements of thought which dissolve them. (I, pp. 128 f.)

What, then, is one's real situation? It is the unconditioned element in historically situated existence which remains despite the relativity and open-endedness of all historically situated knowledge. In other words, Buri claims that there is a point in one's presence to the world which is no longer relative and open-ended even though it cannot be objectively demonstrated. It is the point of the "inwardness of thought" in which the thinker

unconditionally assumes *(übernimmt)* his situation in all its conditionedness. This enactment of the unconditionedness of self-understanding is what we mean by the unsearchable *(nicht mehr erforschbaren)* historicity in the sphere of researchable *(erforschbaren)* history. (I, p. 129.)

This is the point where, so to speak, relativity and open-endedness are dissolved in fact rather than in ideality. It is the point amidst the contingencies of history where a person takes his relative situation upon himself and decides how he will understand himself. It is unconditioned because, located in an objectively relative situation, it is not reducible to any series of relative conditions. While objective reasons might be given for one's understanding, the decision itself cannot be reduced to them.[80] The concept of historicity, thus, serves to indicate that point in knowing in which the relativity and open-endedness of knowledge are transcended by an unconditioned point in the act of knowing itself – even when the result of that act is the acknowledgment of one's relative standpoint.

The notion of historicity is doubly important for Buri's hermeneutic. On the one hand, the concept of historicity is correlative with the concept of self-understanding. Although the epistemological basis for the hermeneutical significance of the concept of self-understanding is the purely empty movement of thought which elucidates the transcendental self in all knowing, a self-understanding itself never occurs as an empty or abstract movement but always in the thickness of historical embodiment. Self-understanding or faith is always qualified by its historicity because it

---

[80]This transcendence of the non-objective self over the objectively determinable conditions of its situation is what Buri means by "unconditioned" and "unconditionedness." It is "unconditioned" only in the sense that no series of conditioned, objective viewpoints can *finally* determine the stance a self takes toward them. That the self is or can be unconditioned in this way is, thus, the basis for personal responsibility. Buri's meaning is reminiscent of Kant's understanding of freedom as unconditioned because it cannot be accounted for under the phenomenal *conditions* of theoretical reason.

is always historically situated. In the case of the Christian self-understanding, this means that faith is situated by the Christian tradition in its objective expressions. Despite the way in which his criticism of objectivity relativizes the absolutistic expressions of theological objectivity, Buri sees no transcendent standpoint from which he can himself make absolutistic claims. All he can do is interpret the objective expressions of the tradition in terms of the non-objective structure of faith. To claim more for his interpretation would be again to fall into a false objectivity.

On the other hand, it is precisely this correlation between historicity and the non-objectivity of self-understanding that allows Buri to appropriate the objective forms of the tradition while avoiding the untenable character of their objectivity. When objectively articulated theological assertions are interpreted without taking account of the historicity they express, the relativity and open-endedness of scientific objectivity dissolves the content of faith into an "infinite approximation process" which falsifies the nature of faith, and, therefore, falsifies the theological content of faith.[81] If, however, the objective form of traditional statements is taken as expressing the historicity of the act of faith itself, then this need not be the case. The same reversal as above again occurs: instead of an independent and, therefore, relativized objectivity being the basis of the historicity of faith, the historicity of faith, the unconditioned point in all acts of knowledge is the content to which admittedly relative objective statements give expression. This does not mean that the objective form (obj-B) of the theologian's own interpretive language escapes the relativity and open-endedness of scientific objectivity. But according to Buri, unlike the objective form of the traditional language, his own interpretive language does not claim an independent and absolute objective status but is rather a reflexive language that points out the true content in the historicity of faith of the putatively independent objectivity of the traditional language. The relativity and open-endedness of the theologian's own language is not debilitating as long as he does not claim any independent objective status for it. Its purpose is to indicate how the objective form of the traditional language expresses not an independent objectivity but the historicity which is the non-objective content in all acts of knowing – even in those which, *per impossible* for theological language, legitimately express an independent objectivity. The non-objective historicity of his own interpretive language appears in the fact that he is

----

[81]This is why Kierkegaard was driven to the method of indirect communication.

a Christian theologian who, in order to articulate the content of faith, cannot transcend the historicity of the Christian self-understanding.[82]

E. BURI'S CLARIFICATION OF THE PROBLEM OF OBJECTIVITY

At the beginning of this chapter, it was stated that any adequate clarification of "the problem of objectivity" in theology must meet two criteria. Buri's analysis of the relationship between various levels of objectivity and knowledge is successful in meeting each of them. The first criterion involved a clear recognition of the difference between the non-objectivity of faith and the inevitably objective character of theological language. There cannot even begin to be clarity over the hermeneutical implications of the problem of objectivity if this distinction is blurred. Buri meets this criterion easily. Indeed, it defines the main problem of his theology. He believes that his most important contribution to the contemporary theological discussion is the recognition of the hermeneutical centrality of the non-objectivity of faith and its content. To develop this recognition into a consistent hermeneutic that covers the entire range of theological interpretation, however, he must deal with the problem of how the non-objectivity of faith can be expressed in the necessarily objective form of theological language. It is now apparent that this problem and, thus, the first criterion stand in the background of all his methodological reflections.

The second criterion, by requiring a delineation of the conditions of objectivity as such, follows closely from the recognition of this problem. Taking the non-objectivity of faith as the hermeneutical norm of theological interpretation allows and requires a criticism of the uncritical objective language in the theological tradition. It is precisely this critical perspective on mythological, speculative, and doctrinal ways of speaking that makes the problem of objectivity so hermeneutically fruitful. But because even a critical theological language must also be objective, it is necessary to specify the conditions of objectivity in general so that it is then possible to show how objectivity as such is a problem even while there is also a legitimate way of speaking objectively in theology. Buri meets this criterion with his distinction between the objective structure

---

[82]Cf., Buri's article "Theologie zwischen — oder mit Jaspers und Heidegger" (*SthUm*, 30 (Juli, 1960), pp. 83 ff.) where he critizes Jaspers' notion of "philosophical faith" for a failure to take seriously enough into account the historicity of the philosopher himself.

of consciousness, the condition of objectivity in general, and the conditions of knowledge which presuppose the subject-object structure. It is then possible for him to show how objectivity as such is a problem for theologies that do not take critical account of the structure of consciousness and, thus, seek to give their objective assertions an objectively independent status; at the same time his discussion of the limits of knowledge lays the foundations for showing how objective theological language is possible in theology without falling into the same pitfalls.

These criteria are not, however, the criteria for an adequate hermeneutic. They do nothing more than lay down the norms that must be met for a clarification of *what* the problem of objectivity is. It is quite another matter actually to develop a hermeneutic on the basis of this clarity. Once it is evident that objectivity presents a theological problem that can be clearly formulated, the really important questions concern the adequacy of the hermeneutic based on it. Only when these questions are answered will it be possible to say how and to what degree the problem of objectivity should form the background of a radical theology.

Buri's discussion of the problem of objectivity and the limits of knowledge is not yet such a hermeneutic but only the beginnings of one. His clarification of the conditions of objectivity in general gives him a basis for criticizing the falsely objective (objectivistic and subjectivistic) forms of the tradition. The decisive question for any radical theology at this point is how the conditions of objectivity in general both allow this criticism and at the same time warrant the theologian's own objective language. A general principle for an existentialist theology would seem to be that an answer to this question can only be given if a way can be shown for the objectivity of theological language to take account directly of the non-objectivity of faith. This is the intention of Buri's treatment of the limits of obj-A and obj-B. At each of the four features of objectivity, he shows how a structure analogous to the non-objectivity of faith is reflected in the use of objectivity itself. These four points converge on a single rule that is the basis of Buri's hermeneutic: *a false objectivity in theological language can be avoided if the uncritical objectivistic and subjectivistic forms of the theological tradition are denied their putative, independent objective status and their sole content is seen to lie in the way they bring to expression various facets of the non-objectivity of faith itself.*

In order to see how Buri develops this rule into an actual hermeneutic it is necessary in the next two chapters to turn to his concepts of faith and revelation and to his theory of symbol and myth. The crucial question is whether Buri can implement this hermeneutical rule in such a way that the objectivity of theological language can give content to the non-objectivity of faith. If he cannot answer this question satisfactorily, then it will be impossible for his theology to avoid the problem of Kierkegaard's indirect communication, and the fruitfulness of the problem of objectivity for a radical theology will be open to serious reservations. This question will increasingly focus the evaluation of Buri's hermeneutic in the following pages.

CHAPTER III

THE NON-OBJECTIVITY OF FAITH AND REVELATION

When Buri criticizes objectivistic forms of traditional theological discourse, he often uses Barth and Schleiermacher to illustrate the modern forms of these problems. His criticism of Barth's "metaphysic of revelation" follows obviously from his position on the subject-object structure of consciousness. But his criticism of Schleiermacher is another matter. Indeed, aside from the general concern to show that the Christian faith can be reinterpreted intelligibly for the conceptuality of modern man, Buri's most obvious continuity with nineteenth century liberalism is his adoption of the same *Glaubenslehre* principle which has been the pervasive methodological theme of all non-speculative liberal theology since Schleiermacher first brilliantly defined it. This principle states that the reference of all religious language is to the self, to the states, dispositions, or self-consciousness of the believing man, rather than to states of affairs independent of the self. To use Buri's language, the task of theology on the basis of the *Glaubenslehre* principle is to interpret all theological doctrines exhaustively in terms of the "self-understanding of faith," not to describe objective matters independent of faith.

The parallel between Buri and Schleiermacher stands out even more sharply on closer inspection. The "self-reference"[1] of theological language in Buri's basic hermeneutical principle seems nothing more than a precise contemporary repristination of Schleiermacher's formula that „Chris-

---

[1] In ordinary English, "self-reference" designates language that refers to itself. The following discussion will depart from this usage and use this phrase as a *terminus technicus* to mean "the *Glaubenslehre* principle that theological language has its content solely in references to the faith of the believing man, hence, in references to the self."

[2] Friedrich Schleiermacher, *Der christliche Glaube*, II Bände herausgegeben von Martin Redeker (Berlin: Walter de Gruyter & Co., siebente Auflage auf Grund der zweiten Auflage und kritischer Prüfung des Textes, 1969), I, p. 105. ET: *The Christian Faith*, tran. H. R. Macintosh and J. S. Steward (Edingburgh: T. an T. Clark, 1928), p. 76. (Hereinafter the German edition will be abbreviated by *DcG* and the English translation by *CF*. Where the translation is mine, the German reference is given first.)

tian doctrines are accounts of the Christian religious affective states (*Gemütszustände*) set forth in speech."[2] And the principles of self-consciousness in the latter and self-understanding in the former both issue from attempts to come to terms with the problem of objectivity.[3] Furthermore, even though Schleiermacher developed his dogmatic system in such a way that he was not restricted to statements about the self alone but also attempted to speak about God and the world,[4] he emphatically stated that in the final analysis the latter two kinds of assertions "must be reduced to propositions of that first form before we can be safe from the insinuation of alien and purely scientific propositions." He continued that in a complete "analysis of Christian piety" the "other two forms might be entirely set aside as superfluous."[5] He justified his own use of all three forms because "at present" the fully consistent procedure would lack historical continuity and ecclesiastical usefulness.[6] One is led to wonder, however, whether Schleiermacher would any longer hold to his "at present" in a more secular time such as our own. Perhaps ecclesiastical usefulness can be attained today only through the fully consistent application from which Schleiermacher drew back. It would appear, at least, that Buri is attempting to apply the *Glaubenslehre* principle without Schleiermacher's reservations.

But if this is the case, how can his own theology avoid his "subjectivistic" charge against such theologies?[7] And if he can, how can he still give an interpretation of the *content* of faith (the "what" of faith and not merely its "that") in the objective language of his own hermeneutic? Having made clear that neither faith nor revelation *in themselves* can be understood in terms of an objective content of doctrinal assertions descriptive of an objectively defined state of affairs either independent of the self (objectivism) or internal to the self (subjectivism), Buri must show

---

[3]Cf., Schleiermacher, *DcG*, I and *CF*, paragraphs 3-5. Cf., also, Paul Löffler, "Selbstbewusstsein und Selbstverständnis als theologische Prinzipien bei Schleiermacher und Bultmann," in *Kerygma und Dogma*, 2. Jahrgang (1956), p. 308.

[4]Cf., Schleiermacher, *DcG*, I, pp. 163-164 (*CF*, pp. 125-126).

[5]Schleiermacher, *CF*, p. 126 (*DcG*, I, p. 165).

[6]*Ibid.*

[7]By "subjectivism" Buri does not mean the same thing as Feuerbach's thesis that theology is anthropology — although Buri would agree that "subjectivism" might have this consequence under certain conditions. It cannot be emphasized strongly enough that, despite attempts to demonstrate otherwise on the part of Barth and others, neither Buri nor Schleiermacher see this *Glaubenslehre* move as the reduction of theology to anthropology and nothing more. Both of them seek to preserve the dimension of transcendence, but they agree that it cannot be treated like an object of cognitive apprehension. Cf., I, pp. 217-219 and II, pp. 19-23, 31-33.

how the objectivity of theological language can *appropriately* grasp the non-objective content of its subject matter. While his analysis of objectivity and non-objectivity may make his understanding of the nature of faith and revelation superior to Schleiermacher's theory, it is still difficult to see how the *theological interpretation* of faith and revelation can avoid the purely formal difficulty of subjectivism for which he criticizes Schleiermacher. It is highly relevant then to compare the self-reference of theological language in Schleiermacher and Buri to see why Buri thinks his existentialist concept of self-understanding avoids the problems in Schleiermacher's interpretation of faith under the concept of self-consciousness. This is particularly important because a common theme running through existentialist theology has been the claim that the existential understanding of faith, made possible by a critical awareness of the problem of objectivity, is what enables a contemporary neo-liberalism to move beyond the shortcomings of nineteenth century liberalism.[8]

A. THE SELF-REFERENCE OF THEOLOGICAL LANGUAGE
IN SCHLEIERMACHER'S CONCEPT OF SELF-CONSCIOUSNESS

As Buri interprets it, liberalism's most important methodological contribution was the argument that theology could no longer take its starting point and its principles of development from a combination of scripture, confession, and natural theology but must turn to general epistemological considerations in order first to provide a hermeneutical framework for interpreting these traditional sources. In Schleiermacher and the heritage of liberal theology that followed him, this approach culminated in the idea of a religious consciousness ingredient in human consciousness in general.[9] Schleiermacher based his understanding of the religious self-consciousness on the concept of *Gefühl* or "feeling" which, as a state of receptivity, is ontologically prior to and the ground of knowing and doing. The prius of relation between man and God then becomes the condition of total receptivity or the feeling of absolute dependence.

[8]Because of the strong reaction against the nineteenth century, contemporary theologians have been extremely hesitant to describe themselves as liberals. But with the perspective of time and despite common roots with neo-orthodoxy in the dialectical theology of the 1920's, it now seems beyond question that almost all Protestant theology outside the direct influence of Barth has been strongly continuous with nineteenth century liberalism. This judgment includes Tillich, Bultmann, Ebeling, Fuchs, the "new quest," and, of course, Buri.

[9]Cf., II, pp. 121-125, 308-317.

Such a state of total receptivity, however, is never given *for conscious-ness* in a pure and unadulterated form because man's determinate states of consciousness are always an intermixture of receptivity and activity. Man's religious self-consciousness or his God-consciousness is always specified, therefore, in terms of determinate states of his general self-consciousness.[10] This supplies Schleiermacher with a basis for distinguishing the God-consciousness of mankind in general into various specific religions. Because the feeling of absolute dependence is never given as such, various religions arise from the different ways the general religious self-consciousness of mankind is specified under the determinate conditions of self-consciousness in diverse times and places. The task of Christian theology becomes that of isolating the uniqueness of the Christian specification of God-consciousness and of interpreting doctrines in terms of it.[11] Since a direct knowledge of God is excluded in this understanding of consciousness, doctrines must be self-referring, having their reference in the expression they give to a determinate form of self-consciousness and the modifications of the self included under it.

Buri argues that the results of Schleiermacher's approach to theology become especially prominent in the doctrine of reconciliation. It is under this heading that traditional, supernaturalistic theology tried to conceive the manner in which salvation had been wrought in Christ apart from its appropriation in faith. Insofar as the more modern approach of Schleiermacher is an attempt not only to escape supernaturalism but also to give a better account of the import of doctrines for the subjectivity of the believer, the changes this approach involves will be nowhere more apparent than in the doctrine of reconciliation. But here Buri sees the subjectivizing tendency of such theology because its systematic principle demands that the reconciling work of Christ not be interpreted apart from the general conditions definitive of human self-consciousness as such.[12]

Following his basic hermeneutical principle, Schleiermacher says that all "statements concerning Christ" must be seen as "immediate expressions of our Christian self-consciousness." Any other treatment of Christ not so related to this self-consciousness is "lacking in purely dogmatic content."[13] Schleiermacher does affirm the "veritable (*eigentliches*) being of God" in Christ "as the constant strength of his God-consciousness"

---

[10] Cf., Schleiermacher, *DcG*, I, and *CF*, paragraph 5.
[11] *Ibid.*, paragraphs 7-15.
[12] II, pp. 123, 127-128.
[13] Schleiermacher, *DcG*, II, pp. 30-31 (*CF*, p. 372).

which distinguishes him from other men,[14] and he does not hesitate to speak of the "act (*Tat*) of the redeemer."[15] In line with this more objective understanding of Christ, he also says that Christ's work (*Geschäft*) consists in assuming "believers into the strength of his God-consciousness."[16] But the peculiarity of the Christian religion is its teleological character which for Schleiermacher means that the stages of Christian piety must "appear in our self-consciousness as our own acts belonging to our individual lives." This characteristic can be reconciled with the other peculiarity of the Christian religion that the challenge (*Forderung*) to the higher stage of religious self-consciousness must also be "grasped in our self-consciousness as the act of the redeemer" only by seeing the redeeming challenge as "*the act of the Redeemer become our own act.*"[17] Concerning this crucial move in Schleiermacher's doctrine of redemption, Buri comments that the "objective moment contained in speaking about the being of God in Christ and about the act of the redeemer is thus completely drawn into the subjectivity of the Christian pious self-consciousness." (II, p. 309.)

The problem Buri sees in Schleiermacher is not this attempt to assimilate the content of doctrines into the inwardness of faith (since this move parallels the basic move of Buri's hermeneutic) but the fact that the conceptuality on which it depends leads him to a false objectification of the inwardness of faith and thus to a loss of the transcending existentiality of faith. Buri does not make the mistake of interpreting Schleiermacher's concept of feeling as a merely psychological category; he sees that for Schleiermacher it was a fundamentally ontological concept. Because this ontological condition is specified for self-consciousness only in terms of determinate states and because only these states are accessible to theological description, the relationship between the feeling of absolute dependence and the theological interpretation of the states of religious self-consciousness in any particular religion is analogous to the relationship in Buri between the non-objectivity of faith itself and the objectivity of theological language which structures faith in the objective forms of a theological tradition. Schleiermacher's error, however, was to conceive of the underlying structure of religion, the feeling of absolute dependence, as an objective ontological condition constitutive of human nature as such. For Buri, faith can never be such a condition because it is an exis-

---

[14]Schleiermacher, *DcG*, II, p. 43 (*CF*, p. 385).
[15]Schleiermacher, *CF*, p. 425 (*DcG*, II, p. 90).
[16]Schleiermacher, *DcG*, II, p. 90 (*CF*, p. 425).
[17]*Ibid*. My italics.

tential process of becoming never given as such but actualized only in the acts of self-definition. Whenever faith is conceived as an ontological condition, it is epistemologically falsified by being brought under the subject-object structure of consciousness (obj-A), and then it is impossible to gain a proper understanding of the existential actuality of faith as a transcending of this structure. Buri claims, then, that Schleiermacher's fundamental theological concept represents a false objectification of the nature of religion despite the rejection of supernatural objectivity which he shares with Buri.[18]

The subjectivism of Schleiermacher's actual interpretations of traditional doctrines (obj-B) follows inevitably, according to Buri, from this fundamental misconstruing of the nature of faith. Even if the feeling of absolute dependence is not a psychological category, Schleiermacher's interpretation of *determinate states* of religious self-consciousness was psychological, Buri argues, because the feeling of absolute dependence receives its specification in self-consciousness only in terms of determinate psychological states which can be theologically interpreted. The specific contents of faith are conceived in terms of objectively definable states of subjectivity, and this is what Buri terms subjectivism, in Schleiermacher's case, a "psychologizing" form of subjectivism. So again as at the level of obj-A, Schleiermacher's lack of an existentialist conceptuality leads to a false objectification of the existential process of faith at the level of theological interpretation (obj-B). Faith is misconstrued by having its content encapsulated in objectively given states of the self.[19]

Buri draws two further criticisms from these basic ones. These center on the German word *verfügbar* which, as Buri uses it, means calculable, given, manipulable, at one's disposal. One of the lasting influences the neo-orthodox theological revolution of the twentieth century has had on all contemporary theology is the recovery of the radical Reformation understanding of the grace of God, and this has meant a renewed appreciation of the *Unverfügbarkeit* of God and of His gift of faith. Existentially interpreted in radical theology, this means that neither faith nor its ground are subject to the control and manipulation of objective consciousness but transcend the very conditions of objectivity. In Schleiermacher, to the contrary, faith becomes *verfügbar* because it is conceived in terms of objectively given states of the self. But faith is an existential process which must be enacted ever anew, and it is, therefore, *unverfügbar* in the sense

[18]Cf., I, pp. 213-215.
[19]Cf., I, pp. 211-216; II, pp. 314-317.

that it is never given as objectively determinable states of the self.[20] The same thing occurs with the ground of faith when it is brought under the conditions of consciousness as an ontological condition. Despite Schleiermacher's attempt to conceive God as transcendent to consciousness, his view of the underlying ground of religion leads him to define the *relationship* between man and God so that it becomes *verfügbar* for the religious consciousness.[21] But in Buri's view, the relational "other" of faith must be as non-objective and *unverfügbar* as faith itself.[22]

There is no question about the cogency of these criticisms of Schleiermacher, and it should be obvious that a conceptuality based on an existential dialectic offers a much sounder understanding of faith than was possible in liberal theology. Still the similarity, at least at a purely formal level, is unmistakable between Buri and Schleiermacher. Having oriented their methodological principles on the problem of objectivity (i.e., the assumption of the complete *Jenseitigkeit* and *Unverfügbarkeit* of God and his acts in contrast to the conditions of human consciousness),[23] they both feel compelled to make the same move, namely, to argue that all doctrines must be interpreted entirely in terms of a factor in human subjectivity which is also transcendent to the *Wechselwirkung* of subject and object. Furthermore, Buri agrees with the theological motive lying behind Schleiermacher's approach. He says:

> If the reconciliation of the sinner with God handed down in the tradition as an objective, saving event is to be that which in all events it also is in essence, namely, a transformation of the inmost situation of the believer, then it must represent a reality in the sphere of subjectivity. It cannot remain the mere objectivity of the divine saving event. (II, p. 315.)

Even though Buri believes his concept of self-understanding is more radical and more adequate than Schleiermacher's concept of self-consciousness, the really crucial question is whether his understanding of faith will permit him to avoid the same criticism he makes of Schleiermacher. If Schleiermacher's "psychologism" is inadequate, is it possible for Buri to

---

[20]Cf., I, pp. 217-223.
[21]Cf., I, pp. 211-223; II, pp. 127-128, 314-317.
[22]I, pp. 219-223.
[23]Cf., Löffler, pp. 308-314. In Schleiermacher the problem of objectivity is construed in terms of the reciprocity of receptivity and self-activity in all determinate states of consciousness. The problem in the awareness of God which leads him to argue for an immediate self-consciousness of total receptivity is quite similar to Buri's problem of the subject-object structure of consciousness. Cf., Schleiermacher, *DcG*, I, pp. 23 ff. (*CF*, pp. 12 ff.).

implement the theological task without some other form of subjectivism at the level of theological interpretation?

B. THE SELF-REFERENCE OF THEOLOGICAL LANGUAGE IN
BURI'S CONCEPT OF SELF-UNDERSTANDING

1. Faith as a General Human Possibility

Like Schleiermacher, Buri also conceives faith in terms of a general human possibility though as a non-objective possibility it is not an onto-logical structure of human being as such. He then, also like Schleierma-cher, interprets the Christian faith as one among any number of possible self-understandings in which this general possibility can receive historis-tic specification. He calls faith a self-*understanding* in order to emphasize both its analogy with and its difference from the liberal idea of religious consciousness. Since Schleiermacher's error arose from his definition of faith in terms of consciousness, a more adequate conception will become evident when self-understanding is contrasted with consciousness.

Human consciousness achieves cognitive form, Buri argues, in two dif-ferent types of scientific apprehension, explanation (*Erklären*) and under-standing (*Verstehen*). Explanation deals with objects quantitatively. Un-derstanding, in contrast, deals with that dimension of scientific objects which does not admit of quantification. It is the proper approach, in par-ticular, to the specifically human spheres of reality, especially to history. It is concerned with the unique and individual. Ideally this means no compromise with the rigor expected in explanation, for understanding al-so seeks to subsume its data under general unifying principles and to place them in the context of encompassing schemas and models.[24] Despite the important differences between them, the crucial point for Buri is their identity when it comes to the objective structure of consciousness. Each is immanent to the subject-object structure. Speaking of under-standing in particular, he says that "understanding as an *under*-standing (*Ver-stehen*) stands in the subject-object dichotomy, presupposes an ob-ject which stands over against a subject as something other and a subject which in making statements about this object does not make statements about itself but makes them precisely about this object." (I, p. 137. My italics.) This is the common feature which makes it possible to charac-

---

[24]Cf., I, pp. 136-137.

terize both by the same generic features of all scientific knowledge, namely, the drive toward "the conceptual-logical objectivity of generally demonstrable *Richtigkeit.*" (I, p. 137.)

Buri argues that faith is not mere emotion or attitude but is a form of cognitive apprehension on a continuum with understanding. It is an understanding of oneself given in the immediacy of being who one is. But the continuum breaks down, and self-understanding receives a logically odd cognitive status because understanding becomes quite different when in self-understanding "the one who understands himself [becomes] the object of his understanding." (I, p. 137.) Here Buri gives classic expression to the conceptual difficulty which lies at the heart of every existentialist philosophy.

Either the knower no longer deals with himself as the one who really enacts the cognitive act but only with an objective representation of himself. Or in understanding, it is really a question of an understanding of himself in and with the enactment of understanding. But then objective cognition ceases because the understanding cannot once again make itself an object of its immediate enactment. Made into an object, self-understanding is already something different from the immediacy of its enactment. (I, pp. 137-138.)

Understanding thus reaches its limit in this conceptual dilemma presented by self-understanding. Yet here, Buri argues, understanding attains its proper authenticity because the conceptually circular statement of the problem can in fact force the thinker out of the realm of conceptual objectivity (i.e., the realm of possibility and unending relativity) and into the actuality of his own existence where he must freely and responsibly decide how he understands *himself*.[25] Self-understanding is given solely in its enactment by the knower himself. As Buri defines it more closely:

That it is up to me that I understand myself, that for all my conditionedness and dependence I am at the same time free, that I am responsible for how and as what I understand myself, that according to whether and how I take this responsibility upon myself I can realize myself or fail to come to myself *(mich verfehlen)*, that depending on whether or not I am a person my existence *(Dasein)* has value and meaning or becomes worthless and meaningless – all that cannot be resolved *(entscheiden)* and justified *(ausweisen)* objectively. Rather, I decide *(entscheide)* thereon precisely in the enactment of my self-understanding, in the manner that I understand myself and am that which I understand myself to be. (I, p. 138.)

Buri believes this concept of a non-objective self-understanding to be a more adequate conception of faith than Schleiermacher's concept of self-

25*Ibid.*, pp. 133 f., 138.

consciousness because it does not stop short with the immanence of consciousness. It is that dimension in the actualization of personhood transcendent to the objectivity of worldly immanence, and consequently, it avoids the subjectivism Buri finds in Schleiermacher. Like Schleiermacher's concept of self-consciousness however, there is nothing intrinsically religious about the concept of self-understanding, up to this point, that would justify as a concept of faith. To equate it with faith, it would be necessary to argue, as Schleiermacher does, that the relationship to God which cannot be located in the *Wechelwirkung* of subject and object can be located in this dimension of human subjectivity. It is necessary, therefore, for Buri to ground the purely general and religiously neutral concept of self-understanding in such a way that it can become the systematic principle of a theology. His theology requires a systematic principle analogous to the feeling of absolute dependence which was Schleiermacher's systematic principle and which gave him a religious ground for the theological assessment of affective states.

2. Human Existence as Grace: Buri's Systematic Principle

Buri bases his systematic principle on the claim that the enactment of self-understanding is not self-positing but is always grounded in a relationship to Transcendence. Writing of the limits of knowledge which lay the foundation for his concept of faith, he says:

> In so far I so [i.e., at the limits of knowledge] become conscious of my freedom, I experience myself simultaneously related *(gebunden)* to a non-objective reality *(ein Ungegenständliches)* which encounters me in my personhood as the truth and for which I must decide in my historistic situation. Here it can occur that the objectively correct and the historically relative *(das Gegenständlich-Richtige, Historisch-Relative)* become transparent for the Transcendence which is other than me. (I, p. 134.)

In the empty movement of thought at the limits of knowledge, objective consciousness founders.[26] "In such foundering of all objective explanation

---

[26]Foundering (*Scheitern*) is a term used by Jaspers to indicate the ultimate impossibility for finite existence and thought to attain any kind of absolute and final ground of security. It is used to describe the final human "situation." Foundering can take place in a multitude of modes one of which is the dialectical movement of thought leading to an objectively empty transcending for thought. This is the particular mode to which Buri appeals here. This movement throws the thinker back into the actuality of his own exis-

and understanding," Buri says, "[this movement of thought] at the same time transcends into the non-objective. But as a transcending into the non-objective, it experiences itself related to Transcendence." Self-understanding is thereby "qualified as faith through its relatedness to Transcendence." (I, p. 138.) Just as Schleiermacher could argue that determinate states of feeling are always qualifications of and are qualified by the feeling of absolute dependence so that these feelings can be interpreted as a relationship to God, Buri can continue with the following statement:

tence. For Jaspers, such a movement out of thought and into existential actuality offers no release from the foundering it is the fate of finite existence to experience, for existential actuality also founders in its limit situations (e.g., death, guilt, struggle). To the agonizing questions which arise in these situations there is no final and unambiguous answer either in thought or existence. Jaspers' metaphysics is an attempt to interpret the various speculative attempts to answer the ultimate questions of being. Because such speculative attempts have been articulated objectively, he argues that their objective, literal form is always ambiguous and subject to debilitating antinomies since being-in-itself or the *Ursprung* of our existential situation can never be defined objectively. Yet such objective forms can be interpreted as ciphers of an unconditioned reality to which existence is related. They are ciphers because the interpretation itself must take an objective form while their final meaning can only be realized in the existence (i.e., what Buri now calls self-understanding) of the interpreter himself. (Cf., Karl Jaspers, *Philosophie*, III: *Metaphysik* (Berlin: Springer Verlag, dritte Auflage, 1956 (1932), p. 218.) Speculative answers to the human questions that arise at the boundary situations can never eliminate existential foundering because it is intrinsic to human existence itself. Interpreted as ciphers, however, such speculative answer can give voice to the question whether being is ultimately trustworthy. As Jaspers says: "Dass mir aber die Transzendenz ausbleibt, dass mein Vertrauen, schliesslich mich selbst in transzendenter Bezogenheit anzutreffen, getäuscht wird — nie weiss ich, was dann meine Schuld war und was ich als mir geschehen tragen muss; *ich kann als ich selbst scheitern*, ohne dass das philosophische Vertrauen und ohne dass göttliches Wort und religiöse Garantie helfen, trotzdem alle Wahrhaftigkeit und Bereitschaft da zu sein schien. In der Vielfachheit des Scheiterns aber ist die Frage, ob Scheitern schlechthin Vernichtung ist, weil das, was scheitert, in der Tat zugrunde geht, oder ob in Scheitern ein Sein offenbar wird; ob Scheitern nicht nur Scheitern, sondern Verewigen sein kann." (*Ibid.*, p. 221.) But the answer to this question can only be realized in existence itself. Ciphers can be the vehicle for the ascertainment of being through existential actuality, but they cannot articulate this being objectively. Consequently, Jaspers' final position on metaphysics is that foundering itself is the final cipher; only so can the true dimensions of the problem of thought, finitude, and existential actuality come to light. (Cf., *ibid.*, pp. 232-236.) As he says: "*Chiffern* können sich für mögliche Existenz *nicht* mehr *fixieren*, und doch brauchen sie *nicht nichts* zu sein. Aber was sie auch sind, objektiv geworden sind sie unendlich zweideutig, und wahr sind sie nur, wenn sie sich erhalten in der Chiffre des *Scheiterns*, welche nach ihrer faktischen Seite mit positivistischer Rückhaltlosigkeit gesehen und existentiell in den Grenzsituationen ernst genommen ist." (*Ibid.*, p. 218.) "Die Undeutbarkeit als letzte Chiffre ist aber nicht mehr als bestimmbare Chiffre. Sie bleibt offen, daher ihr Schweigen. Sie kann ebensogut die absolute Leere wie die endgültige Erfüllung werden." (*Ibid.*, p. 234. All italics are Jaspers'.)

That self-understanding does not relate to Transcendence, that it thus remains only self-understanding and does not become faith is entirely out of the question. In
its actualization, self-understanding is in essence relatedness to Transcendence and
is therefore faith. (I, p. 138.)[27]

This is the decisive move in Buri's theology. On the surface, his concept
of self-understanding might be taken as a religiously neutral interpretation of the existential character of the act of self-determination based on
the concepts of freedom and responsibility. But he is claiming that such
acts are not self-positing movements of human autonomy but are always
posited in an existential dialectic between self and "other."

Despite Buri's strong claim that every self-understanding is grounded
in a relationship to Transcendence, it is particularly important to note
the difference of this systematic principle from Schleiermacher's. Buri
repeatedly emphasizes that the relationship to Transcendence is not an
ontological structure given with human existence itself. The relationship
is never a given feature of existence itself because it occurs only in the
unconditioned acts of freedom and responsibility which transcend the
subject-object structure. The self always has a twofold possibility; it can
actualize its authentic freedom by choosing to take responsibility for itself or refuse this possibility by losing itself in the world and understanding itself entirely in terms of what can be objectively defined.[28] *If* the self
chooses its authenticity in freely taking responsibility for itself, the relationship to Transcendence will occur, but *that* the self will make this
choice is not given ontologically with human existence. The relationship
to Transcendence is, thus, an expression of the transcending existentiality
of human existence that can never be captured in the subject-object
structure which an ontology must assume. From the standpoint of an ob-

---

[27]Cf., also, I, p. 134.

[28]This is the basis for Buri's understanding of sin. (Cf., II, pp. 215-227.) This also accounts for the fact that the concept of self-understanding has slightly different meanings
in Buri and Bultmann. For Bultmann, self-understanding is a theologically neutral term
to designate the existential character of all human possibilities. These can be realized under two basic types of self-understanding: faith and unfaith. For Buri, self-understanding
is already a normative term indicating an actualization of existence which is the opposite
of losing oneself objectively in the world — i.e., what Bultmann calls the self-understanding of lack of faith. Hence self-understanding for Buri is always a manifestation of some
form of faith since it refers to the actualization of one's existence in freedom and responsibility which one can refuse to do. This difference is ultimately a function of Buri's
more thoroughgoing orientation on the problem of objectivity, but the effects of the difference are slight in the long run. For each an existential understanding of the self lies
at the basis of their interpretation of faith and unfaith, and they both interpret the content of faith and unfaith as the acceptance or refusal of certain possibilities of self-actualization.

jective ontology, Buri would say, freedom and responsibility are equally as problematic as the idea of an absolute being-in-itself outside the realm of consciousness.

For a notion so central to the foundation of his hermeneutic, it is strange and perhaps even debilitating that Buri offers little more explanation of or justification for "Transcendence-relatedness" than has been presented here. Since the idea of self-understanding refers to any genuine act of freedom and responsibility, it is an exceedingly strong claim to say that all such acts involve a relationship to Transcendence. This is like telling an atheist that it is impossible for him not to believe in God. Furthermore, the very meaning of "Transcendence" begs for additional clarification which Buri never gives it. Certainly it can be equated with "God" in no straightforward sense because, in line with the reversal his hermeneutic entails throughout, "God" is a mythological concept bound to the subject-object structure and must be theologically interpreted in terms of Transcendence, i.e., in terms of the Transcendence relation *actualized* in the self-understanding of a particular historicity.[29] God cannot, therefore, be used to interpret "Transcendence." Transcendence must interpret "God."

In contrast to this unclarity in Buri, Schleiermacher did seek to establish his systematic principle by the argument that the modes of receptivity, knowing and doing, must be founded on a prior mode of receptivity which was itself grounded in an unconditioned or "absolute" (*schlechthinnig*) relationship. But Buri justifies his refusal to give further grounding to the idea of Transcendence-relatedness for the same reason that he rejects Schleiermacher's ontological interpretation of faith:

> There is no proof for faith external to faith itself. That the foundering of the objective movement of thought is more than mere foundering, that the leap of faith is not a leap into a void, can only be ascertained by him who co-enacts that foundering and risks the leap. (I, p. 139.)

To justify Transcendence would be to draw it into the endlessness and open-endedness of objective movements of thought in the subject-object structure, but this would be to compromise the unconditionedness of Transcendence as it is actualized in self-understanding, for "with every explanation and every understanding, the horizon of what can be explained and understood recedes further and further." (I, p. 139.)

But surely Buri's argument here rests on a confusion. It is one thing

[29] Cf., *HSRG*, pp. 26 f.

to say that faith itself cannot be justified. This is basically what Buri is saying above, and he is correct. *That* a man becomes a man of faith or actualizes his existence in terms of a particular self-understanding cannot be justified by any series of rational arguments but involves a leap into an altogether different level – although rational arguments and clarification may be relevant to his finally making a particular existential decision. This accounts for the religiously unsatisfying character of the arguments for the existence of God. But it is quite a different thing to conclude from this that an analysis of the *meaning* of the terms by means of which faith expresses itself involves the same mistake. In other words, Buri's analysis of the way in which the Trancendence-relation is *actualized* non-objectively gives him no warrant for refusing to say what Transcendence means. This is the case even granting the restrictions the subject-object structure would place on such analysis. One could at least expect him to say more explicitly than he does what Transcendence *cannot* be, or to explain explicitly whether he believes the relation to Transcendence in the actualization of self-understanding warrants the meaning of divinity.

There is, of course, a certain sense in which Buri's approach to the hermeneutical problem requires finally a surd-like element in the foundations of the hermeneutical principle beyond which he cannot go. Having clarified in a general way the problem objectivity poses for both faith and the conceptualization of faith, he argues that all theological ideas have their content only in the non-objective act of self-understanding. This means, then, that all of the objective concepts that might be used to explain the meaning of Transcendence must themselves be interpreted non-objectively in terms of the *act* of self-understanding and the Transcendence-relation it ostensibly involves. One is left simply with a non-objective dialectic of existence, and while an analysis of it may conclude that it is not self-positing, there is no way to move beyond the dialectic itself to establish the meaning of its other term since the meaning of any objective concepts which might establish this meaning would themselves be oblique and could only be interpreted by a circular movement back to the existential dialectic. Although this is scarcely a justification of the unclarity that remains concerning Buri's concept of Transcendence, it does suggest another way in which his systematic principle might be approached. If the concept of Transcendence cannot be grounded independently of the non-objective dialectic, it can, at least, receive some clarification by the way it actually functions as a principle of interpretation.

Looked at from this perspective, Buri's concept of self-understanding involves a structure of choosing and being chosen which can be called a "paradox of grace." The actualization of a self-understanding is entirely an act of freedom; the self realizes its authenticity (and thus in Buri's sense becomes a "person") in the transcending acts of objectively unconditioned freedom in which it takes responsibility for itself. At the same time, Buri claims, precisely in this act of autonomy the self finds itself given or "gifted" (geschenkt) to itself.[30] It is important to note that this "giftedness" does not appear as the conclusion to an argument as though it were an interpretation of the metaphysical structures that must be assumed if the concept of self-understanding is to be adequately grounded. Rather, Buri claims that it is given inextricably and self-evidently with the structure of self-understanding itself. His position is more like a phenomenological analysis than a metaphysical argument. The actualization of self-understanding, then, is an existential dialectic of choosing and being chosen.[31] In this sense, the actualization of a self-understanding is not a simple human possibility, as though Buri's concept of self-understanding could be reduced to willful self-assertion. It involves instead a paradox of grace, a paradox of autonomous freedom and being gifted to oneself in the unity of an existential dialectic.[32]

From this viewpoint, the concept of "Transcendence" functions as a limiting concept which operates in Buri's hermeneutic not to define a transcendent reality objectively but to specify the structure of the existential dialectic. "Transcendence" serves to say, that is, that the actualization of self-understanding includes a "being chosen." It does not, however, specify what this other term of the relationship is, for to do so would be to objectify it. Together the existentiality of self-understand-

---

[30]Cf., e.g., I, pp. 271 f., 298; II, pp. 497 f.; TdE, pp. 20 f., 53-71 (ET, pp. 13-15, 44-61); HSRG, pp. 27-30; DP, pp. 13 ff., 51-55, 62-64, 72, 80; Buri, Denkender Glaube: Schritte auf dem Weg zu einer philosophischen Theologie (Bern: Verlag Paul Haupt, 1966), pp. 49 f., 63 ff. (ET, Thinking Faith, tran. Harold H. Oliver (Philadelphia: Fortress Press, 1968), pp. 42, 55 ff.); Buri, "Sich selber geschenkt werden: Karl Jaspers zum 80. Geburtstag am 23. Februar 1963" in National-Zeitung Basel, Sonntagsbeilage, Nr. 91 (24. February 1963), no page numbers indicated. (Hereinafter Denkender Glaube will be abbreviated as DG.)

[31]For an extremely illuminating discussion in English of the transcending dialectic of choosing and being chosen, cf. Emil L. Fackenheim, Metaphysics and Historicity, The Aquinas Lecture, 1961 (Milwaukee: Marquette University Press, 1961), pp. 75-99.

[32]The phrase "paradox of grace" is Donald Baillie's. (Cf., God Was in Christ (New York: Charles Scribner's Sons, 1948), pp. 114-118.) Formally, Buri's understanding of existence as grace is quite similar to Baillie's paradox of grace, and sometimes Buri uses almost the same locution. (Cf., I, p. 272 and II, p. 498.) Materially, however, Baillie founds his paradox of grace on an objective Heilsgeschichte which Buri would find objectionable.

ing (the non-objective act of self-determination in a particular situation) and Transcendence (the non-objective structure of being chosen which constitutes self-understanding as an existential dialectic) make up Buri's systematic principle, and this principle will then serve as the hermeneutical framework for interpreting doctrines.

This functional meaning of Transcendence becomes apparent in the following statement which is representative of the way Buri articulates the systematic principle throughout his theology.

It remains, therefore, that personal self-understanding in relation to Transcendence and Transcendence itself are non-objectifiable. Here objectifying knowledge comes up against its limits and experiences the revelation of nothingness. It is different with the faith which actualizes this self-understanding and experiences itself therein related to Transcendence. In the enactment of self-understanding, the believer sees just the opposite of being placed before nothingness. In being responsible, he perceives the authentic nature of his being as a person which consists in the fact that he can win himself or lose himself, realize himself or fail himself. He decides what he is just there where he decides how and as what he understands himself. His being is laid entirely in his hands in that he finds himself in this situation as one who has not created himself. He does not awake in this situation but is awakened. And with that the personhood of Transcendence has at once appeared, not as the silence of nothingness and also not as an impersonal power but as the *Persona Dei loquentis,* as speaking person who encounters me in time and so reveals himself to me. (I, pp. 268-269.)[33]

Buri uses a variety of images to elicit this structure of self-understanding. Here he speaks of "being awakened," and in other places, he uses the image of "being graced" or "gifted."[34] He also uses the images of "being called"[35] and "being destined,"[36] and he can even speak of the "voice" that calls into personal responsibility.[37]

The objective character of these images obviously creates problems for Buri's concept of Transcendence just as viewing Transcendence as a limiting concept by no means dissolves all the unclarity over the hermeneutical range Buri gives it. Buri himself seems to equivocate over its meaning. Sometimes it clearly functions as a limiting concept for the structure of the existential dialectic. But at other times, as is even indicated in the above passage and by his use of the various images, Buri

---

[33]Cf., immediately below, pp. 100 ff. for a discussion of Buri's concept of "revelation of nothingness."

[34]I, p. 298; *DG,* pp. 49 f. (ET, p. 42).

[35]HSRG, pp. 34 f., 39.

[36]RF, p. 57.

[37]HSRG, pp. 34 f., 39.

seems to treat Transcendence as *a being* transcendent to the world which discloses itself as personal in the subjectivity of faith. Because of this remaining unclarity, further attention will have to be devoted to the concept of Transcendence below, especially to the claims Buri makes for it in his actual interpretation of Christian doctrines. For the present, however, it is enough to direct attention to the hermeneutical role it plays as a limiting concept. Functionally, this is a role it clearly does have in the foundations of Buri's hermeneutic no matter what additional meaning he might inconsistently give it at other places in his theology.

Buri's proposal to interpret the Christian tradition as an expression of self-understanding becomes more intelligible when his concept of self-understanding is seen to include the systematic principle of a dialectic of choosing and being chosen. On this basis, the self-reference of theological content in Buri's hermeneutic is not merely the willful imposition of an arbitrary philosophical doctrine on the mythological form of the Christian tradition which is now held to be untenable and which can only serve as illustrative material for a meaning entirely different from its original and intrinsic claim.[38] Were this the case, then one would be better advised simply to reject the Christian tradition out of hand and proceed to write a philosophical system. Instead, however, Buri's systematic principle gives him a legitimate claim to be able to interpret the primary intentionality which has always been at the basis of the admittedly objective and mythological language of the Christian tradition. The reason for this is that the paradox of grace in self-understanding is, Buri claims, the existential structure which is expressed mythologically in the most basic assertions of the Christian tradition, in such doctrines as, for instance, creation, providence, the love, mercy, and righteousness of God, the incarnation, and eschatology.[39] If it is once granted that the present situation requires a radical theology based on existentialist interpretation, i.e., on the self-referencing content of theological language in the non-objectivity

[38]This is basically the criticism John Macquarrie makes of Buri in *The Scope of Demythologizing* (London: SCM Press, Ltd., 1960), pp. 127-153. Macquarrie's own prejudices as a result of which he attempts to solve the structural inconsistency in Bultmann by an obscure appeal to paradox makes his discussion of Buri extremely heavy-handed, and he cannot be taken as a reliable guide to the internal logic of Buri's position. Cf., Ogden, *Christ without Myth*, 165-181.

[39]Note, however, that this seems to imply that the structure of self-understanding has a normative significance for the comparative study of religion. In other words, Buri seems forced to claim that it is a *universal* structure of human existence (i.e., in the sense of existentiality) which is given more or less adequate or inadequate expression in various religious traditions, and this would appear seriously to qualify the restrictions Buri attributes to the historicity of any particular self-understanding.

of faith, then Buri's systematic principle is an extremely promising hermeneutical device. A single example, that of creation, will suffice for the
present to show how Transcendence as a limiting concept functions in
this context.

Self-understanding is something which no one else can assume for me but which
I myself must enact – and indeed not by being forced (*gezwungen*), not in the consciousness of being conditioned by something else, but in free responsibility. In self-
understanding I make myself what I am. Therein I can fail myself – or win
myself. It depends on me. And in the midst of all relativity my decision is unconditioned. I am not just partly responsible and partly not – but completely and entirely responsible. In this fateful weight of decision the particular moment receives
the significance of eternity. Still, in every particular moment in which it is
enacted, self-understanding finds itself as a possibility not created by itself. It
finds itself in a situation it did not bring about and in a time all the less at its
disposal. Precisely in the enactment of its free and responsible self-determination,
self-understanding experiences itself, together with its situation in this [particular]
time, as created. Were there no myth of the creator, self-understanding would have
to invent one in order to give this revelation, which has come to it, the expression
appropriate to what has happened. The biblical myth of the creator corresponds to
the self-understanding of faith in that the Transcendence to which it here experiences itself related is no distant, silent Transcendence but a God who comes near to
man and who speaks perceptibly and clearly in his speech. To be with God and to
flee from him, paradise and being driven out of paradise are here actual experiences of the present. In its unendingness, time has a beginning in that which posits
every moment and an end in the same, in that before which we are summoned to
account in every moment. (I, pp. 271-272.)

In this way, the concept of Transcendence functions throughout Buri's
interpretations of the tradition to denude doctrines of their mythological
objectivity and to refer them to the structure of the non-objective dialectic.

When Transcendence is taken as a limiting concept, Buri's statement
that self-understanding as a general human possibility always involves a
relation to Transcendence becomes more intelligible. The paradox of
grace then plays the same role in this theology as Schleiermacher's concept of the feeling of absolute dependence. The feeling of absolute dependence grounds Schleiermacher's concept of religion as a fundamental
structure of human existence whereas the Transcendence-relatedness of
self-understanding grounds Buri's concept of faith as a general human
possibility. The problem for each of them is to show how the specifically
Christian religion is related to their respective systematic principles.
Each answers by saying that the systematic principle is not given in an
undifferentiated form but receives specification by differing historical

modes of human self-actualization.

This is the point, however, at which the problem of objective description of the content of faith recurs in Buri. The actual differentiation of the Christian faith will occur in the self-reference of its doctrinal concepts to the totally non-objective dialectic of existence. Although it is possible to describe the structure of faith as a general human possibility, the question arises whether it is possible to give a theological interpretation of any particular differentiation of that structure in various religious traditions without transgressing the limits Buri imposes on objectification. If not, then the content of any particular faith becomes totally ineffable.

Schleiermacher could respond positively at this point precisely because he was prepared to make objective statements about the self which specified the determinate modes of consciousness in the Christian religion. Immediately following his discussion of the general nature of faith, he offered a criterion for distinguishing the Christian specification of the general principle: "Christianity is a monotheistic faith, belonging to the teleological type of piety, and it is distinguished from other faiths essentially by the fact that everything in it is related to the redemption accomplished by Jesus of Nazareth."[40] He then proceeded to flesh out this criterion by interpreting doctrines in terms of the various states of God-consciousness in Christianity as these arise out of a relation to the God-consciousness of Jesus. In line with his attempt to existentialize all of Schleiermacher's concepts of consciousness, Buri defines faith systematically as "a personal self-understanding which, in its historicity, is aware of a relation to Transcendence revealed to it as truth." (I, p. 134.)[41] The concept of historicity is crucial, then, for the question whether Buri can describe the content of the Christian faith and thereby avoid making it ineffable.

3. Faith and the Christian Self-Understanding

a. The Concept of Historicity

In Buri historicity means the concrete embodiment of the non-objective self; it is the unconditioned point at which the self actualizes itself within the conceptual relativities of any situation. This usage, which has

---

[40]Schleiermacher, DcG, I, p. 74 (CF, p. 52).

[41]The German is as follows: "Glaube ist ein personales Selbstverständnis, das sich in seiner Geschichtlichkeit auf Transzendenz bezogen weiss, die sich ihm als Wahrheit offenbart."

become common in existentialist literature, raises the question why the embodiment of unconditioned selfhood should be called its historicity. Although many thinkers in the history of philosophy have been aware of something like Buri's notion of the unconditioned self, they have been more disposed to see this intrinsic self either as a transcendence of temporality or, at least, as the temporal actualization of structures which are not subject to temporality. What then is the justification for associating the intrinsic self with the notion of historicity?

An answer to this question involves a new kind of awareness of human finitude closely associated with the emergence in the nineteenth century of an acute historical self-consciousness. The historical self-consciousness has brought with it an awareness of the relativity of all human expressions and has resulted in throwing up a challenge to the ancient philosophical notion of a permanent human nature. A new awareness of finitude is associated with this, for it has appeared that all human activity is radically time-bound, and man's temporality cannot be dissociated from his historical situation. Man is nothing more than his history; he *is* what he becomes.

These developments are much broader than existentialism, but they have been particularly important for the existentialist understanding of the self. The existentialists have agreed that man is his history, but the existential dialectic of the self and the criticism of objectivity have led them to raise the question of the subjective conditions of man's history itself. They have argued that a man's history (what he becomes) is constituted by the non-objective actualizations of his existential selfhood which cannot finally be explained by the objectivity of either metaphysical structures (e.g., a permanent human nature) or the external components of objective history. At the same time, a man's historical self-constitution is never in a void. It always stands time-bound in a particular context of external history. But objective history is nothing more than the external expression given to the subjective conditions of other actualizations of selfhood which have then formed the context for one's own actualization. History, therefore, is based on the historicity of existence.[42] The existentialist problem of history becomes the problem of relating the historicity of the individual to the external history which is the context (or "situation") for his self-actualization. Because the tradition and the community in which he stands are the context for his self-actualization, his problem

---

[42]Cf., Heidegger, *Sein und Zeit*, pp. 20-22, 372-404; Jaspers, *Philosophie*, II, *Existenzerhellung*, pp. 118-135.

becomes that of appropriating this history. But it is immediately given to him only in its external, objective form. His problem, then, is to recover its subjective conditions so that it becomes *his* history in the actualization of his historicity.[43]

Buri directly appropriates this development when he says that it is the historicity of the self which "first constitutes history as history, as that which is historical in the genuine sense. It is that which gives history its *Gehalt.*" (I, p. 146.) Discussing it more directly in terms of his epistemological concepts, he says: "Knowledge has its history. But faith is historicity." (I, p. 143.) He then develops the sense in which faith is always embodied in the historicity of the believer by discussing historicity in terms of the now familiar opposition between knowledge and self-understanding. Knowledge has a history because it always builds on the state of a discipline at any given time which is itself the result of a history of research. It has a history because its results are never completed but always open to further refinement and revision in the light of new data. The relation of faith to history is quite different. It is "more positive, immediate, reverent" while at the same time "more critical, sceptical and radical." (I, p. 144.) Faith is historistic because of this double relation to history.

First, the relation of faith to history is more positive and direct. Acts of cognition and faith have in common their occurrence at a specific time and place in history. But scientific knowledge is possible because the content of knowledge is indifferent to its locus in history; knowledge claims can be repeated and checked at any place in space and time by anyone who can meet the necessary conditions for repeating and checking them. With faith, to the contrary, the particular locus in history is not an indifferent matter nor is the content of faith accessible to another through an arbitrary interchange of standpoints toward which it is possible to take a detached and neutral attitude. Faith "is the self-understanding of a single one (*eines einzelnen*) who understands himself in just his (*in seiner je*) particular historistic situation." (I, p. 144.) This more direct relation to history means that

if the understanding-of-oneself does not signify an infinite reflection which dissolves everything [into possibility] but a real coming-oneself in relation to Transcendence, then this can occur only through unconditionally assuming one's partic-

---

[43]For much of discussion of the meaning of historicity, I am indebted to Fackenheim, *Metaphysics and Historicity, passim,* and Otto Friedrich Bollnow, *Existenzphilosophie* (Stuttgart: W. Kohlhammer Verlag, fünfte Auflage, 1955), pp. 112 ff.

ular, concrete, and contingent situation as something inescapably given. (I, p. 144.)

From the standpoint of this more positive relation to history, the historicity of faith is, second, in a position to take a more critical and more radical approach to history. Knowledge sensitive to its nature and limits is aware of its relativity and open-endedness. In this it has a perspective from which it can be critical of claims to knowledge which absolutize themselves and thereby transgress those limits. Yet within its proper limits, scientific knowledge is absolute, i.e., its results are generally demonstrable and valid until new data are discovered or new methods developed. Buri argues that so long as such knowledge stays within its assigned limits, "it has no possibility of seeing its conditionedness as a whole. Within its limits it proceeds with absolute certainty. In the knowledge of its relativity, it has control over its relativity." (I, p. 145.) It is only a transcending movement of thought similar to that which leads to an awareness of the contingent nature of the subject-object structure that can lead to a consciousness of the restrictedness of knowledge as a whole, but such a movement of thought is not an objective movement of scientific knowledge itself. In this way, the unconditioned act of self-understanding relativizes the self-enclosed relativity of scientific knowledge. From the unconditioned point of historicity, it becomes possible to see the conditionedness of history as a whole in the way that it is accessible to objective knowledge. It is this which enables faith to have a more critical (though logically different) stance toward history than knowledge does. Buri emphasizes that such a stance does not call into question the objective *Feststellbarkeiten* of historical knowledge. That type of criticism is the business of knowledge itself. But it does indeed call into question the competence of knowledge "as a whole for that which first constitutes history as history, as that which is historical in the genuine sense." (I, p. 146.)

This double relation of faith to history means that the concept of historicity always indicates a double movement in the actualization of faith – in Buri's words, "a directedness into history and a being beyond history." (I, p. 146.)[44] On the one hand, historicity means that faith is always situated by a history which can be described objectively. In this sense, history is the condition of historicity, and theology possesses no absolute vantage point from which it can assess the relative merits of diverse his-

[44] In Buri's words, "das Angewiesensein auf Geschichte und das Über-alle-Geschichte-hinaus."

torical traditions. On the other hand, the historicity of faith is the condition of history because history itself is constituted by the non-objective existential acts by which men understand themselves. In this sense, historicity refers to the transcending of objective historical determinants in the acts of self-constitution. If faith is always historically situated, the content of faith is nevertheless given in an act which transcends the relativity of objective history while also being the condition for there being any history at all. From the standpoint of objective history, faith is always relative; from the standpoint of faith, this relativity is always suspended by the unconditioned act of appropriating one's historical situation unconditionally as *je meines*. The concept of historicity always has this double focus, and in this way it can serve to define the content of the specifically Christian historicity.

b. The Historicity of Faith

Self-understanding never occurs as a purely abstract existential dialectic but always involves a concrete actualization of the self which must be repeated ever anew. For the same reason there is no general (*allgemein*) Transcendence-relation. It is always one particularized by the concrete historicity of the self. Having a relation to Transcendence (Transcendence-relatedness) is not, therefore, what distinguishes the Christian faith from self-understanding as a general possibility. It is, rather, the historicity of the Christian faith, the concrete mode of existence which results from actualizing the possibility for existing ingredient in the Christian message. To understand the content of faith in Buri's system, it is necessary to examine this possibility, for this is what it means to interpret doctrines as expressions of self-understanding. This historicity will be defined by each of the poles of faith: self-understanding and Transcendence-relatedness.[45]

The historicity of the Christian self-understanding is specified by the relation to the tradition which originated with "the message of God's saving revelation in Jesus Christ" (though this relation has taken multifarious forms throughout the history of Christianity). (I, p. 146.) "Not in any other tradition nor as the original creation of some individual person but only in relation to this history is Christian faith possible." (I, p. 148.) This statement, which is not much more than a tautology (i.e., the

---

[45]Cf., I, pp. 146-153.

Christian faith is the Christian faith), first sets the problem of history and historicity noted above. The self-understanding of faith becomes possible only through specification of the existential possibilities of the Christian message and tradition in a concrete act of epistence. Yet the message and tradition themselves appear only in the form of objectively related accounts or doctrines in objective history. The historicity of faith can only be defined, therefore, through some kind of dialectic between the objectivity of the tradition and the non-objectivity of self-understanding. The question that needs answering is how the historicity of faith can arise out of an objective historical tradition. For Buri, access to an objective tradition can be gained through scientific knowledge using the historical-critical method, so, as occurs time and again in his thought, this question involves the relationship between the objectivity of knowledge and the non-objectivity of self-understanding.

As long as history remains at the level of objectivity, the only possible relationship between self and history is that of an approximation process, i.e., the objective statement that such and such happened or the objective description of the doctrinal content of a tradition. The historical-critical examination of the objective tradition is necessary if the Christian self-understanding is to remain true to its tradition. But such an objective history can never determine the historicity of faith. Giving the example of research into the historical Jesus, Buri notes that

the historical Jesus can neither be believed nor proclaimed; this Jesus becomes an object for science and as such is investigated and proved. If the historical Jesus takes the place of the believed and proclaimed Christ [of the tradition]..., then he becomes something to be believed and proclaimed and therewith scientifically questionable. (I, p. 147.)

This tension between faith and knowledge is insurmountable, and for this reason, the tradition can never be merely objective for faith.

There is one thing every aspect of the tradition has in common despite the diversity that can be isolated by historical-critical examination: "It becomes for the auditor not only an object of explanation and understanding but beyond that *an occasion for self-understanding.*" (I, p. 149. My italics.) This can occur only insofar as one stands in the external history of the tradition

but this possibility ... becomes reality when in the course of this history, which has been objectified and known scientifically, that occurs which is completely non-objective and, for this reason, unresearchable *(das Unerforschliche),* namely, that in relation to the message of God's revelation in Jesus Christ a personal self-understanding originates which experiences itself in its unconditionedness as related to Transcendence and therein as standing in the truth. Such faith can spring up from a dogma or from a result of research .... But when this happens, the knower no longer has to do with history merely as something objectifiable. Then rather, he stands in the specifically Christian historicity. (I, p. 148.)

From its beginning, Buri says, "the Christian faith has always led over and beyond all historical explanation and understanding into the historicity of self-understanding. The decision of faith, whether to understand oneself in terms of the possibilities which here become visible or to refuse them, becomes unavoidable at some point in the face of this tradition." (I, p. 149.) In other words, the historicity of faith is defined by a relation to the external tradition when that tradition ceases to be merely an objective report and addresses the believer as kerygma. It then becomes an occasion for a self-understanding, and its content is absorbed into the non-objective dialectic of existence.[46]

Historicity is much the same with Transcendence-relatedness. In contradistinction from a general Transcendence-relation, this relation occurs in Christianity exclusively in the context of the proclamation of God's revelation in Jesus Christ.[47] It will be recalled that "God" for Buri must be interpreted by Transcendence and that Transcendence is a limiting concept which refers not to a transcendent being but to the structure of the existential dialectic. This is the background against which one must understand Buri's discussion of the revelation of God in primitive Christianity. He argues that an objective, historical-critical examination will show that primitive Christianity did not speak of general revelation or of a corresponding general relation to Transcendence given in and with human existence as such.[48] In primitive Christianity, everything depended on recognizing "that God has revealed himself in Jesus Christ in a decisive way which alone leads to salvation." (I, p. 153.) As Buri continues:

The Christian message places this revelation over against all others – even its own historical prefigurations – as something special. According to it there is a relation to God as father not on the basis of general experience or reflection but solely through the Son of God. Even if the synoptic Jesus – as has been emphasized against this exclusivism – teaches a direct relation of the individual to his father

---

[46]Cf., ibid., pp. 257, 261, 269; TdE, pp. 23-28 (ET, pp. 15-21). As Buri succinctly defines the relationship between faith and tradition: "Geschichtlichkeit bedeutet nämlich: ein durch das Selbstverständnis des Glaubens bestimmtes Verhältnis zu einer Erscheinung der historischen Gegenständlichkeit." (I, p. 417.)

[47]Ibid., pp. 151-153.

[48]Ibid., pp. 152 f.

without the interposition of his own person, still, in view of his special position in the event of revelation, he is the one who proclaims this possibility not as something general but as something historistic. (I, p. 153.)

Thus, the historicity of the Transcendence-relation in the Christian self-understanding is always specified by the proclamation of this particular revelation.

One must be clear that Buri is not advocating an exclusivism with his concept of historicity which the above passage might suggest if taken out of context. By exclusivism is meant the argument that salvation is possible alone through Christ because of an objective act of God at a particular time and place in the past. For Buri all the ingredients in such a claim are mythological, and if taken literally, they lead to an inappropriate, objectivizing understanding of the Christian affirmation. He groups all such claims under the category of objective *Heilsgeschichte* and rejects them repeatedly throughout his theology.[49] He argues that such a position not only misconstrues the nature of revelation in that it considers it on the model of objectivity as something true apart from faith but also that by considering revelation on this level, the non-objective character of faith is falsified. Speaking against such objectifications of revelation, he asserts that "it is not so much the message as the historicity of faith which is not taken here with sufficient seriousness." (I, p. 160.) Again, this statement represents the reversal which is typical of Buri's hermeneutic. One cannot say that the message is not taken with sufficient seriousness when the message itself receives its content only in terms of the non-objective dialectic. And it is precisely the historicity of this dialectic that is denied by the objective interpretation of revelation which leads to exclusivism. Therefore, the exclusivistic assertions of the Christian tradition must function simply as objective expressions for the *historicity* of the actualization of the Christian self-understanding.

On the basis of the non-objective dialectic of existence, this means that any Transcendence-relation must be specified through the concrete historicity of some actualization of existence. In taking this position, Buri is not denying the possibility outside Christianity of appropriate relations to Transcendence. But he is making two positive claims. (i) Such a Transcendence-relation would also be determined by the historicity of that faith; it would not be *allgemein*. (ii) Insofar as one speaks of the

---

[49]Cf., e.g., PaP, p. 117; PuDR, pp. 368 f. (ET, pp. 148-150); EoE, pp. 96-100; Buri, "Die Hermeneutische Funktion der Lehre vom Prophetischen Heilswerk Christi" in *Der Historische Jesus und der Kerygmatische Christus,* herausgegeben von Helmut Ristow and Karl Matthiae (Berlin: Evangelische Verlagsanstalt, 1960), pp. 527 f.

Transcendence-relation distinctive of the Christian self-understanding, one can do so only in terms of the historicity of that faith and that means in terms of the relation determined and structured by the proclamation of this single revelation in Jesus Christ. Buri is saying, if you will, that there is an exclusivism internal to an explication of the Christian self-understanding, but it is an exclusivism that cannot be generalized into an objective doctrine true external to that self-undersanding. It is in this sense and this sense alone that, for Buri, the Transcendence-relation characteristic of any self-understanding receives a special configuration in Christianity.[50]

Buri's notion of the historicity of the Christian faith is exactly parallel to Schleiermacher's specification of religion in general by the particular determinants of sensuous self-consciousness in various religions. The on-

[50]The concept of *Einmaligkeit* itself must, therefore, receive an existentialist interpretation in Buri's theology. When he uses it, as in the above instance, it cannot indicate the once-for-allness of a revelation in the past as any kind of objective reality. It cannot because revelation itself is entirely non-objective. Hence the non-objectivity of revelation demands that the *Einmaligkeit* be absorbed into the internal dialectic of self-understanding. It is a function of an objective revelation in the past only in the historical-critical sense in which every historical event is unique. But in its legitimate theological sense, it is a function of the historicity of self-understanding. In contrast to the generality and abstractness of knowledge, it refers to the utter particularity and unconditionedness of self-understanding. Once-for-allness refers, therefore, to the inner quality of the act of self-understanding (i.e., to its unconditionedness). As Buri says: "Glaube kennt mitten in der Vorläufigkeit der Zeit ein Jetzt der Offenbarung und ein Ein-für-alle-mal der Entscheidung." (I, p. 91.) This absorption of *Einmaligkeit* into the internal dialectic of decision is indicated by the juxtaposition of the following statements from Buri's second volume: "Wie wir in unseren 'Prolegomena' ausführlich dargelegt haben, bildet der nichtobjektivierbare Vollzug des Selbstverständnisses nicht nur die Voraussetzung für das rechtmässige Verständnis des Aussagen des christlichen Glaubens, sondern er stellt auch den Ort dar, in dem sich das von der christlichen Verkündigung gemeinte Heilsgeschehen als solches ereignet." (II, p. 38.) "Einzig und allein im Vollzug des Selbstverständnisses des Glaubens besteht die Wirklichkeit des Inhaltes der Heilsbotschaft." (II, p. 400.) "Insofern wir es im Ursprung der christlichen Versöhnungslehre mit einer Botschaft von einem Versöhnungsgeschehen zu tun haben, wird dem kerygmatischen Charakter dieses Ursprungs nicht Rechnung getragen, wenn sein Inhalt wie eine unabhängig von dieser Botschaft bestehende Objektivität oder wie ein Gegenstand unserer Subjektivität behandelt wird. Der Inhalt einer Botschaft, die ein Glaubenszeugnis darstellt — und mit nichts anderem haben wir es wissenschaftlich nachweisbar im Neuen Testament seiner Intention nach zu tun — besteht nicht unabhängig von seiner Aneignung im Glauben, aus dem die Botschaft entspringt und auf den hin sie ausgerichtet ist. Nur in diesem Angeeignet-werden in Glauben, aus welchem die Botschaft hervorgeht und in dem sie ausgerichtet wird, in dem sie aber auch vernommen und von neuem verstanden sein will, besteht die Wirklichkeit ihres Inhaltes." (II, p. 399.) "Hier ereignet sich das, was mit der Aussage 'Fleischwerdung des Wortes Gottes' gemeint ist, indem sich in dem darauf gerichteten gläubigen Selbstverständnis die Wirklichkeit dieser Aussage erschliesst. Nirgends anderswo als aus der Unbedingtheit des Glaubens kann die Einmaligkeit der Fleischwerdung legitimerweise behauptet werden." (II, p. 431.)

ly difference is that Buri attempts to overcome the methodological short-comings in Schleiermacher's concept of consciousness with the existential concept of historicity. Schleiermacher could describe the specifically Christian religion because he saw no methodological problem in describ-ing the effects of the redeemer in terms of the modifications in the self-consciousness of the believer. Buri, of course, sees this as a psychologiz-ing of faith which denies its existential character. The problem, however, is whether Buri's concept of historicity can permit him to describe the content of the Christian self-understanding. His concept of historicity is important in his theology because it makes clear that a self-understand-ing must always be historistically embodied and that in Christianity this embodiment will be defined by the Christian message and tradition (ana-logous to the relation to the redeemer in Schleiermacher). But he has not yet said *what* the content of this historistic self-understanding is, and it is not clear that he can provide this further definition at the level of theo-logical discourse given his radical orientation to the problem of objectivi-ty.

The concept of historicity contains two poles: the historical situation and the non-objective act of appropriating that situation. Since the possi-bility of a descriptive content of the Christian self-understanding (i.e., a description of *what* this particular self-understanding is) could only arise from the givenness of an objective tradition which occasions and structures the historistic actualization of faith, it is important next to examine Buri's concept of revelation in order to see if it provides this possibility and is thereby a solution to this problem.

C. THE HISTORICITY OF REVELATION IN BURI'S THEOLOGY

The concept of revelation almost never appears in Schleiermacher's *Glaubenslehre*, and, indeed, there is a fundamental sense in which the concept becomes irrelevant after faith is defined as a determinate form of consciousness in an historical community. Because faith arises out of a prius of relationship basic to human consciousness as such, the tradition-al concept is unnecessary. For Schleiermacher, the ground of a particu-lar faith is the distinctive form of religious consciousness which origin-ates in a response to an historical event and to the tradition growing out of that event.[51]

[51]Cf., Schleiermacher's discussion of the originality of revelation, *DcG*, I, pp. 86-94 (CF, pp. 62-68).

In contrast to Schleiermacher, Buri's *Glaubenslehre* does require a concept of revelation although it is one assimilated to his existentializing of theological concepts. After he has tried to conceive the *Unverfügbarkeit* of both Transcendence and faith more radically than Schleiermacher and after he has conceived faith as a self-understanding that can never become a human possession but must be enacted ever anew, he requires a concept of the situation which makes the *unverfügbar* event of faith possible and actualizes it. His concept of historicity demands an understanding of revelation as the disclosive situation which makes self-understanding possible.[52] His problem, again, is to conceive revelation so that it is free from objectifying misunderstandings that would locate the content of revelation apart from the historicity of self-understanding itself. The question is whether this understanding of revelation can provide theological access to its own content and to the content of faith which arises out of it. He develops his concept of revelation in relation to both knowledge and faith.

1. Revelation for Knowledge

Buri treats the problem of revelation for knowledge under the traditional problem of natural theology.[53] Consonant with his understanding of objectivity and the limits of knowledge, he rejects any possibility of an objective, cognitive knowledge of God or revelation. Such knowledge would determine revelation objectively as something apart from the non-objectivity of faith. While he thus agrees with contemporary Protestant theology in rejecting natural theology, "natural theology" takes on a special coloration in the context of his theological principles, and he does insist that there is a revelation for knowledge. But it is entirely negative in content. He affirms a general revelation[54] which he defines as "the disclosure (*Sichtbarwerden*) of the boundaries of all objective knowledge in respect to the ultimate ground of all being."[55]

---

[52]It is important to realize that the disclosure is a situation which opens up the self rather than an objective event of revelation. This is necessary because of the assimiliation of all theological content to the existential dialectic. Cf., I, pp. 45 f., 154-156, 283 f., 291 f.

[53]Cf., *ibid.*, pp. 224-254.

[54]Cf., *TdE*, p. 18 (ET, p. 11). He discusses and rejects four types of traditional approaches to a natural theology: the scriptures, the history of religions, the proofs for the existence of God, and mysticism. Cf., I, pp. 225-252.

[55]Buri, "Das Selbstverständnis des christlichen Glaubens als Prinzip der Dogmatik," in *Theologische Zeitschrift* 10 (1954), p. 369.

Revelation for knowledge he says is a revelation of nothingness (*Offenbarung des Nichts*).[56] By this he means that at the point of statements about the intrinsic self or about being as a whole, knowledge finds itself simply with an empty movement of thought that has no positive content. Referring to Kant's concept of God in the Transcendental Dialectic, he says:

> For knowledge, revelation can only exhibit a limiting concept *(Grenzbegriff)*. Therein is envisaged what cannot become an object, what, however, as limit of objectivity, nevertheless is – only so that it itself cannot become objective. This disclosure *(Offenbarwerden)* of its limits and nothing else is revelation for knowledge. As a limit, this nothingness may not itself again become an object of knowledge – not even a knowledge of an ostensibly higher kind. (I, pp. 253-254.)

From this passage, it might seem that the phrase "revelation of nothingness" means simply that it is impossible to construct a natural theology because of the limits of knowledge. On the question of the status of revelation for knowledge, it seems to say no more than that the content of revelation is inaccessible to objectivity and is a subject matter for faith alone. But Buri seems to want to say something more than this, for, aside from affirming its merely negative character for knowledge he also wants to say that there is a genuine revelation. To grasp this, it is important to pay careful attention to his linguistic usage. He says:

> For knowledge, Transcendence does not become articulate but falls silent. If knowledge supposes that it hears Transcendence speak, that is [only] the voice of the world of objects or its own voice – in any case, not that of Transcendence. For knowledge to think that it has to do here with anything other than with immanence can only lead to muddying what is really knowable. (I, p. 254.)[57]

In another context, speaking of the emergence of the limits of knowledge which do not themselves become cognitive objects, he writes:

> Objective knowledge in concepts no longer stands in the way. But at the same time it is legitimate to speak here of revelation. While for knowledge it remains a purely negative revelation, the apprehension of this limit is still the silencing of Transcendence .... With the concept of nothingness, we refer to a state of affairs in which nothingness is revealed in the dissolution *(Schwinden)* of all objectivity

---

[56]I, pp. 225, 252-254, 292.
[57]The German reads as follows: "Für Wissen schweigt Transzendenz. Dass es meint, die Transzendenz reden zu hören, dann ist das die Stimme der Objektwelt oder seine eigene Stimme — jedenfalls nicht diejenige der Transzendenz. Es hier mit mehr und anderem zu tun zu haben meinen als mit der Immanenz, kann nur zu einer Trübung des wirklich Wissbaren führen."

which can beknown. As the locus of this negative revelation for knowledge, nothingness is a symbol. It is not the language but indeed the silence of Transcendence – and as such, indeed, "an eloquent silence." (I, p. 292.)[58]

While Buri's striking use of such phrases as *nicht sprechend, schweigen, reden, hören, Stimme,* and S*chweigen* must be taken symbolically
or metaphorically, he intends to convey a meaning by their use that can
be articulated in no other way. He means that "revelation of nothingness" is a genuine disclosive situation before which knowledge finds itself brought.

It is therefore possible to extract not one but three interrelated meanings of the idea *Offenbarung des Nichts.* (i) Revelation for knowledge is
negative; knowledge can gain no positive content of revelation.
Revelation for knowledge is merely negative because revelation touches
actualities, the self and Transcendence, which are in principle non-objective whereas knowledge in principle is confined to the objective structure
of consciousness. From within knowledge, it is impossible to say more
about these actualities than what they are *not* for knowledge. (ii) But the
phrase says more because there is also a *revelation* for knowledge. Transcendence does "speak," but this is a disclosure of nothingness for knowledge because if it stays within its proper limits, knowledge is confronted
with an "other," with the unconditioned movement of faith. But insofar as
knowledge continues to understand itself properly as knowledge, i.e., as
bound to objectivity which is its condition, it can give no content *qua*
knowledge to this "other." The proper understanding of knowledge *qua*
knowledge forces it to define the "other" as *ein Nichts.* (iii) This means
that the disclosure consists of the confrontation of knowledge with its limits. This is an important addition to the earlier consideration of the limits of knowledge. It suggests that when Buri criticizes ostensibly objective positions such as metaphysical world-views or the proofs for the existence of God as being a *Wissen des Nichts,* he means more than that
they are merely illegitimate objectifications. While he does mean this –
the first meaning of the phrase shows this – he also means something
more. Once they have been properly criticized, it is possible to interpret

---

[58]The German reads as follows: "Gegenständliches Begriffswissen steht hier also nicht
mehr im Wege. Gleichzeitig aber ist hier mit Recht von Offenbarung zu reden. Wenn es
für Wissen auch bei emer rein negativen Offenbarung bleibt, so ist das Innewerden dieser Grenze doch das Schweigen der Transzendenz . . . Mit dem Begriff des Nichts wei-
sen wir auf einen Sachverhalt hin, in welchem sich im Schwinden aller wissbaren Gegenständlichkeit das Nichts offenbart. Als Ort dieser negativen Offenbarung für Wissen ist
das Nichts ein Symbol. Es ist nicht die Sprache, wohl aber das Schweigen der Transzendenz — und als solches fürwahr 'ein beredtes Schweigen'."

them as mythological forms expressing the legitimate question that is raised *senkrecht* to the ordinary function of objectivity but which would never be raised as such by that ordinary function. In this sense, "revelation of nothingness" itself becomes a genuine, if negative, expression of faith.[59] At its limits, before the question, for instance, of the meaning of being or the question why there is something rather than nothing, knowledge founders.[60] This is a crisis for the knower because it is as though he were held out into nothingness. This awareness occurs not as itself a cognitive object but as a disclosive situation the crisis of which is marked by the dissolution of all cognitive objects. And it is precisely here that the knower is confronted with the question how he will understand himself. But the answer he gives will not be a cognitive movement but a movement of existence in which the non-objective structure of the existential dialectic is actualized. In this sense, then, revelation of nothingness is a genuine revelation and has positive import – but not one that can be given cognitive definition.

A further important point to note is that by affirming a revelation for knowledge, Buri carries his understanding of the negative status of revelation for knowledge far beyond a rejection of natural theology, for the phrase, "revelation of nothingness," applies equally to every *Heilsgeschichte*, to every supernatural theology, and to every objective theology of revelation. In other words, Buri starts from a general consensus in contemporary Protestant theology concerning the illegitimacy of natural theology but then turns this position against every statement of the objective status of doctrines apart from faith. For Buri, all such theologies are exactly analogous to natural theology at the point of the status of knowledge in theology. The question this raises, however, is whether Buri can develop a positive concept of revelation the content of which can be described without falling into the same error.

2. Historicity and Revelation for Faith

From Buri's criticism of objectivity, it is evident that he can understand the positive content of revelation only to the extent that he can absorb it into the non-objectivity of faith itself. To be relevant to the dialectic of faith, the disclosive situation which first actualizes this dialectic

---

[59]For this last point, cf., I, p. 248.
[60]*Ibid.*, pp. 246 f.; cf., *DP*, pp. 13-17, 51-53.

in a concrete situation must somehow be assimilated to the non-objectivity of the dialectic. Revelation can be actual only in the non-objective enactment of self-understanding.

The historicity of self-understanding means that it is not an ineffable and free-floating spirituality but a concrete process of embodiment in a particular situation. Historicity means not merely a kind of serial punctuality of unconditioned decisions without any linear continuity giving them body and texture; it indicates as well the context of embodiment which structures the internal web of action and experience in which the self actualizes itself non-objectively. The self always becomes itself in just this particular history, relative or not. Who the self is cannot be abstracted from its history not merely in the individualistic sense that every particular self is what it becomes but also in the wider sense that who the self becomes as an individual is always conditioned, structured and made possible by the tradition and the community in which it stands.

Buri attempts to understand revelation by relating the non-objective actualization of faith to the objectivity of the tradition which provides the context of continuity for revelation in an historical community. But this move simply recapitulates the problem pointed out with the concept of historicity. How is it possible to relate the non-objective historicity of self-understanding to the objective history which is supposed to define its context? On the one hand, Buri argues that a living faith is always situated by a concrete tradition of revelation. Such a tradition is not constituted by the generality of knowledge but by particularistic myths, stories, and images.[61] In the specific instance with which theology deals, this history is the tradition of objective assertions about a *Heilsgeschichte*. On the other hand, revelation must somehow be assimilated to the non-objectivity of faith. Buri feels that the transcendence of the self over objectivity in its self-enactment allows him not only to escape the mythological and supernaturalistic objectivism of traditional theology but also to solve the classical theological problems which have revolved around the distinction between objective claims independent of faith and their subjective appropriation. But in order to provide the non-objectivity of self-understanding with some kind of content, that is, to prevent its non-objectivity from becoming isolated in incommunicable and punctual acts of an ineffable self, he tries to argue that the non-objective enactment of the self is always constituted by a tradition. The question, then, is if and how he can relate the objectivity of the tradition to the non-objectivity of self-under-

[61] Cf., I, pp. 206-216, 254-256.

standing without either objectifying the self or subjectivizing the tradition. If the unconditionedness and *Unverfügbarkeit* of revelation are preserved only in the enactment of self-understanding, is the objectivity of the tradition any help? This is simply a different version of the same problem discussed throughout this chapter. If the objectivity of the tradition must somehow be assimilated to the non-objectivity of faith in order to arrive at a viable concept of revelation, then does the notion of a positive revelation for faith help to solve the problem of the theological description of the content of faith?

Buri attempts to solve this problem by developing a complex dialectic between the mediacy and the immediacy of revelation.[62] In Protestant orthodox theology and in a slightly different form in Catholic theology, the relationship between a revealed tradition and its contemporary appropriation was defined by the concepts of immediate and mediate revelation (*revelatio supernaturalis immediata et mediata*). Immediate revelation refers to God's original communication to prophets and apostles and to the recording of these disclosures under the guidance or dictation of the Holy Spirit in the canonical writings. Traditionally the period of immediate revelation was said to have ended with the death of the original apostles. Mediate revelation refers to the appropriation of the original revelation by faith. This appropriation is revelatory since the scriptural witness is confirmed as truth by the testimony of the Holy Spirit in the mind and heart of the believer. Despite certain alterations introduced into this schema by the Catholic position on tradition as opposed to the Protestant *sola scriptura*, Protestant and Catholic theologians have agreed in rejecting spiritualist claims of the possibility of a contemporary (i.e., immediate) witness by the Holy Spirit independent of the original traditioned revelation.[63]

This schema makes possible a theological position which can offer some criteria and control over what the church says while at the same time acknowledging the ongoing character of revelation in the appropriation of faith. Buri adopts this traditional distinction as a way of articulating the relation between a tradition expressed objectively in mythical stories and doctrines and the contemporary non-objectivity of self-understanding in which the tradition becomes revelation.

---

[62]*Ibid.*, pp. 258-266.

[63]Cf., *ibid.*, pp. 258 f. As Buri notes, even the Catholic concession of the possibility of "private revelations" and the doctrine of a developing tradition on the basis of the teaching office of the church are not new immediate revelations but are always bound to the tradition already mediated. They are forms of *revelatio supernaturalis mediata*.

He turns the distinction between immediate and mediate revelation into a dialectic constitutive of every revelatory act. Although the self cannot be reduced to that which appears in its external embodiments, Buri argues that the self becomes a person in the community of which it is a part by the appropriation of its tradition.[64] This appropriation is a dialectic involving both sides of the historicity of the self. It must not be divided into something objective, on the one hand, and something subjective, on the other hand. As Buri says:

> Revelation for faith is neither something that happened in the past which stands over against faith as an objective thing nor is it a process in the subjectivity of the believer – neither a *heilsgeschichtliche* factuality *(Tatsächlichkeit)* nor a psychic neutrality *(Zuständlichkeit)*. Rather, it is the eventfulness of revelation itself as the actualization *(Offenbarwerdung als Aktuellwerden)* of personal being in a self-understanding which grows out of a tradition of revelation. (I, p. 263.)[65]

Buri is arguing here that because revelation is an occurrence in the historicity of self-understanding in relation to the history in which the self stands, immediate and mediate revelation ought not to be seen in the usual way as a division into two separated acts. If this happens, the one side is bound to be questioned or even, as he says, usurped by the other side – "here an objectivism of revelation, there a psychologism of faith." (I, p. 263.)

These tendencies to fall over into one form or another of an inappropriate objectivity (objectivism or subjectivism) can only be avoided, Buri argues, by seeing the immediate/mediate distinction as a dialectic of the self. Revelation is never merely immediate or mediate. Every revelation has an immediate element at the same time that it is also mediated.[66] The simple separation between immediate and mediate revelation will work only for the objective point of view appropriate to an historical-critical examination. In this latter sense, immediate revelation is defined either as the origin of a religious tradition or as the report by that tradition that this is the original and definitive communication of God. Mediate revelation is then defined as the historical tradition which has developed from this origin. Buri acknowledges that insofar as a tradition can be communicated only in the objective form of consciousness, this objective form will characterize the witness ingredient in any tradition. But to con-

---

[64]Buri's phrase: "Das werden der Persönlichkeit des Glaubenden an der Überlieferung von Offenbarung für Glauben." (I, p. 261.)

[65]It should be noted that in this statement, Buri is opposing both objectivism and subjectivism.

[66]I, p. 278.

sider revelation under this objective form (as is indeed characteristic in the typical use made of the immediate/mediate distinction) is to misconstrue revelation for faith. Because revelation is an occurrence in the transcendence of the self beyond objectivity, every revelation is immediate; revelation *is* only in the immediacy of its enactment in a self-understanding. At the same time, this immediacy is never in the vacuum of a merely empty and ineffable self-understanding. It is an immediacy of enactment which is always mediated by the tradition in which the self stands.[67]

This means there is another way to look at a tradition than the merely objective way just delineated. Buri argues that viewed from a merely objective standpoint, immediate revelation also will be seen to involve an internal dialectic of immediacy and mediacy. That which is defined as immediate revelation was itself mediated by the concrete tradition in which it occurred. Its immediacy, that is to say, is also the expression of a self-understanding which itself involved the actualization of personhood within a tradition. Thus, quite apart from the objective standpoint, *one can also look at a tradition as the expression of self-understanding.* But this can be done only to the extent that the immediacy/mediacy of the tradition is incorporated into the mediacy/immediacy of one's own self-understanding. Properly understood, therefore, the judgment that a tradition is immediate is not an objective judgment; it is itself an expression of a contemporary self-understanding and involves an immediacy/mediacy dialectic internal to the contemporary witness. As Buri states this complex dialectic:

When, in distinction from the mediacy of all others, an exclusive immediacy is attributed to a revelation in the past, that always occurs out of the immediacy of an unconditioned self-understanding enacted in the present in connection with this tradition of revelation. Thus the immediacy of the *revelatio immediata* can be maintained only in combination with the mediacy which also belongs to it as well as with the immediacy which is also characteristic of the so-called *revelatio mediata*. Immediacy and mediacy belong to the essence of revelation as a historistic appearance. (I, p. 266.)

Actual revelation thus occurs when the non-objective possibilities in principle (which at one time were possibilities in fact for the persons articulating the original expression of self-understanding) mediated by the tradition become possibilities in fact for a contemporary self-understanding. The tradition is not revelation until this occurs in the non-objectivity of a contemporary self-understanding. The tradition is necessary because

[67]Cf., *ibid.*, pp. 259-263.

the actualization of the possibilities ingredient in any particular tradition of expressions of self-understanding is not a simple human possibility. It includes the donative character of faith (Transcendence-relatedness as a limiting concept) in the existential dialectic, but this never occurs in a general form. It can occur only through some particular disclosive situation defining a historicity. Such a disclosive situation is mediated by the tradition when its objective assertions are understood not in their objectivity but as expressions of self-understanding (i.e., as kerygma) offering the possibility for the actualization of another self-understanding.

In this way, Buri succeeds in developing a positive concept of revelation. But while the concepts of revelation for faith and the historicity of the Christian faith solve one problem in Buri's system, they only highlight the problem of the task of theology to which attention has been drawn. To repeat, after he has rejected Schleiermacher's approach through an objectively describable consciousness, Buri's problem is to show how the general concepts of self-understanding and Transcendence-relatedness can receive specification in the Christian self-understanding. This problem is solved with the concepts of historicity and revelation for faith. Those concepts do say *how* the Christian self-understanding receives specification if and when it does appear. It will be a self-understanding specified by the concrete possibilities for existing ingredient in the Christian message as these are mediated by a tradition of objectively expressed, mythological stories and doctrines which can become revelatory to the extent that they are divested of their external objectivity and seen as expressions of self-understanding.

But these concepts do not help in conceiving the theological task of describing *what* these actualized possibilities are. To this point one only knows that there are supposed to be *some* possibilities for existing which define a uniquely Christian self-understanding, that such possibilities are not general but can only be specified in a concrete historicity, and that they become possible through a disclosive situation mediated by a tradition of the objectively expressed doctrines of that self-understanding. In Buri's theology, the content of faith which it is the task of the theologian to describe would be the particular possibilities for existing which define the uniquely Christian self-understanding. But his understanding of revelation for knowledge and his criticism of objectivity make clear that *what* these possibilities are cannot be read off in any *prima facie* way from the objective form of the tradition which serves to mediate them and which also serves as the medium for expressing a contemporary form of the Christian self-understanding. The existential possibilities are not immediately clear from the tradition because its mythological form of discourse is misleadingly objective. And his understanding of the non-objectivity of faith, i.e., of the actualization of these possibilities, seems to make impossible an interpretation of the mythological form of the tradition in terms of a description of the existential possibilities embodied in it. Any such interpretation would only be a transposition of the mythological objectivity into the objectivity of knowledge. That is, it would only be a more cognitively adequate restatement. But it would still be objective and would, therefore, still apparently misconstrue both the nature of faith (its non-objectivity) and the limits of knowledge.

Consequently Buri's concepts of faith and revelation are, up to this point at least, disappointing in solving the problem of how to do theology once the problem of objectivity has been taken with the seriousness he thinks imperative. Far less than solving this problem, they seem to accentuate it. In solving the problem he sees in Schleiermacher, Buri seems to have created a more serious one for himself. Yet Buri is only the most consistent of the existentialist theologians who have oriented theology on the problem of objectivity. He has simply carried the issues raised by the so-called problem of objectivity to their logical conclusion once it has been elevated into a decisive hermeneutical issue. The anomaly arises from the fact that contemporary existentialist theologians, unlike existential theologians such as Kierkegaard, are concerned with carrying out the proper task of theology. They want, that is, to describe the content of the Christian faith in terms of the method of existentialist interpretation. The question that has become clear from this chapter asks, however, whether anything more than the existential problem of how to become a Christian remains after the problem of objectivity comes to the fore. It would seem that Buri must develop some objective way of interpreting the content of revelation in the non-objectivity of faith which does not fall into the errors of an objective understanding of revelation. His theory of symbol and myth is at least partly an attempt to do this.

CHAPTER IV

SYMBOL, MYTH, AND THE DIALECTIC OF OBJECTIVITY AND NON-OBJECTIVITY

It is clear from the preceding chapter that the non-objectivity of faith and revelation in Buri's thought appears to exclude not merely objective, supernaturalistic theology and natural theology but his theology as well. If theology is not the act of faith itself nor proclamation but scientific reflection on the act of faith and on the content of what is proclaimed, then its own discourse must be objective. While the actuality of revelation may not be objective, theological discourse about it certainly is. But if revelation for knowledge is *ein Nichts*, how is any theology at all possible? And if theological reflection is placed in question, then what is to prevent faith and its assertions from becoming capricious or mere illusion?

This is a problem that is wider than Buri's theology, for it touches the man of faith as well. Let it be granted that revelation and faith are non-objective in the sense that revelation is realized only in the act of faith by which it is appropriated. But if the objective tradition only mediates revelation and is not itself, *qua* objective, revelation in some sense, then how is the man of faith to know what content he is actualizing non-objectively? What, in other words, is the content of the internal dialectic of faith itself? Is it possible for the man of faith to know what self-understanding he is actualizing?

These questions come full circle back to the problem of theology. If Buri is going to criticize the objective form of the tradition and to absorb it into the historicity of the self, it would seem that he must at least be prepared to articulate what the content of the non-objective self-understanding is. If, that is, he is going to say that the content of revelation is not the ostensibly objective statement of the tradition but a modification of the self in the actualization of a self-understanding, then theology is possible only if he can, in some way, say what this modification is. Yet it is difficult to see how this theological task can be fulfilled on the basis of his understanding of faith and revelation. Revelation for knowledge is *ein Nichts*; revelation for faith is non-objective and is absorbed into an internal dialectic of the self; and this internal dialectic is understood as the non-objective process of existential becoming.

Buri tries to solve his problem by a process of mediation. He acknowledges the objective form of the tradition which at least provides the context and the continuity for revelation, and he attempts to establish some kind of relationship between *what* is thereby mediated and the non-objective act by which it is appropriated. In this, Buri does develop concepts of faith and revelation which are adequate to his theological purposes given his understanding of objectivity. But while these concepts are adequate in one sense, they do not make clear how the theologian can talk about their content. If it is to be possible to interpret faith and revelation, then there must be some way of mediating among (i) the objective form of the tradition, (ii) the non-objectivity of revelation as it is actualized in faith, and (iii) the objectivity of theological discourse itself. This means that Buri must develop additional hermeneutical principles which allow him to mediate between these various levels of objectivity and non-objectivity. Otherwise theology is impossible on his terms. His hermeneutic can be nothing but an attempt to show how, in the objective form of theology, the theologian can interpret the objective form of the tradition (the assertions of the Christian self-understanding) in terms of the non-objectivity of revelation and self-understanding. Again, the existentialist slogan, "overcoming the subject-object dichotomy," must mean in his theology not a dissolution of objectivity but a dialectic of objectivity and non-objectivity.

A. THE THEORY OF SYMBOLS

Buri addresses the problematic character of language about revelation directly. His answer is that "if the non-objectivity of nothingness, of self-understanding, and of Transcendence are to be allowed for, then the objectivity of statements about revelation for knowledge and faith must be an objectivity of a special sort." What this special type of objectivity is he defines as follows: "It is not merely an objectivity with whose help assertions concerning revelation are made in conceptually scientific and pictorially mythical ways; it is, in addition, an objectivity in and through which revelation simultaneously occurs – as the falling silent of nothingness for knowledge and as the language of Transcendence for faith." (I, p. 286.) Statements about revelation which are either "conceptually scientific" or "pictorially mythological" are illicit because they objectify what is in principle non-objectifiable. In the one case, revelation is reduced to a report about revelation and thereby reduced to the level of relativity appropriate to the historical-critical method. In the other case, revelation is seen as some kind of objective entity having a status apart from faith; but in this form it becomes subject to "conceptually scientific" scrutiny which divests it of its putatively explanatory function. As long as either of these ways of talking about revelation makes no claim to talk about revelation *qua* revelation – i.e., either to grasp its intrinsic reality (myth) or to grasp its intrinsic reality and explain it away (science) – then both of them are appropriate. Mythology becomes a museum piece suitable for various kinds of archeological excavation, and the scientific treatment of reports of revelation finds its appropriate place in the history of institutions and cultures. But the objective form in which assertions about revelation are made can also become the occasion for the occurrence of revelation. In this case, there is a special form of objectivity which can be described neither as mythological (except in a sense to be specified later) nor as scientific. It is a form of objectivity appropriate to the non-objectivity of faith, revelation, and Transcendence. Buri calls this special form of objectivity by the term "symbol." "Symbols are the objectivity of revelation – not merely in the sense that therein revelation is talked about but also so that therein revelation happens." (I, p. 286.)

Buri develops his theory of symbols by contrasting symbols to signs. Signs are the basic tool of concept formation and therefore of conceptual thought. Their basic characteristic is that they are a form of objectivity appropriate to the conditions under which things become objects of consciousness. Symbols, on the contrary, are distinguished by being a form of objectivity in which what is intrinsically non-objective receives objective expression. This is a function ruled out in principle for signs since their only legitimate function is to give expression to what is objective within the limits of knowledge. He develops the theory by contrasting sign and symbol at five points.[1]

(i) Signs are arbitrary conventions. Any sign can be chosen to designate any reality so long as there is clarity about just what it stands for and agreement to use it consistently to refer to just this reality. Thus, in so far as "symbol" is functioning in the present discussion as a sign, one

---

[1] For the following discussion, cf., I, pp. 286-291.

is entirely free to choose some other term such as "cipher," "image," "myth," or "likeness" to designate the meaning-structure to which reference is made. A symbol, on the other hand, is not an arbitrary convention. It derives not from one's own will to apply a convention but from the impact of the object. The symbol participates in the actuality of the disclosive situation; it represents the voice of revelation become spoken.

(ii) Closely related to its merely conventional character, a sign says nothing in and of itself; its whole meaning follows from the function it serves in a particular cognitive context. For this reason, definition is essential to the meaning of signs. In itself, as a vocable, it says nothing until its meaning is defined, and after it is defined, it must be used only in a manner consistent with the definition. While the definition of a sign may accrue to it through long usage, it must be defined explicitly and clarified if it is to serve a clear conceptual function. Scientific knowledge "loses its objectivity and general validity (*Allgemeingültigkeit*) when it 'stands in' or 'under' some sign instead of having free control over the sign in the way appropriate to it." (I, p. 288.) Opposed to saying only what is given to it to say by definition, the symbol speaks out of its own power or remains silent. It does not refer to something lying apart from it but reveals its meaning in and through itself, and there is no possibility of abstracting from its concrete meaning. It is self-interpreting in the sense that it either carries its meaning (i.e., its definition) in itself or says nothing.

(iii) A sign maintains its validity and function only so long as the convention remains in force; with a change in the manner of looking at something or with an advance in research, the convention can be changed or dropped. Revelation which takes place through the symbol does not stand under one's control. Symbols also live and die, but their birth and death is not something over which there is direct control.

(iv) Signs are defined with the intention of giving them a clear and unambiguous meaning so that they can serve a useful cognitive function. A symbol, however, is by nature ambiguous; its meaning can be made unambiguous only by divesting it of its symbolizing function and turning it into a sign. As Buri says:

In its objectivity, it [a symbol] can be an object of knowledge as well as an expression of faith. Accordingly, it can be silent and can speak – and indeed, differently for knowledge and for faith. It does, to be sure, speak unconditionally for the immediate enactment of faith. But elucidated through conceptual thought, this unconditionedness admits of diverse interpretations. Faith would not be decision if the language of Transcendence could be proved as generally *richtige*. (I, p. 291.)

(v) Finally, as was mentioned above, the sign has its legitimate function only in relation to conceptual thought. Consequently, it has no role to play outside the subject-object structure of consciousness. Symbols are also objective in nature, but they do not express an objectivity as such. They have their significance, rather, only in the act of unconditioned decision in which the "truth" expresses itself. Their objective form has no status apart from the non-objective actuality to which they give expression. Abstracted from it, they lose their role as symbols.

Buri's distinction here between sign and symbol reflects ideas that have become quite common in contemporary theology, and the skeleton of his theory seems to add nothing new to the contemporary discussion. It is only in the way that he uses this basic skeleton against the background of his systematic problem of objectivity that his theory receives a distinctive tone. Strangely enough, the first two points of distinction are the places where this distinctive contribution becomes most evident whereas the other three points are self-explanatory.

Buri relates the first two differences between sign and symbol to his understanding of phenomenal consciousness and to the limits of objectivity. As will be recalled from the discussion of the second limit of knowledge, he argues that there are certain givens which are the condition and even the *Gehalt* of knowledge but which themselves never become objects of knowledge. Signs function from within the possibilities of knowledge as these are already given. Because the structure and the *Gehalt* of knowledge are already given, because one is already immanent to the subject-object dichotomy and operating effectively within it, the choice of a sign lies at one's disposal. Reality is already given to be known; and working immanently to this given one exercises a certain control over the environment and has a certain freedom over how it is known. But the choice of a symbol does not lie at our disposal because, to the contrary, it "belongs precisely to that realm which conceptual knowledge tries to designate through its linguistic signs but then thereby comes up against the limits of its possibilities – indeed, not merely relatively but absolutely." (I, p. 289.) In other words, when something is given to be known, a choice of signs to designate it is in order. But *that* there is something given does not lie within the discretion of cognitive apprehension or explanation. It is grounded in that realm encompassing the subject-object structure and offering that structure its possibilities. And not merely the givenness of something to be known stands outside the power of cognition to determine; also that something given *can* be known, i.e., is or is not intelligible, is not open to the free determination of knowledge; it can be known only if it is intelligible. "Cognizability or non-cognizability is an affair of the object, not of the subject." (I, p. 289.) Symbols stand outside our control because their reference is to that realm which is the ultimate origin (*Ursprung*) of all that is given. They stand on the side of the mystery that there is anything given at all; thus, they represent the freedom of being to present itself and not the freedom of the knower to know something once it is presented. As Buri says:

> The arbitrariness of the giving and the use of signs stands over against the freedom of being to show itself or not to show itself, to be cognizable or not to be cognizable. For the knower, that which is freedom on the side of being works itself out as the opposite of arbitrariness and capriciousness: as a being-given-so-and-not-otherwise. At the locus at which being reveals itself for knowledge or faith, the symbol is not replaceable arbitrarily or capriciously. Because of the freedom appropriate to it, it is withdrawn from our arbitrariness and capriciousness – although this locus of the revelation of being must not be separated from the assertions which we make about it. (I, pp. 289-290.)

Symbols derive from this freedom of being to give or withhold itself because the purpose of the symbol is to give expression to the non-objective source of being – the source which is apprehended only negatively in the transcending movement of thought in which one becomes conscious of the contingent character of the structure of consciousness and which is apprehended positively only in the non-objective act of existence related to Transcendence. The symbol is an objective expression of precisely the limits of the subject-object structure whereas signs function legitimately only immanent to those limits.

Symbols have the logically odd function of expressing objectively what cannot be expressed objectively. For this reason they must not be confused with signs. The way of preventing this confusion is to see that their meaning is not intrinsic to their objective form like the sign but to the way in which objective form can become transparent to the non-objective. This means that the purpose of the symbol is not to express an objective meaning but to allow an event to occur, and whatever meaning the symbol has cannot be abstracted from this occurrence. This connects the first point with the second point of contrast between symbols and signs.

The meaning of the sign is contained in the definition which states the convention it serves. Its purpose is to refer to something which in itself it is not but which is given to it by convention to designate. "As against this," Buri says, "the symbol is the revelatory utterance of being itself."

(I, p. 290.) For this reason, the meaning of the symbol is not a conceptual convention attributed to it. Its meaning is self-interpreting – not in the sense of an objective statement but in the sense that in and through the objective form revelation occurs:

> The symbol speaks or is silent from its own power. In it being itself declares itself – as *das Nichts* for knowledge, as self-understanding and Transcendence for faith. *While it is not itself das Nichts, self-understanding or Transcendence, still it exhibits their becoming revealed.* Das Nichts, self-understanding, and Transcendence are for us either as conceptual signs which refer to something not to be conceptually objectified or precisely as symbols in which *das Nichts* itself falls silent (*ausschweigt*) – "*nichtet*" in Heidegger's terminology – or self-understanding and Transcendence declare themselves – as "ciphers" for faith in Jaspers' sense. In that silence as well as in this speaking, symbols are what they are, namely, the revelation of *Nichts* or of the Transcendence-relation of self-understanding. *But they are not a reference to ein Nichts, a self-understanding, or a Transcendence which still lies behind them so that there would have to be a distinction between that which is revealed and that which is not revealed.* In the symbol, we have to do with the revealing *(dem Offenbaren)* itself. Therein the revealing itself falls silent or speaks, obliterates all objectivity for knowledge or becomes objective for faith. (I, p. 290. My italics.)

In other words, Buri is arguing that the function of the symbol cannot be abstracted from the occurrence of revelation in and through it. It is an objective form which has no conceptual status in itself but is the medium or occasion for the actual occurrence of revelation. By interpreting the tradition as a series of symbols, Buri believes he can solve the problem of having self-understanding mediated by an objective form. The form is objective, but in and of itself it has no objective content. The objective form of the symbol is merely the occasion for an event in the subjectivity of the believer.

The distinctive element in this theory of symbols is contributed by Buri's concern with the problem of objectivity. The symbol is an objective form which gives voice to the non-objective ground transcendent to the subject-object structure of consciousness. But because this ground is non-objective in principle, symbols must not be interpreted as having any objective content. To think of them as having objective content would be to see them as making some conceptual claim. But this would be to reduce their function to that of signs, and as signs they would be illicit objectifications because, by attempting to express objectively what is non-objective, they would transgress the legitimate limits within which signs function. If the symbol does give some kind of objective expression to that which is beyond the subject-object structure, it can do so only at that point where there is a finite apprehension of this dimension of being, namely, in the non-objective act of an unconditioned self-understanding. According to Buri, therefore, the legitimate function of the symbol must be seen not in any objective content, but as the occasion for the occurrence of self-understanding. Its objective form cannot be abstracted from the actual occurrence of revelation which it mediates.

B. DEMYTHOLOGIZING, EXISTENTIALIST INTERPRETATION, AND THE SELF-UNDERSTANDING OF MYTH

The theory of symbols is still highly formal and abstract because, like revelation and historicity, there must be some concrete material in the historicity of faith which can become symbolic. Symbols are never given in pure form as symbols but always arise out of the specific tradition in which faith occurs. Buri designates this concrete material which can become symbolic by the concept of myth. A religious tradition always occurs in the form of myth. For this reason, his theory of symbols can only be understood in connection with his understanding of myth.

1. Buri's Concept of Myth

Unlike Bultmann who carefully defines his concept of myth, Buri never offers an explicit definition. Instead he simply uses a concept of myth with a double focus. On the one hand, he assumes that the concept has come to have a common meaning as a category of the history of religions. On the other hand, he also uses the concept in a systematic, philosophical or theological manner.

The history of religions sees myth both as a form of primitive science and as an attempt on the part of primitive man to express his understanding of the source of his existence and of his relation to that source. It serves, that is to say, not only the etiological purpose of explaining astonishing phenomena which cannot otherwise be accounted for but also the religious purpose of expressing man's understanding of the source and goal of his existence which is beyond his control and calculation. In doing this, myth usually takes the form of a double history. In addition to this world and its history, there is another, supernatural world and its history, and the relation between them is seen in the form of a history of the gods in which there are supernatural incursions into the natural world.[2]

The connection between this historical account of myth and Buri's systematic use of it is the concept of objectivity. The various characteristics of myth can be summed up as objectifications into worldly objects of that which is the ground and source of our existence. In this, transcendence is reduced to immanence in the two senses that it is conceived in images appropriate only to worldly phenomena and that a supernatural world is seen as running parallel to the finite world. In both cases, a qualitative difference is reduced to a difference in degree only.[3] Buri's systematic definition is that *any objective discourse about that which is non-objective in principle is mythological.*[4]

This systematic definition is much wider than the descriptive one, for in addition to the primitive idea of myth, it allows Buri to speak of *Wissenschaftsmythos* and of *Pseudowissenschaft.*[5] He notes that the origin of the category of myth is inseparable from the rise of modern *Wissenschaftlichkeit.* For the man who lives in a mythological world-view, the category of myth in the strict sense does not exist, and the development of such a category means that myth itself has already been demythologized and overcome.[6] Once science has developed the concept, it is impossible to retreat behind it and live once again in the immediacy of such a world-view.[7] But science itself can become mythological. This happens in

---

[2]Cf., Paul Tillich, "Mythus und Mythologie," in RGG[2], IV, Sp. 363; Bultmann, "Neues Testament und Mythologie," pp. 15 f., 22 and 22, note 2 (ET, pp. 1 f., 10 f., and 10, note 2); Ogden, *Christ without Myth,* pp. 24-27.

[3]Cf., *ibid.,* p. 26.

[4]Cf., I, pp. 203, 223; *TdE,* p. 101 (ET, p. 91). Buri himself nowhere makes this definition as a systematic principle except parenthetically. It does function for him as a systematic concept, however, for only so is it possible to understand how he uses "mythological" to describe positions, such as speculative metaphysics and a false understanding of science, which do not fit the merely descriptive use.

[5]Cf., I, pp. 201-204, 209-211, *et passim.*

[6]*Ibid.,* p. 198. Buri, of course, does not overlook that the category of myth was used by the New Testament writers to criticize heathen religion. This would seem to suggest that some kind of critical consciousness had been attained in the New Testament. But as Buri correctly notes, the concept of myth used there was not one arrived at through a critical self-consciousness as he means it. It was used, rather, simply in a pejorative sense to define the uniqueness and superiority of the new religion. As Buri here writes: "Wenn der Mythosbegriff auftaucht, so ist das ein Zeichen dafür, dass der Mythos selber in Frage gestellt oder schon überwunden ist. Das ist noch nicht der Fall, wenn im Neuen Testament vor den Mythen gewarnt wird (1. Tim. 1:4, 4:7. 2. Tim. 4:4. 2. Pet. 1:16), oder wenn die alte Kirche die gnostische Mythologie bekämpft; denn hier wird einfach fremden Mythen der eigene christlich-kirchliche Mythos entgegengestellt." *Ibid.*

[7]*Ibid.,* Cf., EoE, pp. 94 f.

either of two ways. Either science demythologizes the myth and tries to replace it with a more intellectually adequate conception of the ground and source of existence, or science dispenses altogether with the reality to which myth points and claims that reality is exhausted by what objective consciousness can determine legitimately. The first form is mythological because there is an obvious transgression of the limits of knowledge; being-itself is still objectified, and the qualitative difference between time and eternity is reduced to a matter of degree within immanence – not in intention but simply because of the conditions of finite consciousness. Buri consequently designates speculative metaphysics and ontology as having the same conceptual status as mythology. The second form is no less mythological and no less a transgression of the limits of objectivity, for the accession to objectivity within immanence is accompanied by the claim that this limited objectivity is all. This is a transgression of the limits of objectivity because in staying within the proper limits of objectivity, science still does not acknowledge that the structure of objectivity itself is limited, contingent, and non-exhaustive. This systematic definition of myth as an objectification of that which is non-objective thus allows Buri to combine under a single concept the descriptive notion in the history of religions and a misunderstanding of itself on the part of science.

2. The Reappropriation of Myth in Self-Understanding

a. Demythologizing and Existentialist Interpretation

In terms of this combined notion of myth, Buri now states his own position in the contemporary demythologizing debate. Here he develops the position he only suggested in 1952 by the negative concept of dekerygmatizing.

Demythologizing is necessary once the mythological form has been recognized as mythological; indeed, the very recognition of it as mythical is already a demythologizing.[8] But the mythical self-understanding still remains untouched by the essentially negative task of criticizing the objective form of the mythological claim. For this reason, Buri is in full agreement with Bultmann that demythologizing must be accompanied by existentialist interpretation. To remain merely at the level of a negative criticism by a type of thinking which sees itself as "come of age" would

[8] I, p. 198.

be to fail to recognize the important function myth does play in the lives of people even if its objective claim must be discounted. Furthermore, on Buri's terms it would amount to an absolutization of the scientific perspective and, consequently, a transgression of the limits of knowledge. It is possible for scientific thinking to make a negative criticism of myth because the mythological form has attempted to answer final questions at a level appropriate to the structure of scientific thinking. But scientific thinking is no more able to give an objective answer to the question of the source and goal of our existence than is mythological thought. So, to stay merely at the point of a negative critique would amount either to a refusal to grant the legitimacy of such questions or to a claim that reality is exhausted by what can be known about it. Demythologizing can be complete only if it is followed by an attempt to understand the force of the question which myth can ask and answer only in an inappropriate way. Following Bultmann, Buri agrees that the proper way to approach this question is through existentialist interpretation. Mythological statements must be interpreted exhaustively as statements about the non-objective self-understanding of the believer and not as stating something objectively true apart from that self-understanding.[9]

But Buri argues that demythologizing and existentialist interpretation are also insufficient.[10] Just as demythologizing requires existentialist interpretation if it is not to end in a false scientism or a scientific mythology, so also, existentialist interpretation is inconceivable without demythologizing. There must be a critical stage of reflection attained (demythologizing) before the move can be made toward interpreting mythological statements as expressive of a self-understanding, as self-referring statements about the existence of the believer (existentialist interpretation). But because existentialist interpretation is so closely tied to the scientific criticism of myth, it is difficult to free it from being dominated by a scientific conceptuality. If this happens, then existentialist interpretation itself falls under the sway of a false objectivity instead of seeing that the force of saying that mythological statements are expressions of self-understanding is the insight that they are expressions of faith. Insofar as they are expressions of faith, they must be interpreted in terms of the non-objective dimension of faith, and this dimension cannot be grasped as *allgemein ausweisbar* by a scientific conceptuality.[11]

---

[9]*Ibid.*, p. 199.
[10]*Ibid.*, pp. 198 f.
[11]*Ibid.* Cf., *ibid.*, pp. 175-178, 203 f., 299-301.

Buri accuses Bultmann of having fallen into this error.[12] Bultmann's attempt to found his existentialist interpretation on an objective and scientific ontology of human being results in the attempt to make an objective description of self-understanding in terms of "given" structures of human existence. Despite Bultmann's emphasis on the problem of objectivity and his understanding of the necessity for existentialist interpretation, Buri claims that his dependence on a scientific conceptuality leads him to overlook the "transcending" dimension of human existence and to reduce the non-objectivity of faith to something objectively given. Bultmann's problem, according to Buri, is that he has not understood the problem of objectivity radically enough, in terms of the discussion of Bultmann in the second chapter, that he has not carefully enough considered the conditions of objectivity in general. The objectivity he criticizes is that form of objective thinking dominated by the modern, scientific world view which defines thought in terms of objectifications of "things"; but in agreement with Heidegger, Bultmann still feels it is possible to make an objective, scientific description of the self with special concepts ("existentials") appropriate to subjects. This is a failure to see that no matter what kind of concepts are employed, the intrinsic self is never something "given" so that it can be described objectively; and it is a failure to see that faith and the content of doctrines reside entirely in this non-objective dimension.

Bultmann's refusal to free himself from the scientific conceptuality, which is appropriate at the level of demythologizing, leads him into a twofold error. In the first place, he remains bound to the notion of a descriptive, scientific ontology. In this he has not conceived the problem of objectivity radically enough, and he is insufficiently aware of the nature of consciousness and of the limits of knowledge. In the second place, his dependence on an objective ontology allows him at the crucial point in his system to fall back on the orthodox, objective *Heilsgeschichte*. His refusal to demythologize the Christ event means that there is a mythological remainder in his program. In 1952, Buri pointed out this contradiction in Bultmann's program. He still adheres to this criticism, arguing that this accounts for the orthodox, *heilsgeschichtlich* root of Bultmann's thought which stands in contradiction to many of his other statements about the nature of faith. But Buri now goes a step farther and argues

---

[12]Cf., *ibid.*, pp. 199, 203, 222; PaP, pp. 116 f.; Buri, "Das hermeneutische Problem in der protestantischen Theologie der Gegenwart" in *SthUm*, 17 (Dez. 1947), p. 31; EoE, pp. 93-100; Buri, "Theologie und Philosophie," pp. 123-126.

that the reason for this contradiction abides in Bultmann's inadequate grasp of the problem of objectivity.

Many interpreters felt that Buri's dekerygmatizing proposal would mean a total exclusion of the particularity of the Christian kerygmatic claim and of the reality of grace. He was criticized for reducing the Christian message to a simple human possibility which could be stated as a general truth.[13] It is because of this misleading aspect of the term "dekerygmatizing" that Buri now rejects it as a systematic proposal. But as was suggested in the first chapter, he still adheres to the force of dekerygmatizing as a negative criticism of the mythological remainder in Bultmann's position. It is now evident that the kerygma Buri wanted to eliminate in dekerygmatizing was the kerygma that was tied to an objective event in the past taken to have some kind of status as the ground and possibility of salvation apart from the non-objective actualization of faith itself. Buri denies that this rejection means the reduction of the Christian affirmation to a simple human possibility the content of which can be stated as a general truth. This would be an equally false objectification – a transgression of the limits of objectivity and a misunderstanding of the nature of faith. The kerygma cannot be grounded in any reality apart from the non-objective dialectic of faith itself. Insofar as Bultmann grounds existentialist interpretation of the kerygma in a kerygmatic event of the past essentially independent of self-understanding, Buri would still argue that demythologizing must be understood to include dekerygmatizing. But he would insist that this does not mean a reduction of the Christian message to a general truth. The Christian message is still constituted by a kerygma which cannot be stated generally but which can only be actualized in the non-objective historicity of faith. The *essential meaning* of every Christian doctrine is *kerygmatic* – but not as an objective truth (in the sense either of a proposition *or* a *Heilsgeschichte*), rather as the appeal to a possibility of existence. In other words, the alternative, event or general truth, is misplaced if event is understood as an objective event of the past. For Buri, the content of faith is still an event, but it is one that cannot be isolated objectively (either in the past or the present) external to the existential dialectic in which that content becomes a reality in faith.

Both now and when he made the original dekerygmatizing proposal, Buri has been consistent in insisting that dekerygmatizing also does not

---

[13]Cf., e.g., James M. Robinson, *A New Quest of the Historical Jesus* (London: SCM Press, Ltd., 1959), pp. 80-85, and Macquarrie, *The Scope of Demythologizing*, pp. 148-153.

mean a reduction of the possibility of faith to a simple human possibility. His only point is to insist that the sense in which faith is not a simple human possibility is one that cannot be grounded in an external event of the past (or in an external event of any kind, for that matter). The sense in which faith is not a simple human possibility can be gotten at only through the non-objective dialectic of existence itself. It is in and through this dialectic of its self-actualization that the self both comes to itself in its autonomy (in its freedom and responsibility) and also realizes that its self-actualization is a gift.

In view of this criticism of Bultmann's version of demythologizing, Buri now argues that besides demythologizing and existentialist interpretation still a third element in the method is needed. He calls this "the self-understanding of myth." (I, p. 199.) If existentialist interpretation is used solely in connection with the scientific conceptuality necessary for demythologizing, it is inevitable that some false form of objectivity will result. Existentialist interpretation can be properly employed only if the non-objectivity of faith is kept constantly in sight. And this means that over and beyond the quite necessary demythologizing of myth, it is necessary to adhere to myth as the most adequate objective form for expressing self-understanding. Self-understanding, if you will, lives but does not have its being in myth. If existentialist interpretation binds itself only to demythologizing, it cannot help but eliminate myth in favor of some other objective form taken to be more adequate – an ontology of human being, a general truth, a metaphysic, a mythological remainder. A legitimate existentialist interpretation that holds fast to the non-objectivity of faith will mean a re-appropriation of myth on the far side of the demythologized myth. Only in the mythological form of objectivity, which has now been lifted into a critical consciousness, can "the self-understanding of myth" be preserved.

b. The Dialectic of Myth

This means that theology must take a highly dialectical position on the problem of mythological forms of speaking. Buri articulates this as three forms of myth which theology must take into account (i) "myth in its pre-scientific objectivity," (ii) "myth as an objective scientific mythology," and (iii) "myth as the objective expression of a non-objectifiable faith." (I, p. 199.)[14]

14Cf., I, pp. 199-206.

The first form of myth is the proper subject of scientific criticism (demythologizing both because it tries to be explanatory as primitive science and because it attempts to answer the question of the source and goal of finite existence in an inappropriate manner. It is at this point that Buri acknowledges one of the primary functions objective thought does have to play in theology despite the non-objectivity of faith and revelation. But he also fears that, unless scientific thinking is sufficiently critical of itself, its criticism of myth can lead to an imperialism of scientific thinking in which it totally eliminates myth and sets itself up as an exhaustive explanatory model. Beyond science, it is philosophy which can hold science within its proper limits. The function of philosophy is not to provide new facts about the world or to construct comprehensive metaphysical systems objectively descriptive of everything that happens. Its function, rather, is the formal one of elucidating the structures of consciousness themselves, of disclosing the place of knowledge within the contingency of consciousness, and of pointing to the non-objective dimension within human existence.[15] It is only here in the reciprocal criticism of myth by science and of science by philosophy that existentialist interpretation can function legitimately, for the philosophical elucidation of consciousness holds existentialist interpretation fast to the non-objectivity of faith and Transcendence.

The elucidation of the limits of objectivity makes it possible to assess the function of myth anew. Demythologizing is necessary because myth is an inappropriate objectification. But existentialist interpretation must be a legitimate interpretation of faith, and this means it must respect the non-objectivity of faith. It is necessary to guard existentialist interpretation from itself falling into a false objectivity. When this has been done through philosophical transcending, there is the problem how any interpretation of the non-objectivity of faith can be made at all. It then becomes possible to see that as long as myth is divested of its own false objectivity it can serve, as no other objective form can, to give expression to this non-objectivity.[16] Just because a proper understanding of faith and

---

[15]Cf., *ibid.*, pp. 35 f.

[16]Buri defines the function of philosophy at this point in the following manner: "Wohl löst die Wissenschaft den Mythos auf, indem sie ihn als Mythos erkennt. Aber gerade dadurch, dass sie meint, ihn wissenschaftlich erledigen zu können, wird sie seinem Wesen nicht nur nicht gerecht, sondern wird selber zu einer Art Mythos: zum Mythos der alles erklärenden Wissenschaft. Die philosophische Besinnung dagegen überwindet den Wissenschaftsmythos, indem sie die Grenzen des gegenständlichen Wissens aufdeckt, und wird so fähig zu einem tiferen Verständnis des Mythos als Ausdruck für das Ungegenständliche des Glaubens. Aber gerade darin versteht sie den Mythos anders, als er sich selber

Transcendence is aware of their non-objectivity, "the mythical tradition within which faith arises does not come into question for faith *in its mythical objectivity.*" (I, p. 204. My italics.) In its objectivity

it is demythologized for faith which elucidates itself scientifically. But because it is faith and not self-absolutizing science, the mythical objectivity of the tradition can become faith's expression for that which cannot be brought to expression in the objectivity of science because it cannot be grasped in scientific categories and for science is therefore not there. So, faith proceeds through demythologizing to a new mythical thought. The objectivity of myth becomes the expression for faith which is essentially non-objective. (I, p. 204.)

In other words, once the limits of every scientific conceptuality have been brought to consciousness, the reality of what is essentially non-objective can be given objective expression for existentialist interpretation only through a form of speaking which is essentially unscientific. The depths and mystery of the non-objective relation between faith and being can be given expression through the mythological form of discourse in a way that cannot be touched by the dry and leveling consistency of scientific objectivity. But this can be done only so long as mythological discourse is not confused with the literally objective claim it makes in its pre-scientific form. For this reason, the appropriation of myth must be highly dialectical. It can serve as an expression for the non-objectivity of self-understanding only under a critical consciousness directed both at its pre-scientific articulation and at the scientific objectivity which denudes its pre-scientific form. But properly understood, myth can give expression to the transcending dimension of human existence which can be captured in no form of objective discourse. Only as the "self-understanding of myth" can existentialist interpretation achieve its legitimate role beyond demythologizing.[17]

---

versteht, insofern er noch nichts von der wissenschaftlichen Aufklärung weiss, durch welche die philosophische Besinnung hindurchgegangen ist und die — als in ihre Grenzen gewiesene Wissenschaft — vom philosophischen Glauben aufbehalten wird." *Ibid.*, pp. 198 f.

[17]Buri makes no pretensions that this interpretation of the self-understanding of myth is necessarily equivalent to the understanding of myth maintained in the unbroken mythological consciousness. He says: "Ob dabei das, was am Mythos dem Glauben an Offenbarung zuteil wird, dem historisch ursprünglichen Sinn des Mythos entspricht, ist eine historisch wissenschaftliche Frage, deren Beantwortung für den Glauben nicht gleichgültig ist, von der er aber in seiner Wahrheit grundsätzlich unabhängig ist. Lebendiger Glaube ist nicht historisch, sondern geschichtlich. Das Gegenständliche ist für den Glauben nicht in seiner Gegenständlichkeit, sondern als Ausdruck seiner — des Glaubens — Ungegenständlichkeit wesentlich." *Ibid.*, p. 204.

C. MYTH AND SYMBOL

The relationship between myth and symbol in Buri's thought seems, at first glance, to present a problem. According to the systematic definition of myth which Buri employs, it would appear that myth and symbol are identical since each is defined as an objectification of that which is non-objective in principle. If their definitions are so similar, what can be the systematic gain in making a terminological distinction between them? While Buri's systematic definition of myth is quite similar to his understanding of symbol, his understanding of mythological forms of discourse as a whole is highly dialectical so that symbol cannot be identified in any straightforward way with myth although there is a systematic relation. To see this it is necessary to examine the relationship between self-understanding and both myth and symbol.

While the mythological form of speaking can serve as an *expression* for self-understanding, Buri is quite clear that self-understanding itself is not mythological. He says:

Revelation for faith always stands in tradition. Tradition precedes it and tradition proceeds out of it once more. Personal being which is aware of its relation to Transcendence originates in the context of tradition. But since, *in distinction from myth* in which they come to expression, personal being and Transcendence themselves ar non-objective, tensions are also inevitable here between the mythical tradition and personal faith. The appropriation of the tradition of faith is enacted precisely in overcoming these tensions. (I, p. 257. My italics.)[18]

No matter what its form – whether still pre-scientific or critically appropriated as an expression of self-understanding – myth is an objectification of that which is non-objective whereas self-understanding is the non-objective actualization of a relation to Transcendence. Because of its peculiar logical status, myth can be an appropriate expression of self-understanding only in the third form of myth, in the self-understanding of myth. On the far side of its uncritical objectivity and of the uncritical absolutization of rational objectivity in a scientific mythology, myth can serve as the appropriate expression for self-understanding. At this point it is held in a critical consciousness in which its objective form is no longer a problem, for (i) it has been divested of its ostensibly objective

---

[18]Cf., also *ibid.*, p. 177: "Was jedoch von keiner Wissenschaft zum Gegenstand ihrer Forschung gemacht werden kann, und worüber sie deshalb, ohne ihre Grenzen zu überschreiten, keine Aussagen zu machen imstande ist, das ist das Ungegenständliche des Selbstverständnisses, das sich im Mythos nur ausspricht, das in seinem Vollzug der Mythos aber gerade nicht ist." Cf., *DP*, pp. 56-58.

claim, and (ii) the movement of philosophical transcending in criticism of the absolutization of scientific objectivity makes it possible for faith to hold fast to the non-objectivity of self-understanding and Transcendence.

The relation between symbol and self-understanding has two aspects. (i) Symbol is an objective form peculiarly appropriate to the non-objectivity of self-understanding because it serves to express it. But in order to serve this function, (ii) its form must be seen not as making an objective claim but as the medium in and under which revelation itself occurs. It receives its only content, therefore, in the modification of existence which eventuates from the disclosive situation in which it becomes transparent to the possibility of an existential self-understanding.

Symbol, then, has a basically normative function for Buri whereas myth is a basically descriptive term. Symbol and myth are related to the extent that the mythological form of the tradition becomes a symbol. This occurs when the myth serves legitimately to give expression to a self-understanding. But myth as such is not symbolic. Only when it functions in Buri's third form of myth to give expression to a self-understanding does it become a symbol. Buri never says that the tradition is symbolic; he always says that it is mythological.[19] In the first instance, the tradition within which faith lives is a mythological world of stories and images which can be defined objectively as mythological from an historical-critical perspective. It is from this vantage point that the need for demythologizing first arises. Myth thus has several levels, and at the first level, the level of tradition and expressions of faith, it is not symbolic. It is only in terms of a critical consciousness on the problem of objectivity that it becomes possible to appropriate myth as a legitimate expression of faith. When this occurs, myth is functioning symbolically because, from a normative point of view, it can be seen as the medium for an appropriate understanding of faith and revelation. While both symbol and myth are defined systematically as objectifications of the non-objective, not all such objectifications in the mythological form are legitimate. Only in the critical consciousness of the dialectic of myth does myth become symbolic.

The concepts of myth and symbol play an important role in Buri's theology because they show how he can take a positive approach to the objective language of a religious tradition which appears absurd from a

---

[19]Cf., e.g., I, p. 256: "Offenbarung beginnt mit dem Mythos und lebt im Mythos. Mit dem Mythos schwindet auch die Offenbarung für Glauben."

purely scientific perspective. His concept of myth provides him with an objective form which mediates faith and in which faith can express itself. And his concept of symbol shows how the literal objectivity of myth *can* serve this function without the theologian or the believer having to take the myth at its face value. But a close examination of each of these concepts will reveal that neither the dialectic of myth nor the theory of symbols explain how the theologian can interpret the mythological objectivity in order to articulate its content or its true meaning for faith.

Once he has restricted scientific objectivity so that it is inappropriate to faith, Buri needs some form of objectivity which can serve to articulate faith. This he finds in myth. He argues that, when myth is held in a critical consciousness, it can serve to give legitimate expression to faith as no other objective form can. Only the essentially unscientific form of myth can give expression to the non-objective reality of faith. The problem here, however, is with the critical consciousness. Myth can serve this function only when it is divested of its primitive, uncritical objectivity. This means that, when myths express a self-understanding, *what* they express is not the literal, objective content of the myth in its pristine form but some other content (i.e., that of an existential self-understanding) which comes to expression in and through them. This position on myth serves perfectly well to explain Buri's view of how myths function in the lives of religious people. But it does not explain how the theologian can explicate the content of the self-understanding coming to expression in the myth. This content is itself non-mythological.

Presumably the normative concept of symbol provides access to the content of self-understanding. Myths become symbols when their objective form is understood not in the literal sense of the original myth but as expressing a self-understanding. The symbolic understanding of the myth should give the theologian a way of interpreting the true content of self-understanding expressed in the myth. But Buri's theory of symbols does not allow this.

Symbols are a special form of objectivity which is supposed to provide the objective vehicle the theologian needs to carry out his task. But this special form of objectivity operates legitimately as a symbol only when it mediates the actual occurrence of revelation (and thus faith). It has no status apart from this occurrence. To see the objective form of the symbol itself as articulating the content of the self-understanding would apparently be to reduce the symbol to a sign. So again with symbols, there is an explanation of how religious concepts might function in the lives of religious people but no explanation of how the theologian can explicate their content. How is the theologian to *interpret* symbolic assertions? If he avoids reducing them to signs, are his interpretations also symbols? They obviously cannot be because this would involve his existentialist interpretation in an infinite regress, symbols interpreting symbols interpreting symbols with no resting point for the content of any of them. Does Buri, then, leave any room for such interpretations in his strictures on objectivity in relation to the non-objective actuality of revelation in faith?

Because of this problem with the content of symbols, one is tempted to ask again whether revelation and faith can have any content. If symbols cannot have an objective content but can serve only as the medium in which something non-objective occurs, then how is one to say *what* occurs? Does not faith become ineffable? And if it does not, then is not the statement of the content a reduction of the symbol to a sign?

It is apparent, therefore, that Buri's concepts of myth and symbol does not answer the question how theology is possible in an existentialist theology such as his. This discussion of myth and symbol does sharpen the question, however. It is clear that if theology is possible in Buri's terms, there must be a hermeneutical principle which makes it possible for the theologian to interpret the content of symbols in the objective form of consciousness (obj-B). In order to avoid an infinite regress, such a principle would have to be non-mythological and non-symbolic offering some point of reference in terms of which expressions of self-understanding could be explicated to arrive at a theological interpretation of their content. The one point in Buri's theology which seems to meet these conditions is his systematic principle which defines the structure of the existential dialectic.

D. THE HERMENEUTICAL SIGNIFICANCE OF THE SYSTEMATIC PRINCIPLE

Even though Buri's systematic principle is not an ontological structure, it does describe a structure of human existence in its existential actualization.[20] The principle is non-mythological because it refers to the non-objective dialectic of existence rather than to objective or subjective states of affairs given independently of that dialectic. In this sense, the systematic principle represents the existential structure which seeks to express itself inappropriately in various kinds of myth. It is also non-sym-

[20] Cf., I, p. 172; II, p. 141.

bolic because it does not represent the actual mediation of the existential dialectic through the symbolic use of objective doctrines but describes the structure of what occurs when that mediation takes place. Hence, it can serve as a non-symbolic principle to interpret the symbolic (not mythological) content. Myths are the objective form in which faith expresses itself; symbols represent the legitimate content of myths; and the systematic principle is the hermeneutical device by means of which this content can be interpreted.

The crucial problem with the systematic principle is whether its hermeneutical function will result in an anthropologizing of theology, a reduction of the content of all theological assertions to man alone. Buri stringently denies that this is the case.[21] Despite the fact that the content of all theological assertions must be interpreted in terms of the existential dialectic that occurs in the self, Buri believes that the Transcendence-relation, which is the basis of the systematic principle, prevents the reduction of this content to the self alone. The problem, however, is what to make of "Transcendence" if it is only a limiting concept descriptive of the existential dialectic, of the structure of choosing and being chosen which constitutes the "paradox of grace." It might be admitted on the basis of an existentialist analysis that the existential self is relational in structure, that is, that who the self is is always realized in a dialectical relation to something which posits its possibility as a self. But the objection could be raised that this "other" need be nothing more than something internal to the world as a whole – e.g., the "social self," the neighbor who lays claim on the self, or even the transcendent dimension of the self.[22] In other words, the transition is not at all self-evi-

---

[21]Cf., I, pp. 217-219; II, pp. 19-23, 31-33.

[22]Buri and Jaspers are fond of quoting Kierkegaard's famous statement that "the disrelationship of despair is not a simple disrelationship but a disrelationship in a relation which relates itself to its own self and is [therein] constituted by another, so that the disrelationship in that self-relation reflects itself infinitely in the relation to the Power which constituted it." (Søren Kierkegaard, *The Sickness unto Death*, tran. Walter Lowrie (Garden City, N.Y.: Doubleday Anchor Book, Doubleday & Co., 1954), p. 147. Cf., I, p. 217; PuDR, p. 265 (ET, p. 146); Jaspers, *Philosophie*, I: *Weltorientierung*, p. 15.) What Buri and Jaspers do not seem to realize is that taken in context this statement by Kierkegaard does not necessarily imply that the relational other by which the self is dialectically constituted is the equivalent of their Transcendence. It is equally compatible with any number of other relational concepts. In particular, it would be compatible with Heidegger's notion of *Existenz* according to which the self is indeed posited relationally. But the "other" to which the self is related is nothing more than the trancendent or ecstatic dimension of itself. Heidegger articulates this through his analysis of the "call" to authenticity. Cf., *Sein und Zeit*, p. 38 where Heidegger understands being as *transcendens schlechthin* in the sense of "fundamental ontology" as a disclosure of the being of

dent from the claim that the self non-objectively realizes itself in relation to an "other" to the claim that this "other" is not some worldly object or objects or a dimension of the self. And it is difficult to see how Buri could establish this transition.

Buri, however, seeks to deny that Transcendence can be identified with anything immanent to the world. Any such identification, he argues, could only be made by a false identification of Transcendence with an objective reality within the subject-object structure. This would contradict the character of the existential dialectic itself and would be a transgression of the limits of consciousness. Consequently, Buri seems to claim that Transcendence must be genuinely transcendent and in some sense represent, in the existential dialectic, a finite, though non-objective, relation to being-itself:

To see the answer to the question about the why of Being in this unconditioned of personhood, as has happened in all constructions of an "Absolute I" as the "World-Ground," would not only contradict the unconditionedness to which the I is destined, but would also have to be expressed in the subject-object schema and would thus confirm that it is Being-for-us rather than Being-in-itself. Just as the self-absolutization of the "I" is impossible in the subject-object schema, so certainly in the recognition of its boundaries does it encounter Being as the Naught (das Nichts). For thought which is within the subject-object schema, Being which is not simply Being-for-me is identical with the Naught. But, on the other hand, this is not the sole statement with respect to Being which is possible for thought. Just as certainly as Being is inaccessible to this schema, and every attempt to go beyond it leads further into the Naught of the non-objectifiability of Being, so the Naught is not the only reality which we confront here. For when we take seriously the fact that we are unconditionally destined for personhood, we encounter in the midst of the Naught and outside of it the non-objectifiable reality of "being called and destined" for personhood. If this being-destined occurs in the sphere of our personhood and has to be realized in it, then we are dealing not merely with a possibility immanently demonstrable to human existence as such, but with a nonobjectifiable reality of one who destines, which is to be distinguished from the non-objectifiability of the reality of human personhood.[23]

Thus, while functionally Transcendence must play the hermeneutical role of a limiting concept for the structure of the existential dialectic and while the content of theological assertions is limited to this structure, Bu-

Dasein and pp. 267-301 where conscience is analyzed as the seat of the "call" to authenticity.

[23]RF, p. 57. I have followed the convention of translating das Nichts as "nothing" or "nothingness" which I believe to be a more adequate English rendering than "the Naught." However, the essay from which this quotation is taken was written by Buri in English, and there is no published German version. I have, therefore, quoted it in its only published form.

ri believes that the reference of Transcendence is not entirely vacuous or non-restrictive. There are certain criteria which define its proper use.

For this reason, Buri dissociates himself from those sides of the radical theology movement which speak of the death of God or which are content with a totally secularized and anthropological interpretation of God-language.[24] In all of these cases, Buri argues that an insufficiently critical concern with the problem of objectivity leads either to an illicit objectification of the self in faith (e.g., Paul van Buren) or to the adoption of a new mythology to replace an old one (e.g., Thomas J. J. Altizer).[25] Consequently, as an application of the reappropriation of myth in self-understanding, he holds that theology cannot dispense with language about God, for only so can the donative character of faith be brought to expression and an anthropologizing of theology be prevented. God-language is mythological, of course, and there can be no immediate identification of Transcendence with "God." But against Herbert Braun, Buri says that what is meant by being-in-Christ must not be interpreted without reference to God as though it refers simply to a "relation between men."[26] "We must speak of [being-in-Christ] as the transcendent dimension of our personhood, the voice which calls us to responsibility."[27] Therefore, mythological language about God is essential to bring to proper expression the existential structure that is the genuine content of the Christian confession of Christ.[28] In the same context, Buri says: "God is the mythological expression for the unconditionedness of personal responsibility."[29] On this view, "God" is more than a merely anthropocentric concept because the existential structure which God-language serves to express requires an unconditioned ground for the unconditionedness of personal responsibility.

The actual reference of Transcendence in Buri's theology still begs for additional clarification. In particular, Buri needs to specify much more fully the relationship between his systematic concept of Transcendence and the mythological concept of God since it would seem that the full force of the anthropologizing criticism can be avoided only if it can be shown that existentialist interpretation does not systematically exclude theological reference to God. It will be necessary, therefore, to turn

---

[24]Cf., HSRG, pp. 16-25.
[25]Cf., ibid., pp. 11-15, 31.
[26]Ibid., p. 27.
[27]Ibid.
[28]Ibid.
[29]Ibid.

again to the concept of Transcendence in the discussion of Buri's application of the systematic principle to the interpretation of traditional doctrines. For the present, it will be enough to grant Buri's claim that even as a limiting concept, Trancendence provides sufficient protection against the reduction of theology to nothing more than the self. The important question which must be answered here concerns how the systematic principle provides rules of interpretation in the context of Buri's hermeneutical theory.

Buri believes that Schleiermacher is subject to the anthropologizing criticism because he reduces revelation entirely to the immanence of human consciousness.[30] Buri claims that his systematic principle avoids this danger and, at the same time, offers a way out of the dilemma of subjectivism and objectivism. Referring the content of all theological assertions to the non-objective dialectic of the self can make clear both that the Christian message has to do with something that happens to the self and is not its own creation and that the intelligibility of what happens cannot be abstracted from the self. The objectivism of a supernatural *Heilsgeschichte* falls away because the meaning of such language is interpreted exhaustively in terms of the dialectic of the self. But the subjectivizing danger also falls away because such interpretations are not objective descriptions of immanent states. They are elucidations which ultimately have no objective content since they refer to that which has no reality outside of its transcending actualization.

Buri clearly acknowledges that all theological thinking and speaking must be an objective reference (obj-A) to either a subjective or an objective reality (obj-B). For this reason and because he has argued that mythological and speculative forms of discourse are appropriate forms to give expression to the non-objectivity of self-understanding, he sees no other way to interpret theological doctrines than through the various objective forms (subjectivism or objectivism) they have taken in the history of theology. The procedure by which he actually applies the systematic principle is, hence, a dialectical discussion of the various subjectivizing and objectivizing interpretations in the history of theology. He discusses the history of each doctrine thoroughly showing the various problems and tensions occasioned by giving such doctrines an independent objective status in themselves. But because he has no other form of discourse by which to interpret and because he thinks such forms are appropriate to express faith if held in a critical tension, he does not simply criticize

[30]Cf., II, pp. 309-317.

such positions. By playing one off against another he seeks to attain a position where it can be seen how the traditional forms do give expression to the systematic principle. The purpose of his critical treatment is to prevent objectifying mis-interpretations (either subjectivism or objectivism) so that the objective form of his own discourse can be seen to elucidate the non-objective actualization of faith.

The historicity of faith and revelation is particularly important for the way in which subjectivistic and objectivistic interpretations of doctrines express various aspects of the systematic principle. In relation to the systematic principle, the concept of historicity has the role of indicating that the non-objective process of choosing and being chosen is never an abstract movement but an existential act in a particular situation. The material in which the historicity of faith expresses itself will, for reasons shown above, always be a set of myths and doctrines the objective form of which requires existentialist interpretation. When these objective assertions are interpreted in terms of the structure of the existential act of faith, i.e., the systematic principle, the formal concept of historicity gives rise to two hermeneutical rules by means of which traditional objectivity finds its true content in the structure of the existential process. The first of these rules has to do with the distinction between the formal structure of the systematic principle and its actual embodiment, the second with the distinction between the form and the content of the objective assertions to be interpreted.

Buri's concept of self-understanding as a general human possibility makes evident that, for analytical purposes, the systematic principle can be separated from any of its historistic manifestations and described abstractly as something like a structure of human being. Buri insists, however, that it not be seen as "generally establishable and demonstrable *Beschaffenheiten*" of human existence given with human being as such. (II, p. 216.) It is never a general possibility but always *je meines*. For this reason, one must speak of it in relation to some historicity and, thus, in relation to some *Verwirklichung des Personseins*.[31] Nevertheless, in any

---

[31]Cf., *ibid.*, p. 97: "Sofern die Anthropologien menschliches Personsein voraussetzen, handelt es sich dabei um eine allgemeine Möglichkeit — wobei von der Verwirklichung des Personseins noch abgesehen ist. Wenn wir jedoch darauf hinweisen, dass durch die Beantwortung der Frage nach dem Menschen dessen Wesen erst noch bestimmt wird, so bezogen wir uns bereits auf die Verwirklichung des Personseins." Buri's most important difference with Jaspers' "philosophical faith" originates here. Jaspers' philosophical faith elucidates the problem of objectivity and thereby recognizes the transcending dimension of the self and the non-objective relatedness of self and "other" in transcending. But according to Buri, Jaspers stops short with this general structure and does not see that it

analysis of a particular self-understanding, it will always be possible to separate the purely formal structure from the mode of its actual embodiment. Buri turns this fact on the actual content of traditional doctrines. He shows that many difficulties in the relationship between various facets of particular doctrines or between different doctrines can be resolved when one doctrine or a part of a doctrine is seen to have its content in a reference to the general structural features of human existence whereas others must be interpreted in terms of the concrete actualization (i.e., the historicity). In this way, various aspects of traditional doctrines symbolize the formal features of the existential dialectic.

The same rule can be applied to the form and content of traditional objectivity. Buri believes his systematic principle avoids the anthropologizing criticism. The self is not the source of its own realization; it is posited in a dialectical relation to an "other" which does not, however, abrogate its freedom and responsibility. In the application of the systematic principle to the interpretation of doctrines, the historicity of faith itself becomes a symbol for this graciousness of faith. That the systematic principle occurs in a concrete history and never as an abstract movement points to the fact that faith is not a possibility immanent to human selfhood as such. It always confronts the self as something lying outside its power to control. The historicity of the systematic principle is a purely formal feature of the existential dialectic prior to the application of the principle to the interpretation of doctrines. But this purely formal feature is itself symbolized by the formal character of the Christian message. The mythological form of the Christian message is kerygmatic; it speaks of a saving act of God in a particular event of the past. Quite apart from its content, this mythological form symbolizes the donative character of the existential dialectic. This application of the systematic principle is illustrated by the following passage where Buri plays off subjectivizing and objectivizing misconceptions of the reconciliation of the believer. He says that

because of their necessary objectivity, all statements about the self-understanding of faith are exposed to the misunderstanding of subjectivism. Just so, the impres-

---

is never given except in a concrete historicity. Despite his emphasis on some historicity, Jaspers fails to interpret the actualization of the self in a particular historistic situation. Instead he ranges over the whole *philosophia perennis* as merely illustrative of the general principle. But the self must be interpreted in terms of its actual historistic embodiment because the systematic principle is not a generalized structure. It receives its content only from some concrete embodiment. Cf., I, p. 172 and Buri, "Theologie zwischen — oder mit Jaspers und Heidegger," pp. 89-92.

sion could arise on the basis of this subjectivistic misunderstanding of the self-understanding of faith – which transcends all objectivity in its enactment – that it is a possibility which lies at the disposal of the one who enacts the self-understanding and is, accordingly, a matter of arbitrary realization. But such an interpretation would not only fully misconstrue the nature of faithful self-understanding which as faithful does not present an objectively demonstrable and applicable structure of human subjectivity either according to its form or its realization. In addition, it would overlook the specific peculiarity of the Christian faith which consists in the fact that one cannot speak of reconciliation in faith without a relation to the proclaimed event of reconciliation in Christ.... This indispensable relation of the self-understanding of faith to a statement concerning a saving event which does not lie at our disposal testifies quite sufficiently that the divine graciousness of this event of reconciliation is recognized – even though in this manner this self-understanding could fall under the equally unwarranted suspicion of being a false, supernaturalistic or naturalistic objectivism of salvation. To be sure, the suspicion of neither the subjectivism nor the objectivism of our understanding of the doctrine of reconciliation can be refuted in a generally comprehensible way. It is refuted only for the faith which actualizes itself in a fashion appropriate to the method of our interpretation of this doctrine. (II, p. 406.)

Thus, one aspect of the historicity of any doctrine will be its kerygmatic character, and this aspect can be taken as symbolizing the formal feature of the systematic principle that the paradox of grace is always realized in a concrete history.

Taken by itself, however, the formal character of the Christian message is not enough because it would only point to the equally formal character of the systematic principle, i.e., *that* it will be realized in some historicity. For this reason, the content of that historicity is equally important, and it will be necessary to see how this content distinguishes the Christian self-understanding from other possibilities. But again, at the purely formal level, the content of the Christian message is a symbol for the historicity of faith. That the Christian self-understanding is always actualized in response to the proclamation of Christ symbolizes the historistic structure of the systematic principle.

Buri's systematic principle, therefore, provides the hermeneutical rules for interpreting the content of the theological tradition. It is a non-mythological and non-symbolic principle which can interpret the content of myth and symbol. Buri's other hermeneutical principles, the concepts of faith, revelation, symbol, and myth, say only that faith is an existential process and that the content of faith must be interpreted in terms of this process. They do not, however, specify how interpretation can occur, and given the problem of objectivity which is the background against which each of these other concepts is developed, there is some question wheth-

er a theological interpretation of the content of the existential process
is possible. Only with the systematic principle is there a hermeneutical
principle which offers the possibility of interpreting the content of faith,
revelation, symbol, and myth in a non-mythological and non-symbolic
way. When the subjectivizing and objectivizing content of traditional
doctrines are interpreted in terms of the structure of the systematic principle, Buri believes he avoids reducing this content to ideas, theories or
general principles while at the same time avoiding the untenable mythological meanings they have in their uncritical objective form. Because the
systematic principle itself points to a historistic actualization, the content
of doctrines is not an idea or principle but an act structured by the tradition. In this way, Buri thinks that his method of interpretation avoids
making objective doctrinal proposals either about objective states in reality apart from the self or about subjective states of the self (which as
objective would still have a status apart from the actualization of faith itself).

There can be no question that Buri's systematic principle does provide
him with a hermeneutical principle and with hermeneutical rules for interpreting the content of faith. This is not the point at which the hermeneutical value of the problem of objectivity comes into question. *The
problem is whether the hermeneutical application of the systematic principle permits Buri to articulate the specifically Christian content of the
Christian self-understanding.* The hermeneutical rules discussed above
show how the content of traditional objectivity can be taken to symbolize
aspects of the systematic principle. But in each case *what* is symbolized is
only a purely formal characteristic of the systematic principle in general
– *that* faith is always an existential actualization of a paradox of grace
and *that* it occurs in a specific historicity. But Buri claims that the material (and not merely formal) significance of the concept of historicity is
to differentiate the content of various self-understandings from one another. The question is whether the systematic principle allows him to specify this historistic content. If it does not, then the content of the Christian faith becomes ineffable, reduces, that is, to nothing more than self-
understanding in general.

Should this be the final judgment on Buri's hermeneutic, the cause
will rest with his analysis of the problem of objectivity. In order to avoid
the subjectivizing and objectivizing dangers in his own interpretation,
Buri must emphasize that his hermeneutical principle points to a non-objective act. It would then follow that the only content interpretations on
the basis of this principle permit is the purely formal content of its gener-

al structure. Actually to specify the historistic content of its actualization, which is where the differentiation of one self-understanding from another occurs, would be to transgress the limits on objectification. Buri's systematic principle will work, in other words, only if the content it permits is more than the merely formal features of self-understanding in general, or only if it specifies the content of the Christian historicity and not merely the formal idea that every self-understanding is actualized in a particular history as a purely general paradox of grace. This is the criterion against which the fruitfulness of the problem of objectivity for a radical theology must be tested, assuming that Buri has given the most thoroughgoing analysis of the problem. The next step is to examine Buri's implementation of the systematic principle in the interpretation of doctrines to see if it meets this criterion.

PART II

THE PROBLEM OF OBJECTIVITY IN THE IMPLEMENTATION
OF THE HERMENEUTICAL PRINCIPLES

CHAPTER V

HISTORICITY AND THE SYSTEMATIC PRINCIPLE IN THE INTERPRETATION OF DOCTRINES

Buri's interpretation of the person of Jesus Christ will be taken as a case study in the application of his systematic principle. This particular doctrine has been chosen for two reasons. It is an interesting doctrine for testing the hermeneutics of any radical theology because traditionally the attempt to define the God-manhood of Christ represents a classic example of the type of doctrine a radical theology would find difficulty in either accepting or reconstructing. It will be interesting, therefore, to examine how Buri interprets its objective, mythological form as a symbol entirely representative of the structure of an actualized self-understanding. But Buri's Christology is also important because it illustrates with particular clarity the kinds of modifications in the organization of and approach to traditional doctrines which he believes to follow from the orientation of his prolegomena on the problem of objectivity. The comprehensiveness and consistency of Buri's approach to the problem of developing a radical theology is nowhere more impressively demonstrated than in this reorganization of traditional *loci* which he sees to follow from his hermeneutical principles. Before turning directly to his interpretation of the person of Christ, it is necessary first, then, to see how this doctrine fits into the total system.

A. ANTHROPOLOGY AND CHRISTOLOGY IN THE DOGMATIC SYSTEM

The first volume of Buri's system after his prolegomena is entitled *Man and Grace*. The selection of topics indicated by this title is a significant departure from the traditional order of Christian theology. The traditional order – dating at least from the *Sentences* of Peter Lombard in the twelfth century – considers the doctrine of God first followed by the doctrine of creation. Theological anthropology is dealt with under the doctrine of creation because man, as the image of God, is considered to be the peak of God's creation. Since natural man is fallen and since the Christian message deals essentially with God's redemptive act on behalf of fallen man, not only man's original condition but also his fallen nature is treated in this section on creation. The third part of the theological system then deals with the doctrine of redemption, the person and work of Christ, followed by a section on the church and eschatology. Theological anthropology thus precedes soteriology and is the presupposition of the latter.[1]

Because of the consequences it has for anthropology, Buri challenges this traditional arrangement on both formal and material grounds. Formally, he says, it would appear appropriate to speak of God first and then of creation and redemption since man is God's creation and God has acted to save man only after his fall from his created status. This holds, however, only so long as it is assumed that God can be known either on the basis of an objective revelation or through the natural capacities of human reason. Yet both of these avenues to knowledge of God have become highly problematic since the Enlightenment. With its traditional epistemological presuppositions called into question, it became necessary in the nineteenth century for theology to preface its interpretation of doctrines with extensive methodological introductions justifying both the avenue and the type of knowledge it claimed. In some instances of liberal theology, these prolegomena became the major part of the theological system (e.g., Hermann Lüdemann), and today methodological debates are still at the center of theological argument and occupy significant portions of theological systems.[2] Buri argues that where prolegomena have received this importance a change in the traditional order has already taken place, for reflection about man and his capacities has received *de facto* priority.

Not only has anthropology replaced the doctrine of God as the first object of theological reflection, but, in addition, this should have occasioned a re-thinking of the doctrines following the prolegomena. If the doctrines of God and man maintained their traditional arrangement this was "because otherwise one feared through such a transposition of anthropology to come all too dangerously close to Feuerbach." (II, p. 23.) "But where prolegomena attain such a previously unknown length and impor-

---

[1] II, p. 21.
[2] *Ibid.*, pp. 21 f.

tance, and anthropologizing of theology has, in fact, already occurred....A transposition of anthropology was not at all necessary any longer. That it was not undertaken is, to be sure, understandable in view of the precarious situation of this theology; but for all that, it is still an unjustified inconsistency." (II, p. 23.) In Buri's mind, leaving the traditional order untouched after the prolegomena was highly questionable because, after the type of epistemological considerations demanded by modern thought, the traditional way of treating anthropology could only "appear as attempted justifications of a mythology which in itself had become antiquated and superfluous." (II, p. 23.) For purely formal reasons, then, Buri thinks that the modern theological situation demands a re-thinking of the arrangement of traditional theological *loci*.

Buri draws his material criticism from the content of classical theological anthropology. But this has implications for the formal problem because the way traditional anthropology was arranged in the dogmatic system already raised questions for other doctrines, especially soteriology. The classical procedure was to describe man's original condition and then his nature after the fall. The Biblical text for this was taken from Gen. 1-3. But because there is not enough information here for a full anthropology, other Biblical passages were used to ground it. A classical procedure was to turn to the New Testament understanding of man's perfection in Christ in order to infer details about the condition of fallen man presupposed by his new perfection. Because, however, the Biblical statements about the original and the perfected states are completely independent of each other and because certain concepts such as the loss of an original condition do not even appear, it is extremely difficult to ground Biblically the systematic anthropology which seems demanded by the theologian's attempt to conceive the significance of God's saving act in Christ.[3] The systematic problems occasioned by the attempt to conceive a separate anthropology as the presupposition of an equally separate doctrine of redemption had particularly difficult implications for soteriology.

The reformers' emphasis on the *sola gratia* demanded that the fall be conceived as a total corruption of an original perfection so that all possibility of man's contributing to his own salvation could be excluded. While this did allow full expression of the *sola gratia,* it also made it impossible to conceive man's humanity or his personhood after the fall. It thus resulted in a fully non-historical understanding of man; precisely that

[3]Cf., *Ibid.,* pp. 25 f., 62 f.

which constitutes man as man must be conceived as lost if the *sola gratia* is to be preserved. Because of this problem, protestant orthodoxy retreated from the original Reformation position and re-conceived theological anthropology along more or less Catholic lines according to which only some part of the original perfection, but not that which constitutes man as man, was lost in the fall. But, Buri argues, this necessarily results in falling back into some form of synergism which it was the purpose of the *sola gratia* to eliminate. If the *sola gratia* is maintained, then salvation can only be a magic *Fremderlösung* which does not touch man's real personhood. If man's nature as man is somehow taken into account, then it seems impossible to avoid a synergism or a *Selbsterlösung*. Buri maintains that for the traditional way of treating theological anthropology, this dilemma is impossible to avoid.[4]

Still another material problem which results from the traditional structure is the development of anthropology without any reference to the new man in grace. This structure is justified because the new man is a proper topic for soteriology, anthropology providing the presupposition for the former. Buri's response, however, is that

this means nothing less than that in the form of theological anthropology typical in the past precisely that cannot come to expression which constitutes the central content of the New Testament message of salvation: the redemption of man through Christ. In these anthropologies man is spoken of as though Christ and the new being in him had nothing at all to do with their presentation. (II., p. 26 f.)

Thus, Buri feels not only that the traditional treatment of the original condition and the fall must be reconceived in view of soteriology but also that the uniquely Christian view of man must have some intrinsic connection with a thological anthropology, with a definition of who man is.

As might be expected, Buri locates the center of the above mentioned problems in a false understanding of the objective status of theological assertions:

When the original perfection of Adam, his fall, and its results in his descendents are considered objectively and when, then, in the same objectifying way a *Heilsgeschichte* is set over against an *Unheilsgeschichte* which began with the fall and either the exclusive efficaciousness of grace or its co-operation with the capacities of man remaining after the fall are explained like a mathematical calculation (*Rechenexempel*), then the only thing that can result is the presentation of an external redemption or a self-redemption or some mixture of the two. In such conceptions of

4*Ibid.*, pp. 27, 29.

redemption neither the nature nor the realization of the grace of God are adequately articulated but, in ever new variations, are only placed in question. (II, p. 29.)

Buri proposes that these various problems can be solved only if theological assertions are not interpreted objectively but seen as expressions of self-understanding. As long as the problem of objectivity is not clarified in terms of the existential dialectic, theological claims cannot but be conceived in a merely external fashion that neither solves the objective problems themselves nor properly conceives the reference of the objective form of theological statements to the actualization of faith. By interpreting all theological assertions in terms of the immediate dialectic of the actualization of faith, Buri claims he can overcome the oppositions that tend to arise in the history of theology.[5]

But this position also demands that the order of the theological system be reconceived. Buri follows the modern preoccupation with epistemological questions and continues the anthropoligical focus of his prolegomena by making theological anthropology the first substantive section of his system. And because it is the Christian kerygma which differentiates the Christian self-understanding, he no longer separates soteriology into a separate section but makes it integral to every section.[6] As Buri says:

When the assertions of the Christian tradition are conceived as witnesses to faith and when the nature of faith is seen in the *existentiell* enactment of self-understanding, that demands that man as the "subject" of this self-understanding must be placed at the beginning in the construction of the dogmatic system. We do not have to do with just any understanding-of-oneself but with the self-understanding defined by the message of God's decisive saving act in Christ. Because we believe that the attested Christ-event is not a saving event without the man who understands himself in terms of it but can become a living reality only in a hu-

---

[5]*Ibid.*, pp. 28-34.

[6]This statement reflects Buri's earlier presentation of a soteriology under the heading "existence as grace." (Cf., *TdE*, pp. 53 ff., ET, pp. 44 ff.) This understanding of existence follows logically from his systematic principle and might still be used to characterize not only his anthropology but his theology as a whole. The departure from the earlier position consists in his now conceiving soteriology entirely in terms of Christology. In the earlier position Christology served a quite subordinate role. The dialectic of sin and grace was developed before Christology and independently of it, and Christology was of mainly historical interest exemplifying in its various forms the mythological expression which could be given to the basically independent dialectic of existence as grace. The change in his thought represents his complete break with consistent eschatology (except as an historical hypothesis) and his much greater willingness to appropriate the entire tradition as a legitimate expression of faith. The basis for this change was Buri's thinking out to the end the implications of his concepts of self-understanding and historicity. The concept of historicity, in particular, now accounts for the centrality of Christology as the organizing principle of his entire system.

man self-understanding, therefore, we can present anthropology only in dependence on soteriology and soteriology only as one with anthropology. (II. p. 19.)[7]

The consequence of this re-thinking of the arrangement of *loci* is that no separate section is devoted to Christology. Instead, because he is interpreting the Christian self-understanding, every particular section – including that on the fall and sin – is interpreted Christologically.[8] In the

---

[7] Buri thinks that by interpreting all doctrines in terms of this historistic embodiment of his systematic principle and not as any kind of objective theory having a status apart from self-understanding, he can overcome the dilemmas resulting from such objective theories. The following statement shows how he thinks this notion of an anthropological soteriology and a soteriological anthropology can overcome certain objectifying problems at one crucial point in the tradition. In brief compass this is a paradigm of the way the systematic principle and the concept of self-understanding work in the interpretation of every doctrine. "Wo Anthropologie und Soteriologie der Intention und dem Inhalt nach zusammengehören", kann die Problematik neu in Angriff genommen werden, die mit dem Kernstück der von der Reformation herkommenden Theologie, der Lehre von der Erlösung als Rechtfertigung und Heiligung, verbunden ist: wir meinen die schon erwähnte Schwierigkeit, dass durch Fremderlösung oder Selbsterlösung und auch durch jeden Kompromiss zwischen ihnen das Zurgeltungkommen der christlichen Heilsbotschaft in Frage gestellt ist. Indem wir zeigen, wie die Gnade der göttlichen Heilstat in Christus nicht anders als in einem darauf bezogenen Selbstverständnis zur Auswirkung kommen kann, wird eine magische Fremderlösung ausgeschlossen. Weil sich das Selbstverständnis des neuen Seins in Christus als ein Geschenk der Gnade Gottes versteht, ist seiner Deutung Als Selbsterlösung ein Riegel vorgeschoben. Auch um einen Kompromiss zwischen beiden und ein entsprechendes Rechnen mit fremder und eigener Gerechtigkeit kann es sich nicht handeln, weil hier mit dem Selbst des Selbstverständnisses ebenso radikal ernst gemacht wird wie mit dem Gnadencharakter dieses Selbst-werdens im Akt des Glaubens." (II, pp. 33 f.)

[8] Cf., *ibid.*, pp. 38-40. Buri is quite aware of the formal similarity with Barth's Christocentric system. He is also aware that Barth has sought in this way to solve many of the same substantive problems in the history of theology that he sees. But Buri objects to Barth's objective interpretation of doctrines apart from the self-understanding of faith. Buri says: "Bei Karl Barth nun ist nicht nur die Anthropologie durch eine solche christologische und soteriologische Grundstruktur bestimmt, sondern die *Kirchliche Dogmatik* in allen ihren Teilen. In dieser christologisch-soteriologischen Ausrichtung liegt der Wesenscharakter dieses epochalen Werkes. Nun hält sich freilich Barth in der Verteilung seiner Dogmatik an das klassische Einteilungsschema der theologischen Summen und Systeme aller Zeiten und entfaltet infolgedessen seine Anthropologie bereits in der Lehre von der Schöpfung. Aber nicht erst dieser Teil der Dogmatik, sondern schon ihre ausführlichen Prolegomena sind orientiert an dem von Gott in Jesus Christus gesprochenen Wort der Versöhnung." (*Ibid.*, p. 36.) But then Buri comments: "Barth kann bei aller Betonung des Eingehen Gottes ins Fleisch freilich nicht verhindern, dass immer da, wo dieses Eingehen Gottes ins Fleisch in seinen Darlegungen — z.B. in der Anthropologie und Soteriologie — aufgezeigt werden sollte, es letztlich bei einem blossen Geschehen in Gott selber bleibt. Wird gesagt, dass Jesus Christus der wahre Mensch ist und sich in ihm die Versöhnung des Menschen mit Gott ereignet habe, so bleibt zu fragen: Wenn der Mensch nur der in Christus geschehenen Versöhnung aus gedacht wird, wie kann dann die Wirklichkeit des einzelnen Menschseins in der Welt und die Versöhnung als in diesem Menschen geschehende Wirklichkeit ernstgenommen werden? Besonders in den ethischen Partien wird of-

context of his systematic principle and the concept of historicity, this meaus that Christology itself is taken to function as a symbol for the non-objectivity of faith. Quite apart from any material content Christology might have in the Christian self-understanding, Buri sees it also as a symbol for a purely formal point true of any self-understanding whatsoever. In this way, the Christocentric emphasis serves to focus the meaning of all doctrines on the methodological principle of self-understanding.[9] But aside from this formal result of the logic of Buri's position, the Christological emphasis also means that the historistic content of any particular aspect of the Christian self-understanding will be structured by the message of God's saving act in Christ. In this way, the person and work of Christ structure different aspects of the Christian self-understanding and do not constitute a separate unity of dogmatic *loci* as in the traditional doctrine of redemption. The work of Christ serves to structure the self-understanding of reconciliation and the new being. But the person of Christ serves to structure the concrete Christian embodiment of the statement that man is the image of God, i.e., theological anthropology in a narrow sense. Thus, to see how Buri's systematic principle applies to the person of Christ, one must consider what man as the image of God means as a symbol expressive of the Christian self-understanding.

B. THE IMAGO DEI AND THE HISTORICITY OF THE
CHRISTIAN SELF-UNDERSTANDING

Since the primary aim here is to show how Buri interprets the person of Christ, most of the complexity and detail of his historical-critical discussion of the traditional conception of man may be ignored in order simply to show how his anthropological proposal is bound up with his interpretation of the God-man Christology. He orients his interpretation on

fensichtlich, dass unter diesen Voraussetzungen nicht von dem wirklichen Neuwerden des Menschen im Sinne des Neuen Testament gesprochen werden kann. Solches spekulative Überspielen der menschlichen Wirklichkeit ist die Folge eines Denkens, das alles Heilsgeschehen als eine metaphysische Gegenständlichkeit interpretiert. Indem das Böse zum Nichtigen erklärt wird, wird im Grund nicht nur die Ethik, sondern auch die Notwendigkeit des christologischen Heilswerkes illusorisch. Ein Nichtiges braucht nicht erst noch durch Gott oder den Menschen überwunden zu werden." (*Ibid.*, p. 37.)

[9]Cf., *supra*, pp. 133-135; cf., also, e.g., II, pp. 222-227, esp. 226, 248-251, 379-387.

three basic problems which arise out of the traditional attempts to ground theological anthropology.

First, there is the relative indeterminateness of the Biblical notion of man as the likeness of God. Except for Genesis 1-3, it is seldom mentioned again in the Bible and then in such a way that the content is not specified.[10] The Genesis account, however, does not provide the sufficient basis for a theological anthropology.[11]

Second, the Bible makes use of the likeness notion in two different senses. On the one hand, it speaks of a likeness which originates in creation, and it nowhere asserts that this likeness is lost. On the other hand, in the New Testament it is not man as such but Christ who is the image of God (2. Cor. 4:4; Col. 1:15), and "only through him can man be transformed into the likeness of God (Rom. 8:29; 2. Cor. 3:18; Eph. 4:24; Col. 3:10; 1. John 3:2)." (II, p. 46.)[12] In the light of the first problem, it became common for theologians to attempt to solve this second one by specifying and systematizing the notion of the likeness deriving from creation by inference from the more detailed descriptions of the likeness in Christ. But Buri maintains that such systematic interconnections can not be supported because the two notions of likeness occur in entirely different Biblical contexts. "A unification of these ideas of the likeness of God grounded in Christ and that corresponding to man from creation is difficult," Buri says, "for in the idea of the created likeness neither its loss nor its restoration is considered." (II, p. 46.) And the systematizing attempts to interpret the likeness in Christ and the new and old Adam as a restoration of an original condition fit the New Testament contexts as little as they can be unified with the Old Testament.[13]

Finally, there is the problem arising out of the former difficulties of conceiving the created condition of man and the fall without qualifying either soteriology or man's nature as man. Buri argues that at least this can be derived from the Bible: those places where the likeness is referred to apart from the creation account make it clear that however the likeness is specified it is preserved even in the *status corruptionis*. In this at least the outlines of the Catholic interpretation of man's nature is Biblically correct.[14] The problem is how to conceive theological anthropology on this basis without calling into question either sin or the *sola gratia* or both.

10*Ibid.*, pp. 45 f., 104 f.
11Cf., *ibid.*, pp. 62-66, 105.
12Cf., *DP*, 37-39, 42-49, 56-64.
13II, pp. 67 f.
14*Ibid.*, pp. 66 f.

Again Buri sees the source of these problems in the uncritical objectivity of anthropological assertions as though what is being described has some independent mythological or speculative status in itself. "But the 'object' of this discourse is precisely that which is finally no object at all." All theological anthropologies "designate that essence of man concerning which every objective assertion is inadequate because in this conception it is a question of a reality which is what it is only in its occurrence (*Geschehen*)." The "appropriate relation" between such a reality and objectifying discourse about it is attained only "when the statements concerning this 'object' are no longer merely a calculable objectifying (*verfügbarmachendes Objektivieren*) but when in this unavoidable objectifying the non-objectifiable itself is brought to expression. Then assertions concerning the likeness of God can be interpreted as an expression of a being in the likeness of God manifested in such an understanding." (II, pp. 69 f.)

Buri's proposed solution is, therefore, to collapse the objective form of anthropological discourse – e.g., the objective idea that the created condition was a state of an original pair in the past which was changed by the original sin, the corrupted condition then being passed on to all future generations by some objective process – into the immediate, non-objective dialectic of the self. Only when the objective (mythological and speculative) theological statements about man are interpreted as expressions of a basically unitary self-understanding can the traditional problems be overcome. The method Buri follows in proposing this solution directly involves the relation earlier observed between the systematic principle and its historistic embodiment.

The problems of the indeterminateness in the description of the likeness, the disparate concepts of the likeness from creation and in Christ, and the continuity of the likeness after the fall as that which constitutes man as man are solved by seeing the created likeness as a mythological expression for the structure of self-understanding in general (i.e., the reality of existence as grace described by the systematic principle) and the likeness in Christ as an expression for the concrete *Verwirklichung* of the likeness in the Christian self-understanding.[15] The *schöpfungsmässige*

---

[15]It is extremely important to note that by "historistic *Verwirklichung*" Buri does not just mean that the systematic principle receives a concrete modification and structure in its Christian form. Were this all he meant then the application of his systematic principle would be precisely parallel to that of Schleiermacher. Theology would consist in a "subjectivism" of objective descriptions of states of the self occasioned by the Christian manifestation of the systematic principle. The problem of objectivity demands that *Verwirklichung* mean not merely a particular embodiment of the systematic principle; it

Gottebenbildlichkeit is thus a purely formal concept definitive of man's possibility of personhood.[16] This possibility consists in the fact that man is a creature who is self-reflexively aware of himself and who, therefore, first determines who he is by the way in which he understands himself.[17] Quite apart from the specific content of any anthropology, it is this basic possibility which is presupposed by all anthropological theories, even those (e.g., naturalism and materialism) which end up trying to deny man's fundamental personhood.[18] "Even the denial of man's spirituality can only be enacted by the denied spirit." (II, p. 52.) Thus, insofar as the created likeness defines nothing more than this general possibility of man's personhood, it provides a way of affirming the continuity of man's being as man after the fall. But this is an expression of nothing more than a purely formal possibility. Seen merely as an expression of the systematic principle, it says nothing yet about the historistic actualization of personhood in a particular self-understanding. It thereby accounts for the indeterminateness of the biblical definition of the image.[19]

The systematic principle cannot, of course, be understood apart from its historistic embodiment. While it must necessarily be articulated objectively as a possibility of human being, what is thus articulated is the possibility of a specific actualization and not a general or formal *Vorfindlichkeit* ingredient in human being as such.[20] Consequently, the formal possibility of personhood never occurs in its formality but only in an actualized historicity. Because the *schöpfungsmässige Gottebenbildlichkeit* is an expression of the formal possibility of self-understanding (i.e., personhood), it also involves a relation to Transcendence. But because it is an abstraction from any particular historicity, the likeness here expressed and its Transcendence-relatedness is entirely empty. For this reason, Buri says that the "concept of creator" in the likeness from creation is purely a "limiting concept." (II, p. 107.) The significance of this statement is to point to the merely formal character of the likeness from creation. At the same time, Buri emphasizes that the statement of the formal character of the created likeness is not the result of a natural theology nor is

---

must also mean that the concrete content of this embodiment is given only in the non-objective act of its realization. Everything in Buri's attempt to overcome the problem of objectivity hangs on this implication of *Verwirklichung*. As has already been suggested, the central problem of his theology also rests here.

[16]II, pp. 104-106.
[17]Cf., *ibid.*, pp. 50-52.
[18]*Ibid.*, pp. 50-52, 93-95.
[19]*Ibid.*, p. 106.
[20]*Ibid.*, p. 216.

the statement of the God (or Transcendence) in whose likeness man is said to be created.[21] In other words, the understanding of the likeness from creation is not, even in its formality, independent from a specific historicity of which it forms the presupposition. The statement of the formal meaning of the likeness is itself abstracted from the historicity of the Biblical self-understanding, and seen in its abstractness, it is as though it were "directed at a mere *Nichts*" about which nothing can be said. (II, p. 107.) Properly to understand the formal likeness from creation, it must be seen that this formal possibility is itself an expression of faith abstracted from some concrete historicity.[22]

In the Old Testament this formal principle is historistically embodied in the self-understanding of a covenantal people and a covenantal God. It is in this historicity that the formal possibility of personhood (the likeness from creation) and the corresponding relation to Transcendence receives some positive convent in the actualisation of this self-understanding. In the Christian faith, this formal possibility of the created likeness receives its content through the historicity defined by the proclamation of the kerygma of Jesus Christ (which stands in continuity with the Old Testament self-understanding):

The relation of the believer to this, his God, now takes on a new form in the New Testament. In the New Testament, the God of the covenant becomes the creator and the Lord of history in a quite specific way. Now, as its creator and ruler, he encompasses not merely the world and that which belongs to it and occurs in it. Rather, within this universal guidance, he reveals himself as the Lord of history in that he intervenes in it through the sending of his Messiah. This Messiah is not now seen simply as one who stands ready in heaven to be expected in some event in the future but in closest connection with the earthly appearance of Jesus of Nazareth. Jesus is recognized as he who knows himself as the Messiah expected in the near future, or, in the earthly form of Jesus, there is already envisioned the incarnation *(Fleischwerdung)* of this heavenly being. Through his death and resurrection the eschaton is set in process and the new world is already breaking in. Jesus gathers the community of the new aeon, and the community of believers who, after his death, await his parousia understand themselves as placed in the realm in which the new creation occurs. (II, pp. 111 f.)

This is all stated in mythological language which must, of course, be interpreted as the expression of a self-understanding. But its significance for Buri is that it is precisely this mythological eschatology of Jesus Christ which defines the historicity of the Christian self-understanding.

[21]*Ibid.*, pp. 107 f.
[22]*Ibid.*, p. 109.

It must be seen not in its mythological objectivity bus as the expression for the self-understanding of the original Christian community. As such, it constitutes the historicity which defines the self-understanding of every Christian community. The formal possibility of self-understanding receives its historistic content as the particular actualization of self-understanding which is determined by response to this kerygma. For the Christian, then, the formal possibility of personhood (the image of God from creation) receives its concrete historistic embodiment in terms of the image of God in Christ. As Buri describes this connection:

> As the inaugurator of this new creation, Christ is the likeness of God, and participating in this new creation, believers are transformed into the image of Christ and thereby into the likeness of God. Christ's likeness of God thus consists in his being the mediator of the new creation, and the God-likeness of the believer rests on his becoming a new creature through the new creation mediated by Christ. On the basis of the historistic realization *(Verwirklichung)* of the new being in Christ experienced in its own being *(Dasein),* the New Testament proclaims the possibility, contained *(beschlossene Möglichkeit)* in this historistic situation, of a new self-understanding *(Sichverstehens)* which can actualize *(verwirklichen)* itself in the hearing of this message. (II, p. 112.)[23]

Thus, it is through his distinction between systematic principle and historicity that Buri resolves the problem of the disparate references to the image of God in the Bible. While the image of God from creation is a mythological expression for nothing more than the formal possibility of personhood and is, therefore, only a limiting concept, the image of God in Christ defines the specific historistic actualization of this possibility in the Christian community. To ascertain what the content of the image of God is in the Christian self-understanding it is necessary to refer to the person of Jesus Christ as a symbol expressing the Christian self-understanding. In this way, Christology in the narrow sense is, in Buri's theology, an aspect of anthropology. It has no other status outside its function of giving symbolic expression to a non-objective self-understanding actualized as a paradox of grace, the historicity of which receives its specific content or structure from the kerygma of Jesus Christ. In Buri's theology, the ostensibly objective doctrine of the person of Christ can only be interpreted by showing the structure the formal image of God receives when actualized as a self-understanding in response to the Christian kerygma. Its purpose is to show how the systematic principle is actualized in relation to one particular aspect of the Christian self-under-'

[23]Cf., also *DP,* pp. 39-49, 62-64.

standing, namely, the equally mythological and symbolic statement that man is the image of God.[24]

This background in the organization of the substantive parts of Buri's system makes it possible to turn to his actual interpretation of traditional Christology. With this particular doctrine as an example, one must enquire how Buri's systematic principle operates when he applies it to the historicity of the Christian self-understanding (i.e., to the actualization of a self-understanding which expresses itself objectively through the mythological and speculative statements of traditional Christology).

C. THE PERSON OF CHRIST AND THE CHRISTIAN SELF-UNDERSTANDING

Everything in Buri's hermeneutic depends on his notion of historicity—understood in its double dimension of non-objective act and structuring of this act. The problem of objectivity forces this emphasis. In order that the systematic principle and his interpretation of doctrines not be understood as another objective theory, he must emphasize the reference of everything he says to an *act* of existence transcending the subject-object relation. Since everything turns on concrete actualization and not on a general theory, he must be able to specify the content or structure of this actualization. That is, he must be able to specify what the historicity of the systematic principle is in any particular instance of its actualization. But here the central problem of Buri's theology emerges again: *When he specifies the historicity of the Christian self-understanding, the content of this historicity turns out to be nothing more than a restatement of his systematic principle.* In other words, he does not really solve the problem of how to do theology in his system since the solution to this problem depends on his providing some description of the content of the specifically Christian self-understanding. While this thesis applies to almost the entirety of his substantive treatment of doctrines, it is particularly disturbing with the doctrine of the person of Christ because the symbolic function of this doctrine is to define the content of the specifically Christian self-understanding.

Following his procedure of developing his own interpretation out of

---

[24]Cf., II, pp. 112 f., 134. In this sense, Christology refers to a fairly narrow aspect of the structure of self-understanding. However, it must be recalled that all doctrines are interpreted as expressions of self-understanding and that this self-understanding is differentiated Christologically. It then becomes apparent that this particular section serves as the foundation for the Christological orientation of all other doctrines in Buri's thought.

the subjectivizing and objectivizing objectivity of the tradition, Buri fo-
cuses his discussion on the classical Christological formulations. The classical problem in Christology is to articulate the God-man unity. In the history of the problem the conceptual difficulties have worked to the particular disadvantage of the humanity of Christ. "Because the one side, the
divinity of the Son, stands unquestioned, these [conceptual] difficulties
work their whole force on the other side, on his human personhood."
(II, p. 119.) Buri argues that on conceptual grounds alone the problem
in the Trinitarian-Christological statements cannot be solved.[25] He sees,
however, in this conceptual "foundering" of a merely objectifying attempt to understand the meaning of the dogmatic statements more than
simply a negative justification of his criticism of the objective status of
theological statements. Precisely in their conceptual impossibility there is
a confirmation that what is at stake here is not finally an objective theory
bu a kerygmatic statement of the significance of Christ for faith:[26]

> Insofar as the trinity and the doctrine of the two natures restate the logical pa-
> radox of the kerygma and are not meant to explain it and make it intelligible,
> then they represent legitimate attestations of the self-understanding of the Christian
> faith . . . . This foundering of Christology has significance insofar as thereby the im-
> possibility of this objectifying undertaking comes to light, and with it a new under-
> standing of the doctrine of the person of Christ, which is not enslaved to objectifi-
> cations, becomes necessary. (II, p. 131.)

The paradox of the kerygma to which Buri refers here can be stated objectively as the paradox that in a single event of history God has acted
decisively for man's salvation. But Buri distinguishes the kerygma from
an objective truth-claim in order to point out that the kerygma is a claim
on faith, a call to decision, and not an objective statement of a fact.
The kerygmatic nature of theological statements can only be properly interpreted by seeing them in terms of the self-understanding to which they
lay claim. Consequently, the true paradoxicality of the kerygma lies not
in any form of an objective claim but in its giving expression to the paradoxical character of self-understanding itself – that the act of self-understanding is at once assumption of responsibility and being gifted to oneself. In this sense, the two sides of the paradox of traditional Christology, the *incarnation* of *God* in a man and the *humanity* of this man, must
be interpreted in terms of the two sides of the paradox in the dialectic of

[25]Cf., II, pp. 119, 121, 131.
[26]Cf., *ibid.*, pp. 117, 127 f.

the self, *Transcendence-relatedness* and *historicity*.[27] The two sides of the original dogma, which tend to fall apart when taken as objective theories, can be properly interpreted when seen as symbolic expressions of a single self-understanding, and this means as particular expressions of the dialectic of the self defined by the systematic principle. Because this dialectic is a unitary act, each side of the paradox will give expression to the unity of this act, though from different perspectives. The God side, the symbol of the incarnation as expressive of the Transcendence-relatedness of the act of self-understanding, will be taken up first.

1. The Divinity of Christ in the Christian Self-Understanding

Buri says: "In the primitive Christian kerygma of the saving act of God in Christ, the particular relation to Transcendence in Christian faith comes to expression." (II, p. 130.) But when one asks what the cash value of this particular Transcendence relation is, the reply is a purely circular statement: "Through the Trinitarian concept of God and through the doctrine of the God-man, we are asked whether, in our personhood, we are prepared to acknowledge ourselves related to a personal Transcendence as it confronts us in God's becoming man in Christ." (II, pp. 137 f.) This statement is circular because instead of defining the his-

---

[27]*Ibid.*, p. 130. Buri divides the history of Christology into two major stages: the supernatural theory of classical Christianity which failed to do justice to the humanity and the dissolution of classical Christology in liberalism which took account of the humanity by conceiving Jesus merely as an expression of the religious self-consciousness of man but which thereby lost the non-objectivity of Transcendence-relatedness in the act of self-understanding. As Buri formulates his own proposal: "Wie die altkirchliche Christologie und alle ihre Verwendungen an den Schwierigkeiten zerbrachen, die für sie an der Menschheit Christi erwuchsen, so führte im Neuprotestantismus der Versuch, die Jesusauffassung im menschlichen Selbstbewusstsein zu begründen, zu der Auflösung des Kerygmas von der Heilstat Gottes in Christus. Hier wie dort ist die Problematik am menschlichen Personsein Christi aufgebrochen: im trinitarisch-christologischen Dogma infolge seiner Verbindung mit einer objektivierten Gottheit, in der neuprotestantischen Jesusauffassung infolge der Nichtbearbeitung der Geschichtlichkeit jeder Art menschlichen Bewusstseins. Der erdachte Zussammenhang Jesu mit der objektivierten Gottheit und mit den Objektivationen menschlichen Bewusstseins ist zu ersetzen durch den Hinweis auf Transzendenzbezug und Geschichtlichkeit. Transzendenzbezug und Geschichtlichkeit stellen aber Erscheinungen menschlichen Personseins dar und wollen auch in ihren Objektivierungen von Personsein aus verstanden sein." (*Ibid.*) This statement is also a particularly good example of Buri's material principle. Since the totality of the doctrinal tradition is the material context for the Christian self-understanding, Buri must always seek a unity by relating different sides of the tradition. Usually he does this, as here, by a typology of orthodox and liberal positions.

toricity of this self-understanding, it simply repeats "as it confronts us in God's becoming man in Christ." But the significance of this "as . . ." is precisely what is at stake.

If this sentence makes any sense at all, then apparently the distinctiveness of this Transcendence-relation is its *personal* character. The mythological symbols of traditional Christology are appropriate to it because God reveals himself as personal insofar as he incarnates himself in a person. Below and in the next chapter it will be necessary to consider what this ascription of personhood to Transcendence might mean. First, however, it is necessary to see how this distinctive characteristic of the Christian relation to Transcendence becomes concretely significant in terms of actualization of the historicity of faith. In contrast to metaphysicau theories that God is a person, Buri says that the situation is different

when we speak of God's becoming man *(Menschwerdung Gottes)* not otherwise than in connection with our personhood. Then we know that we first perceive *(innewerden)* our personhood in being related to a personal God and at once therewith that this personal God is reality for us in that we know ourselves responsible before him. To God's becoming man in Christ *(Menschwerdung Gottes)*, as the dogma formulates it, corresponds man's becoming man *(die Menschwerdung des Menschen)* as the awareness *(Innewerden)* of personal responsibility before a personal God. God's becoming man attested in the dogma becomes an occasion for us to understand ourselves as persons because it is an expression for the Transcendence-relatedness of personal being which becomes a reality in history. (II, p. 138.)

Thus, Buri interprets the objectively stated doctrine of the incarnation entirely in terms of the internal dialectic of the self.

But what is the distinctively Christian historicity of this Transcendence-relation? As the final sentence of the last citation makes all too clear, *when the doctrine of the incarnation is seen as a symbol for the historicity of the Christian self-understanding, it does nothing more than re-state the systematic principle.* That principle says (i) that what it means to be a person cannot be articulated as an objective anthropology but is a definition of the self in the non-objective act of its self-realization and (ii) that this non-objective act is at the same time posited by an act of grace in a relation to Transcendence. Buri's interpretation of the incarnation does nothing more than re-state this principle. It would seem that the only significance of this doctrine is not to *differentiate* a particular modification of the systematic principle in its actualization but to serve as an *occasion* for its realization. But Buri places great stress on the fact that the systematic principle itself is never realized. It is, rather, the presupposition of its various modifications in the non-objective actualization of various historicities.

The only distinctive *differentia* seems to be the claim that Transcendence is personal in the Christian self-understanding. A moment's reflection will show, however, that if this is considered consistently with some of Buri's other principles, it also reduces to a statement of the systematic principle.

What does it mean to say that God is personal when this statement is taken as an expression of a self-understanding? Buri seems to be saying that while such a claim is not an object of knowledge established on the basis of proof or of a metaphysical scheme, it is a reality revealed to faith in the historistic actualization of the Christian self-understanding. The first thing to be said about this interpretation is that it is not a real *differentia* of the Christian faith. There are other possible self-understandings (i.e., not theories) both religious and philosophical which could make the same kind of affirmation. But more important to note is that if this is his meaning, Buri seems to violate his strictures on objectivity. Even if one refuses to say that the statement is an object of knowledge or a theory, it is still an objective statement no matter what the *source* or *grounds* for the claim – i.e., though it may not be justified under the canons of knowledge, it is still a statement of faith about the *nature* of Transcendence. Accordingly, if Buri adheres strictly to his understanding of the subject-object relation, then "God is personal" cannot be a claim about the nature of Transcendence. According to his own principles it must itself be interpreted in terms of the non-objective dialectic of the self. What would be such an interpretation?

Here two points made earlier should be recalled. First, Buri has clearly and consistently stated that "God is the mythological expression for the unconditionedness of personal responsibility. . . . We must speak of it as the transcendent dimension of our personhood, the voice which calls us to responsibility."[28] Second, he has claimed that in the purely formal understanding of self-understanding, the relation to Transcendence may be interpreted both as a gift and as a call to or a claim upon one's responsibility. In other words, the actual non-objective enactment of personhood is not a self-positing but a relationship, defined by an indicative and an imperative, to that which is transcendent and remains unknown. Taken together, these two points establish the earlier point that Buri cannot consistently use Transcendence as more than a limiting concept. On this

[28]HSRG, p. 27.

account, "God is personal" can only be a symbolic expression for the indicative and imperative in the dialectic of the self's non-objective enactment of personhood. On a consistent interpretation, therefore, this statement must not be taken as a description of the *nature* of Transcendence (even in the historicity of a particular self-understanding) but as the only· adequate way to give expression to the *relationship* of the self to an unknown "other" in the existential dialectic. Not Transcendence (or God) is personal but the relationship between the self and that to which it is related (an "X, we know not what") in its transcending. For a proper understanding of the actualization of the self, it is necessary to define the relationship in personal terms (i) because in it the self becomes a person and (ii) because only such personal categories as "call," "response," and "voice" are appropriate to describe the relationship. This argument is valid no matter what Buri's intensions are in the above passages.[29]

If Buri's statement, "God is personal," cannot be consistently interpreted as a claim about the nature of Transcendence, then this one distinctive aspect in the historistic expression of the divinity of Christ reduces back to a restatement of the systematic principle. It says nothing about the distinctive modification of the dialectic in the historicity of the Christian self-understanding. It turns out that instead of being a distinctive specification of the systematic principle in its concrete actualization,

[29]This argument represents an attempt to apply Buri's principles consistently. It does not represent what seems *prima facie* to be his intention. He seems, that is, to want to say that in the Christian self-understanding, Transcendence *is* personal as though he were making an ontological claim grounded in the historicity of this particular faith. (Cf., e.g., I, pp. 140, 278 ff.; II, pp. 104, 111 ff.) For this reason, it will be necessary to return to this difficult notion of Transcendence in the next two chapters and to raise more systematic questions about it. In at least one place in the present context, however, Buri makes this claim about the personal character of Transcendence in a way that inadvertently confirms the argument of this study. He says: "Vom urchristlichen Kerygma her kommt der Lehre von der Person Christi zu, Gott nicht als das letzte, unfassbare, allem Begreifenwollen sich als Nichts erweisende, überpersönliche Geheimnis hinzustellen. In der Lehre von der Person Christi geht es um den Gott, den sich durch seine Offenbarung in Jesus Christus als auf das Personsein des Menschen bezogen erweist. Was sich im Anschluss an diese Botschaft als Mythologie oder Spekulation im Dogma und seiner Geschichte entfaltet, bekommt positive Bedeutung als ein glaubensmässiges Verständnis des Kerygmas, in dem der Mensch auf diese Aussagen hin sich von diesem Gott als Person persönlich angeredet, gewollt und berufen versteht." (II, p. 132.) The many conflicting statements in Buri's theology which can be appealed to on either side of the interpretation — Transcendence as a personal God or Transcendence as a limiting concept — show that Buri himself seems uncertain concerning the full range of his principles. The important point to note here is that this uncertainty is directly a function of the status accorded to the problem of objectivity. Bluntly put, the problem concerns the answer Buri would give to the question: "Is it your position that Christians believe in God, and, if so, can this belief be affirmed without making an objective claim?"

what Buri calls the historicity of self-understanding in this particular doctrine is nothing more than a mythological way of stating an abstract principle about the self. The same applies to the other side of Christology, to the humanity of the God-man as an expression of self-understanding.

2. The Humanity of Christ in the Christian Self-Understanding

Buri interprets the history of the Christological debates about the personhood of Christ as ending in either monophysite or dyophysite tendencies. The monophysite tendency came to preponderance through acceptance of the "an- or enhypostasis of the Logos by which the human nature of Christ does not represent an independent person – is anhypostatic – but possesses his personhood only in the person of the Logos – enhypostatic, 'innerwesentlich'." (II, p. 120.) This position tends toward monophysitism because the human nature threatens to become completely absorbed into the divine nature. This failure to take full account of the humanity is the great problem in classical Christology. Despite its problems, the an- and enhypostasis did guard against dyophysitism, i.e., "the sundering of the two natures of the God-man." In this fashion, it "established the unity of his divine-human person in the *unio personalis seu hypostatica* – but at the cost of the humanity of the redeemer." (II, p. 120). The two tendencies-re-emerged, according to Buri, in the Lutheran and Reformed camps of protestant orthodoxy. In connection with its concern for the ubiquity of Christ and its position *finitum capax infiniti,* Lutheran theology gave renewed expression to the an- and enhypostasis and thus to the tendency toward monophysitism.[30] The Reformed opposition to the Lutheran position tended in the direction of dyophysitism:

The humanity of the person of Christ becomes no less questionable where on Reformed ground the Lutheran *finitum capax infiniti* is opposed by the *finitum incapax infiniti.* The so-called *Extracalvinisticum* lays down that the Logos can be fully absorbed by no finite appearance – neither by the earthly person of Jesus nor by the elements of the eucharist; rather, despite its entrance into the finite, at the same time, it always remains *(weile)* outside the finite as the exalted one with God *(der Erhöhte bei Gott).* (II, pp. 120 f.)

Again it is Buri's contention that such problems, falling now on one extreme and now on another, are the fate of all purely objective at-

[30]Cf., II, pp. 120, 140.

tempts to conceive that which defies objective articulation.[31] His proposal is to take not just one or another of these alternatives but to interpret the entire *Lehrgegensatz* as an adequate mythological expression for the significance of the person of Christ. He admits that his own interpretation will be no less a theory than the mythology he is rejecting in its objectivity. The form of objectivity is the only way to speak or think at all. But in his mind, precisely the purpose of the Lutheran and Reformed positions (seen in their totality and not as exclusive alternatives) is "to bring to expression" that "the reality of human personhood can be converted into no theory." (II, p. 140.) In other words, Buri claims that his own theory about the significance of Christological formulations will be a theory denying the adequacy of any theory; it will be a self-negating theory.

Insofar as this is the meaning of the Christological assertions, then Buri has already done nothing more than re-state his systematic principle. That is, Christology becomes nothing more than a symbol for his problem of objectivity in the context of the systematic principle: man's being is a non-objective reality which cannot be conceptualized but only enacted. Christological statements in this sense are nothing more than a way of *denying* the theoretical adequacy of cognitive statements about man. Therefore, they symbolize not a particular modification of man's historicity but historicity itself. In this way, they are nothing more than a statement of that part of the systematic principle which emphasizes that it is not a general theory about man's nature but points to the fact that man's nature is only in his "to be" which he must assume in his concrete historicity.

Still, Buri goes on to say that such statements also indicate a content for that historicity:

> While the discussion of the Chalcedonian doctrine of the two natures endangers the full humanity of Christ or calls into question his personal unity so long as the humanity and the divinity of Christ are taken as objective things, in this doctrine is to be seen an illuminating insight into the basic structure of human personhood when objectivities of conceptual knowledge are no longer sought therein. (II, pp. 140 f.)

The various aspects of traditional Christology as they receive definition in Lutheran and Reformed thought should serve, then, to give particular historistic content and differentiation to this basic structure. Unfortunate-

---

[31]*Ibid.*, pp. 121, 140.

ly, however, one finds, as indeed this statement already hints, that they do nothing more than restate that structure in mythological form.

The *Extracalvinisticum* serves to bring to expression the transcending and, therefore, non-objective dimension in the basic structure of human being:

> The incompleteness of personhood without relatedness to Transcendence and the reference *(Bezogensein)* of personal being to Transcendence are in no way scientifically demonstrable *(nachweisbar)* – neither psychologically nor historically. All the less are they to be grounded as supernatural givens of revelation in a doctrine of a God-man or in his presence in the cult. The The *Extracalvinisticum* guards against precisely such an objective demonstrability of faith contents in that it emphasizes the *finitum incapax infiniti* and therewith lays down the autonomy of the incarnated Son of God in heaven. (II, p. 141.)

If this statement is taken seriously, then the *Extracalvinisticum* does nothing to give content to the Christian actualization of the systematic principle. Its cash value is solely in stating the nature of the self in relation to the subject-object scheme, and this is an essential part of the systematic principle. *It says nothing about how the Christian self-understanding is differentiated as one among many possible self-understandings in which that systematic principle is actualized.* When it is combined with the symbolic meaning of the divinity of Christ, the two together simply re-state the principle that the self becomes who it is only in a transcending (i.e., non-objective and therefore indemonstrable) act of self-determination which is at the same time an equally non-objective positing of the self by a transcendent "other" which can never be identified with anything objective in the world.

The same applies when the *Extracalvinisticum* is combined with the Lutheran position. Having given what can only be seen as a restatement of his systematic principle, Buri returns to the notion of historicity and emphasizes that this actualization never occurs in abstraction but always concretely. "We must take into account," he says, "that we are not interpreting just any faith but the self-understanding of the Christian faith. Christian faith knows itself related to the transcendence of God revealed in Christ, and it understands the humanity of the God-man to the effect that personhood is realized only in relation to the transcendence of God revealed in Christ." (II, p. 141.) This leads, then, to the following significance for the an- and enhypostasis:

> In this case, *anhypostatis* means: the Christian faith is not in a position to justify itself *(sich auszuweisen)* as a general human possibility in the sense of a natural

theology as though the human soul were by nature Christian or Christ had entered so into history that one could somehow demonstrate *(nachweisen)* him therein in his supernaturalism *(Übernatürlichkeit)*. Enhypostasis signifies, however, that Christian faith realizes itself in no other way than in the assumption of its historistic situation that is defined by the message of Christ. Its essence consists in this historicity. But in the sense of the *Extracalvinisticum* we continue to maintain that also, in this *enhypostasis* of the self-understanding of the Christian faith in the kerygma, it is a question of a reality occurring only in the enactment of self-understanding. The confessional statements of this faith are just as different from the faith itself as the elevated Christ in heaven is from each of his earthly hypostaseis. (II, pp. 141 f.)

The anhypostasis is a purely negative doctrine guarding the historicity of faith. By saying it rules out natural theology, Buri means to point out that the possibility of faith is not something given as such to or found as such in human existence but is something which the self must realize in the concrete actualization of itself. In this respect it gives expression to that implication of the concept of historicity which denies the notion of a permanent human nature. Human being is not constituted by certain essential structures which are simply actualized in *concreto* in a multitude of different modalities. It is, rather, a self-making process which cannot be defined in advance. Who the self is is first decided by how the self understands itself. Human nature cannot be defined in advance of the self-making process by which it actualizes itself.[32]

But this negative function guarding the historicity of faith does no more than articulate another aspect of the systematic principle. It emphasizes that feature built into the principle itself that it should not be taken as a general theory about human being but that its sole function as a principle is to point to that "to be" character of human existence which can only be realized in the specific transcending act by which the self first actualizes itself. The anhypostasis does nothing in the way of defining the content of the uniquely Christian actualization of the systematic principle.

Presumably the positive character of the enhypostasis is to perform this function. But the significance of this doctrine is purely circular, and in its circularity, it only restates the principle of historicity but does not give it any content. In the light of the anhypostasis, it says that the general possibility of historicity is defined in the Christian self-understanding by the message of Christ, i.e., by the Christian historicity. But at a point where one expects to learn precisely what this definition is, this is like

[32]Cf., Fackenheim, pp. 13 ff., note 9, *et passim.*

saying that the Christian faith is the Christian faith. If the anhypostasis gives expression to the general principle of historicity, the enhypostasis now says that the historicity of the Christian self-understanding is specified by the Christian kerygma. But beyond this it does not say what this specification is. It goes no further than the systematic principle which already says that every general possibility of self-understanding will be specified by the historicity appropriate to it.

In this context, the *Extracalvinisticum* is a reminder of the subject-object problem in relation to historicity. It reminds that historicity is not a principle but an act, and as such, a transcending of all objectivity. Assertions on the part of any particular historistic self-embodiment (i.e., confessions of faith), therefore, have no independent objective status but serve only to extent that they can be referred back to the dialectic of the self. The objective statements of a self-understanding cannot be identified with that self-understanding itself. This, however, again does nothing more than state the significance of the systematic principle in relation to the problem of objectivity in general.

One is forced to conclude, then, that the ostensible content of the Christian self-understanding turns out to be nothing more than a restatement of the systematic principle. Although this conclusion follows from an analysis of only one of Buri's interpretations, the same conclusion is forced upon the reader of his theology almost without exception in every doctrine he treats.[33] The reason for this conclusion, as will become evident below, follows with a certain necessity from the centrality of the problem of objectivity in Buri's thought. And the exceptions are as significant as the conclusion, for if the loss of historicity turns out to follow necessarily from Buri's analysis of objectivity and non-objectivity, then any success in specifying the historicity of the Christian self-understanding will be inconsistent with the position on objectivity. Such an inconsistency at the very center of Buri's theology will, of course, have far-reaching implications for the hermeneutics of a radical theology, in particular, for the role the problem of objectivity should play in such a theology. Since the above conclusion is to be given this weight, it will be helpful to support it more fully in terms of certain points made earlier.

D. THE FAILURE OF HISTORICITY

One of the hermeneutical rules showed that both the form and the content of the Christian kerygma must be interpreted in terms of the his-

---

[33]Cf., e.g., II, pp. 222-228, 245-251, 385 f., 387-391, 401-406, 493-496.

toricity of the systematic principle.[34] The form of the Christian kerygma is important because its form as the proclamation of a saving act of God in an event of the past symbolized the formal concept both that the possibilities of human existence are nothing more than its "to be" which the self must actualize in a once-for-all historicity and that the actualization of this "to be" is nevertheless not a self-creation or a self-positing. Quite apart from its particular content, the kerygma itself is a symbol for the general principle of historicity. It is extremely important that this meaning be seen to be *intrinsic* to the formal nature of the Christian message itself (and not arbitrarily imposed on it) because the general principle of historicity is crucial in the hermeneutics of existentialist interpretation. On the content side, the Christian kerygma was supposed somehow to structure the particular actualization of the systematic principle in the Christian self-understanding. But analysis has now shown that a specification of the content tends to reduce it back to nothing more than a general statement of the systematic principle. This means that instead of specifying the content of historicity, doctrines do nothing more than state the general principle of historicity as such. This, in fact, appears to be the only significance Buri can give to Christology.

This conclusion is substantiated by a particularly enlightening section in Buri's prolegomena. In his discussion of the general nature of revelation, he treats in a provisional way contents of revelation for faith. He deals here with certain positive features in the Christian revelation of God, Christ, and the Holy Spirit when these are seen in terms of the non-objective dialectic of the self. The section on Christ is entitled significantly: "The special revelation in Christ for faith as the historicity of Christian faith." (I, p. 280.) He concludes this discussion in the following way:

> The special revelation in Christ for faith is not represented by what may be drawn cognitively about it out of the New Testament sources. That is only a matter of a tradition of revelation which can become revelation for us insofar as it becomes an occasion for a new self-understanding. For us in our historistic situation, the particularity *(Besonderheit)* of this redeeming self-understanding in relation to the message of Christ becomes actual precisely in this and not in some other relation – e.g., not to Buddha or to Mohammed or to any other reality of the history of religions. But one should beware of deriving from that a *religionswissenschaftlich* or dogmatic proof for the uniqueness *(Besonderheit)* of the revelation of Christ. On the basis of the history of religions only relative but no absolute uniqueness *(Besonderheit)* can be established in relation to the appearance of

---

[34]Cf., *supra*, pp. 135 f.

Jesus. Judgments of faith are precisely judgments of faith which, if they are not to become false dogmatic assertions, have validity only for the faith expressing itself in them as statements of its self-understanding. But they have no validity independent of that faith. The doctrine of the special revelation of God in Christ for faith is to be proven neither out of the history of religions (in the sense of an "absoluteness of Christianity") nor on the basis of the Bible in the form of a *heilsgeschichtlich* theory; rather, it is the expression of the historicity of the Christian faith which at one time arose and again and again arises at just this place and not at any other. (I, pp. 281 f.)

The problem with this statement of the particularity of the revelation of Christ for self-understanding is that it says nothing about *what* the particular self-understanding is that arises at just this place and at no other. Here Christology documents only the notion of historicity in general. It provides no content for the self-understanding which is actualized in relation to it but only says that whatever self-understanding does arise will be historistic, i.e., will be defined by just this revelation. This is nothing more than to say that the meaning of faith in Christianity can only be grasped in terms of the meaning of the concept of self-understanding and that self-understanding is self-understanding, i.e., is historistic.

Another observation documents the same point. When the hermeneutical role of the systematic principle was first analyzed, the doctrine of creation was cited as a mythological form of objectivity which can be existentially interpreted in terms of the dialectic of the self.[35] According to Buri, then, this doctrine has nothing to do with an objective world creator. As an expression for the systematic principle in abstraction from any particular historicity, however, the doctrine of creation remains merely empty. Buri makes this clear in his discussion of the likeness of God from creation. Because the created likeness only symbolizes the general possibility for the non-objective actualization of personhood which constitutes man as man, the mythological notion of a creator is nothing but a limiting concept. To define the specific Transcendence-relation in any particular actualization of a self-understanding, presumably it would be necessary to refer to the historistic content of a self-understanding. This would be a historicity defined by Christ in the Christian self-understanding. It calls to mind the mythological idea of the Logos or the Son as the principle of creation. The specific modification of the doctrine of creation would be historistically defined in this way by a Christological concept. Buri did, in fact, make this move. But at just that point it also became evident that existentialist interpretation of the doctrine of crea-

[35]Cf., *supra*, pp. 87-89.

tion in Christ does no more than restate the doctrine as a limiting concept in its form of expressing the systematic principle.

Buri has not yet developed his doctrine of creation in detail. But in another context, he does refer to its historistic modification in the Christian faith. Speaking of Paul's interpretation of "being in Christ," Buri writes:

> Because of the person-forming, creative power [of his interpretation] of the preached Christ, Paul had probably not yet attributed a world creative potency to this Christ. But his immediate followers did indeed do this in that they confessed that God had created the world in Christ (Col. 1:16; cf., 1 John 3:10). With that they brought to expression that for those who understand themselves in their personhood in terms of the message of Christ, God is not otherwise God than he is God for them in this self-understanding as persons in the new being in Christ. With this understanding of Christ as the world-creative principle, an assertion is won through which all absolutizations both of a general possibility of human personhood as well as of every historistic realization of such personhood – even a possible absolutization of a self-understanding of the Christian faith – are excluded. In terms of its possibility as well as its realization, personhood is a creation of God in Christ. And indeed, precisely this statement is to be understood as a statement of faith, i.e., as a statement concerning a reality which exists only in the enactment of the self-understanding corresponding to it and which thus represents something different from every theory of world creation – even personalistic ones. (II, pp. 225 f.)

The meaning of this statement is, first, that personhood is not its own creation and, second, that it is realized in the Christian faith only as a concrete response to the kerygma which cannot be absolutized into an objective claim about the nature of things. But *what* is realized is nothing other than the dialectic of the self exposited by the systematic principle. To be sure, it says that this systematic principle is actualized only in a concrete historicity, one defined by the kerygma in the Christian faith. But it does not say that this actualization is any kind of distinctive modification of the systematic principle. What is actualized is nothing more than the formal dialectic even though the actualization of this principle may be occasioned or caused by any number of possible historistic self-understandings. This means that the historistic concept of creation in Christ reduces to the doctrine of creation expressing the systematic principle. It only says that for the Christian this merely "limiting" notion will be actualized in response to the Christian kerygma. But it in no way specifies any unique content for this actualization. *What* is actualized is only the systematic principle.

Buri's discussion of symbols of Transcendence in his prolegomena can serve as a final point of documentation for this thesis.[36] In his discussion of various symbols of Transcendence, he claims that Christ is a symbol of Transcendence because, in the historicity of the Christian self-understanding, it is Christ who provides the appropriate symbol for the configuration of Transcendence-relatedness in that tradition. The statement of what this content is, however, turns out to be surprisingly formal: "In this way, the Christ-myth can serve as a symbol for the self-understanding of faith, that for all its self-activity, its realization is still experienced as a gift which is not at its disposal but which occurs to it." (I, p. 298.) Here in a single sentence is an exact confirmation of the thesis concerning the loss of genuine historicity in Buri's interpretation of doctrines.

E. THE SYSTEMATIC PRINCIPLE, HISTORICITY, AND THE DILEMMA OF OBJECTIVITY

It seems necessary to conclude that even Buri's systematic principle does not solve the problem of how to do theology in his system. Initially, it looked as though this principle would give him one non-symbolic point of reference from the perspective of which it would be possible to specify the content of the Christian self-understanding after it seemed that his concept of faith, revelation, symbol, and myth had made this specification difficult if not impossible. But now even the systematic principle does not solve this problem because the content of doctrines becomes a restatement of the pure formality of the systematic principle. In a moment it will be shown that this conclusion has devastating consequences for the theological task. First, however, the question must be raised whether the above interpretation of Buri's principles has been accurate to his intentions.

Instead of criticizing Buri from assumptions alien to his own, the conclusion to this analysis has been reached by a direct reading of Buri's own statements. First it was shown why a self-understanding must be specified by its distinctive historicity, and then it was argued that Buri's interpretation of the actual historicity of the Christian self-understanding fails to achieve this specification. With a thinker as systematically rigorous and as methodologically self-conscious as Buri, the procedure by which this conclusion was reached should give pause. Perhaps Buri intends the concept of historicity in an entirely different way, and perhaps

[36]Cf., I, pp. 296-299.

the "content" of a self-understanding has quite different ramifications for Buri from the ones the argument of this study has assumed. In this case, the evaluative framework of this study would be misplaced. The content of the Christian self-understanding, the thrust of existentialist interpretation, and the basic character of Buri's conception of a radical theology would be entirely different and would require evaluation in totally different terms. Might he have meant something else with the concept of historicity?

There is at least one possible alternative reading of the notion of historicity which Buri's actual interpretation of doctrines sometimes seems to suggest. It might be nothing more nor less than a purely formal concept. In this sense it would give expression to the concept of *Existenz*. As has been noted, this concept refers to the transcending nature of human personhood. Who the self is cannot be defined in advance of how the self decides to understand itself in a concrete situation. The purpose of the "concept" of *Existenz* is to throw the notion of a permanent "human nature" into question by defining man as a self-making process. Because the self *is* its "to be," what the self is is, strictly speaking, non-cognitive, non-discursive, indemonstrable. What the self is is the transcending *act* by which the self first determines itself. This concept does not mean to deny the relevance of objective thought for how the self decides. But at the point of actualization itself, it is "passion" and not objectivity that is at stake. Buri calls the actualization of self-understanding "unconditioned" not because in this act the self somehow becomes God-like or because it is somehow free from its historical situation. It is unconditioned because precisely in its finite, conditioned, and relative situation, the relativity of objective thinking is transcended in the decisive act for just "this" or "that." Insofar as the systematic principle delineates the structure of *Existenz,* historicity points out that this structure should not be taken as an essential quality (*Beschaffenheit*) given in human nature as such but that it is a possibility which must be actualized. Historicity means that the systematic principle is always actualized in a concrete situation.

If historicity means nothing more than this, *then the content of the Christian self-understanding is the systematic principle.* The historicity of this self-understanding simply means that the concrete situation in which the systematic principle is actualized is a response to the kerygma of God's act in Christ. The historicity of the Christian self-understanding would not involve any concrete specification of the systematic principle but would, rather, simply be a documentation of the existentiality of the systematic principle. It would indicate that the systematic principle should be understood neither as a principle nor as an ontology of human being but as a structure which must be actualized in the non-objective act of self-definition in a concrete situation. And the sole content of Christianity would be this structure.

Against the assumption made throughout this study that the Christian self-understanding involves some specific content, this interpretation would imply a *causal* relationship between the systematic principle and the historicity of the Christian self-understanding. Since historicity would mean no more than the transcending actualization of any self-understanding in its particular situation, the historicity of the Christian faith would consist simply in the kerygma and the Christian tradition being the objectively historical occasion or cause for the enactment of the systematic principle. In this way, the abstractness of the systematic principle would be avoided because the notion of historicity would still show that it is not a general theory about human nature as such but a possibility which must be actualized. But there would be no *structural* relation between this actualization (i.e., the historicity of the systematic principle) and the content of Christian doctrines (i.e., what the Christian says). On this interpretation, there would be no contradiction between Buri's hermeneutical principles and his actual interpretations. This meaning of historicity would correspond exactly with the above presentation of his Christology, but there would be no conflict with the intension of his principles.

This is a plausible interpretation of what historicity means, and in many places Buri seems to accept it.[37] But it cannot be brought into agree-

---

[37]In a recent book which is in part a reply to an earlier version of the present study, Buri seems to confirm this interpretation, but without being aware of the conflict it occasions with his other principles. He says: "Wenn sich sodann herausstellt, dass sich die Interpretation, die sich mir aus meinem Verständnis der christlichen Überlieferung ergibt, nicht von einer allgemein menschlichen unterscheidet, sondern sich grundsätzlich auch unter Absehung von seiner besonderen Prägung durch die christliche Überlieferung als Wahrheit des Personseins, zu dem sich der Mensch gnadenweise berufen erfahren kann, erweisen lässt und als solche neue, über geschichtliche, speziell konfessionelle und religionsgeschichtliche Grenzen hinausführende Gemeinschaft zu stiften vermag, so steht dies gerade nicht im Widerspruch zur Geschichtlichkeit menschlichen Selbstverständnisses, sondern bedeutet vielmehr dessen Wahrheit und Erfüllung, wie sie im Symbol der Imago Dei in Christus gemeint ist." (*Gott in Amerika*, p. 249.) And further: "Gleichzeitig vermerkt er auch, dass es in meinem System kein eigentliches Lehrstück von der Person Christi gebe, weil die Paradoxie der Menschwerdung als Symbol der Paradoxie von Gegenständlichkeit und Ungegenständlichkeit im Selbstverständnis des Glaubens das Strukturprinzip der ganzen Dogmatik darstelle. Diese Funktion der Christologie als Strukturprinzip nimmt freilich Hardwick zum Anlass, mir noch einmal Auflösung der Dogmatik

ment with the thrust of Buri's most important principles. Since, however, this purely formal meaning of historicity is the one that actually results from his interpretation of doctrines (and the one he explicitly seems to adopt at times), it can also be shown that, even if this meaning did not contradict other of his basic principles, it nevertheless has debilitating consequences for any proper execution of the theological task. Each of these points will be taken up in turn.

First, the formal interpretation of historicity conflicts with many of Buri's own statements and with certain important principles he has laid down. To be sure, Buri sometimes suggests that the mythological content of Christian doctrines provides "an illuminating insight into the basic structure of human personhood," as though their content did nothing more than elucidate the purely formal dialectic of the self. (II, p. 141.) Also, in various passages, he sometimes says that the Christian kerygma is the *occasion* for a self-understanding the content of which is understanding ourselves as persons related to Transcendence.[38] Such statements would suggest the merely causal interpretation of historicity. Nevertheless, Buri almost always speaks in these connections as if the "illuminating insight" or the sense in which the kerygma is an "occasion" receives a particular modification insofar as it is defined by the message of Christ. He continually suggests that there is some structural relationship between the message of Christ and the historistic self-understanding that is a response to it. For instance: "In the primitive Christian kerygma of the saving act of God in Christ, the *particular* relation to Transcendence in Christian faith comes to expression." (II, p. 130. My italics.) Or: "We do not have to do with *just any* understanding-of-oneself but with the self-understanding *defined* by the message of God's decisive saving act in Christ." (II, p. 19. My italics.) Such qualifying phrases as "defined by," "in relation to," or "particular self-understanding" are replete in all of

---

in bloss formale, inhaltlose Bestimmungen zum Vorwurf zu machen. Davon, dass das Prinzip zur sachgemässen Interpretation des christlichen Überlieferungsstoffes verwendet wird, nimmt er merkwürdigerweise nicht Notiz, und auch nicht von dem andern Umstand dass von diesem Stoff, der der christlichen Dogmatik vergegeben ist, deren Christlichkeit herrührt. Statt dessen meint er, ein derartiger Ausweis der Christlichkeit auf Grund des Bezogenseins auf die christliche Tradition genüge nicht — wobei er nicht beachtet, dass er damit gegenüber der Dogmatik eine Forderung erhebt, die mit deren von ihm doch sonst anerkannten Geschichtlichkeit unvereinbar ist." (*Ibid.*, p. 250.) The problem, of course, concerns *how* this principle does in fact interpret the Christian tradition, and this Buri's reply does not touch. Furthermore, to say that the Christian material is pre-given does not help much if its content is so formal as to have nothing to do with its pre-given historicity.

[38]Cf., e.g., *supra*, pp. 156-159.

Buri's actual statements of the content of the Christian historicity.

If this is not enough, certain features of Buri's prolegomena demand that the historicity of the Christian self-understanding be differentiated by some content. His concept of self-understanding itself demands this. It will be recalled that the only way he can differentiate self-understanding as a general human possibility from the Christian self-understanding is by arguing that this general structural possibility of human existence receives a distinctive modification and realization when it is defined by the historicity of the Christian message. Buri's distinction between revelation for knowledge as *ein Nichts* and the positive content of revelation for faith assumes it also. Revelation for faith is positive not simply because it is a concrete actualization transcending the subject-object relation but also because in that actualization it is situated by a faithful self-understanding in a tradition. If the content of its actualization were only a general possibility of human existence and nothing more, then revelation for faith would itself be reduced to *ein Nichts*.

Buri's practice, of course, is in contradiction to these principles, so it is also important to consider the consequences of allowing historicity to become merely formal. The first problem, is, ironically, that Buri has not and cannot articulate the content of the Christian self-understanding. The content of the Christian self-understanding in Buri's interpretation of doctrines does nothing more than restate the systematic principle for interpreting any self-understanding whatsoever, the purpose of its historicity being to indicate the existentiality of its actualization. In relation to any particular self-understanding, however, Buri has clearly affirmed that the systematic principle is formal and empty. It merely states the presupposition of any concrete actualization or modification. Insofar as the content of the Christian self-understanding does nothing more than restate this principle, it also becomes empty. It states nothing more than the formal dialectic of self-understanding as a general human possibility. If this is what the content of the Christian self-understanding turns out to be, one must conclude that there is some Christian historicity within this Christian historicity, a Christian self-understanding within the Christian self-understanding. The formal meaning of Christian doctrines would point to historicity in general; that is, like the systematic principle, their meaning would be to indicate that the systematic principle is not an abstraction but always a concrete actualization. In this case, the *actual historicity* of any particular Christian self-understanding would depend on what a particular Christian actualized in his concrete situation, and this could not be defined in advance. Thus, within the general Christian self-understanding which does nothing but restate the systematic principle, there would be a multitude of Christian self-understandings depending on what any individual Christian actually did. And there would be no structural relation between the Christian self-understanding in general and the individual Christian self-understandings. The Christian self-understanding in general would say no more than that there will be *some* historistic actualization by individual selves.

To the extent that this interpretation is unavoidable, to the same extent the Christian faith has been evacuated of any content save that of the merely abstract dialectic of the self. It is important to observe the consequences that follow. One serious result is that all Christian doctrines would end up saying the same thing because faith's only content would be this abstract statement that, in its transcending self-definition, the self is both responsible freedom and gracious gift. Of course, there is a profound sense in which all Christian doctrines do have the intention of saying the same thing. But there is more than one Christian doctrine precisely because the same thing they all say contains a multiplex richness which encompasses all the diversity and the complexity of human experience. They do not say the same thing in the sense that their total content reduces to the repetition of a single abstract formula.

Furthermore, the single thing that all Christian doctrines say is the material content of a particular view of human life and destiny which is a real alternative to other views. In contrast to this, the systematic principle is purely formal. The single thing that all doctrines say if they merely express the systematic principle makes it impossible to differentiate the Christian self-understanding from any other since self-understanding as a general human possibility is simply the structural presupposition of all particular self-understandings. This is an even more serious consequence. The content of Christian doctrines becomes nothing except a formal statement of the concept of self-understanding in general. Any actual historicity (i.e., actualization) of a self-understanding would be so concrete and multifarious from individual to individual that it could neither be anticipated in advance nor defined by any general structures. The Christian self-understanding would then be as broad as any particular self-understanding, and there would be no way at all to differentiate it from the concrete manifestation of any other religious or philosophical self-understanding – Buddhist, Islamic, humanist, atheistic, or what have you.

Finally, this last conclusion leads to still another debilitating consequence. Above it was already suggested that if the only content of Christian doctrines is to restate the systematic principle then it seems the only significance for the particular Christign historicity is cgusal. It is a keryg-matic claim that brings about or occasions the actualization of the dia-lectic of the described by the formal principle. But if the relationship is only causal, then there is ng intrinsic relation between *the content of the mythological symbols* which cause this effect and *the content of the effect itself*. The mythological content of the Christian tradition would thereby have not intrinsic relation to what, according to Buri, is the fun-damental truth of human existence; that mythology would be merely one among presumably many causative ways to bring about the actualization of that fundamental truth. On this basis, not only would there no longer be any basis within theology for interpreting the content of the Christian tradition in one way rather than in another, but more important, the question would be obvious: why these mythological stories at all? It is not enough to say that one cannot transcend his historically relative si-tuation as a Christian or a Westerner. This response would not only leave the question of truth completely in the air. It would even make the question of meaning irrelevant. There could be no basis for the theolo-gian or the believer to say one thing rather than another unless it could be empirically established that one tradition or interpretation causes the desired effect more often than another. The result would be a magical understanding of the content of Christian affirmations! The only role left to them would be in a crude form of worship, the ritualized mumbling of strictly unintelligible formulas whose only function is to produce cer-tain effects. A radical theology that set out to interpret religious meaning for modern man would end with an understanding of the content of Christianity more primitive even than myth.

Both from Buri's basic principles and from the consequences that fol-low an alternative view of historicity, one is forced to conclude, then, that the historicity of the Christian self-understanding must indicate some specific range of content for the self-understanding defined by the Chris-tian message. But Buri's actual practice in interpreting doctrines is open to the criticisms that result from a purely formal understanding of histo-ricity. Is there a way out of this conundrum within the limits of Buri's theology? To begin to answer this question it is necessary first to exa-mine how this apparent contradiction in his hermeneutic comes about.

Ultimately, the failure of historicity in Buri's theology follows with a certain necessity from his treatment of the problem of objectivity. Be-cause of his analysis of the subject-object relation, he excludes objectivi-ty (obj-B) from the intrinsic self and being-itself. At only one point is there any relationship between finite being and absolute being, and that is in a non-objective, transcending actualization of the intrinsic self. Because the Christian faith is concerned with each of these non-objective dimensions, Buri must conceive revelation and the interpretation of revelation solely in terms of the dynamic of the self in which there is some relatedness between the two. For this reason, he proposes to interpret the content of faith entirely in terms of self-understanding. That there is such a finite relation accounts for his argument that the turn to self-understanding is not a total anthropologizing of theology or a loss of all transcendence. *But this finite relation is equally non-objective.* This means that objective descriptions are equally as inappropriate here as with being-itself. Consequently, he turns to mythological forms of objectivity as appropriate non-literal and symbolic ways of talking about the finite relation between two non-objective realities. But because every objective statement, not only the mythological symbols but also *the objective interpretations of symbols*, must continually be qualified in view of the non-objective, existential *actualization* of the relationship, his substantive theological statements continually threaten to become entirely vacuous.

At only one point does he seem to come down on an adequate objective statement about the transcending relatedness of the intrinsic self, and that is the systematic principle. He claims that while the relation between self and Transcendence is entirely non-objective, this relation does have certain structural characteristics. These he defines by the abstract dialectic of the self in the systematic principle. If this dialectic is the *only* objective, yet non-mythological and non-symbolic thing that can be said about the non-objective dimension of the self, then it follows with a certain necessity and consitency that all interpretations of particular doctrines expressing the Christian self-understanding will only be able to repeat this abstract principle. In this way the contradiction in Buri's hermeneutic follows from his orientation on the problem of objectivity.

It would seem that a radical theology based on existentialist interpretation has an essential stake in regaining the historicity Buri loses in his interpretation of doctrines. Yet this would involve repudiating some of the restrictions he has placed on objective description. Since Buri's analysis of the problem of objectivity, the epistemological grounds of the existential method, is the most cogent among the radical theologians, the problem in his hermeneutic is a paradigm of the problem at the root of any radical theology which adopts existentialist interpretation. Such a theology is faced with the following dilemma. Either it holds fast to the restriction on objective description in relation to faith and thereby ends with a loss of historicity and with the debilitating consequences that involves. Or it preserves historicity as the differentiating principle for the Christian self-understanding and violates the restrictions on objectivity. The above analysis indicates that only by taking the latter horn of the dilemma can the task of Christian theology be implemented. The question is whether this option is possible without contradicting in another sense the principle of existentialist interpretation. In the present context this question concerns whether such a modification is possible within the limits of Buri's hermeneutic.

The historicity of the Christian self-understanding could be preserved only to the extent that it was possible to show how the abstract dialectic of self-understanding as a general human possibility receives distinctive specification when it is actualized historistically as a concrete response to the message of Christ.[39] Could this be shown, then the relationship between the Christian self-understanding and the symbolic assertions which occasion and express it would be more than causal. The specification of self-understanding (its content) would be structurally related to the content of the Christian kerygma and to the doctrines which develop it. This would not at all necessitate a retreat from Buri's demand that objective doctrinal assertions be interpreted exhaustively in terms of self-understanding. It would, thus, not qualify the program of a radical existentialist theology. But it would mean that *the distinctive content of the Christian self-understanding would have to be accessible to some form of objective description.* The content of doctrinal symbols might still be restricted from having any objective descriptive force in relation to the world or to transcendent reality. But at least in relation to the man of faith, it would be necessary to specify objectively the dynamics, the states, and the structures at work in the distinctively Christian actualization of self-understanding.

The assumption on which this position is based is that the Christian faith involves an understanding of human existence to which there are real alternatives. Once it is settled that the content of all Christian affirmations requires exhaustive existentialist interpretation, then the only way to show how being a Christian involves a real alternative to other possibilities is to describe the content of Christianity in terms of the existential modes of being it involves. If an absolutism and exclusivism which are alien to the existential method and to demythologizing are to

---

[39]The parallel with Schleiermacher should not be overlooked. By "specification" the same thing is meant as Schleiermacher's idea of the Christian modification of his systematic principle, the feeling of absolute dependence.

be avoided, one must be extremely careful how this point is formulated. To say that the doctrinal content of Christianity is exhausted by its reference to a distinctive mode of existence is not to say, in turn, that this mode of existence is a possibility only because of the Christian doctrinal tradition – as though one had to express one's self-understanding by means of Christian affirmations in order to actualize the existential posture which is the content of the doctrinal tradition, or, to put it more bluntly, as though these existential possibilities were possibilities in fact only for Christians.[40] The Christian myths express certain existential possibilities, but these possibilities themselves are logically separable *from any particular* mythological framework, including the Christian one, that might give them expression. At the same time, however, the Christian myths have no other content than these possibilities of existence.[41] And whether in actualizing these possibilities a person confessed himself a Christian or not, there are certainly other existential possibilities by means of which men can actualize their existence to which these possibilities constitute a real alternative.

To put this into Buri's terms, this means that the content of the Christian self-understanding expresses only one possible way of being a person since Buri's concept of "personhood" simply refers to the purely formal dialectic of existence in which the self first takes hold of itself in freedom and responsibility.[42] There must be different ways of being a person in this sense, that is, different modes of existence under which men freely take responsibility for themselves. Of course, one might argue that a truly fulfilled humanity will involve the actualization of certain modes of existence to the exclusion of others. Then fully personal being would be limited to those modes, and the concept of person would take on a normative significance. If the content of the Christian self-understanding

40Cf., Ogden, *Christ without Myth*, pp. 115-125, 141-146.

41This means that there is no necessary relationship between actualizing the existential content of the Christian myths and actually confessing oneself a Christian. Certain existential possibilities are the necessary and sufficient condition for the content of the Christian doctrinal assertions, but the Christian doctrinal assertions are only a sufficient condition of the existential possibilities which are their content.

42"Personhood" does, of course, have a normative significance at the purely general level of the systematic principle in that a man can refuse his freedom and responsibility and understand himself simply as the world objectively defines him. But surely Buri would not want to say that *every* actualization of freedom and responsibility expresses the content of Christianity — especially since some ways men freely take responsibility for themselves are obviously mutually exclusive. Is it not true that in a purely general sense (i.e., short of some material norms of what constitutes authentic human behaviour), both Eichmann and Bonhoeffer freely took responsibility for themselves?

were identified with these possibilities of existence, then there would be a sense in which the content of the Christian self-understanding was universal, absolute, and exclusive. But it is important to observe that one could argue this case only from the standpoint of some material vision of the actualized possibilities of human existence which constitute truly fulfilled humanity as against certain other equally material conceptions. One could not make this case from the purely formal conception of human personhood in general since every actualization of self-understanding (including the excluded modes of existence which fall short of fulfilled humanity) will presuppose it. And in this case, it would still be true that the material vision which constitutes a truly fulfilled humanity would be expressed in terms of certain existential possibilities which are logically independent of any particular mythological framework, including the Christian one. The content of the Christian self-understanding would be universal, absolute, and exclusive not because a fulfilled humanity is limited to confessing Christians but because the content of the Christian confession is nothing other than the existential possibilities which constitute a fulfilled humanity but which may also be actualized by non-Christians.

It must be possible, then, to specify those possibilities of existence which distinguish the content of the Christian tradition from other possible ways in which men can actualize themselves as persons – even though, again, this content, precisely because it is constituted by existential possibilities, could not be restricted to the Christian tradition. And the only way this could be done would be by an objective description of existential possibilities. Of course, such a proposal would violate Buri's restrictions on objectivity. He has argued that self-understanding is an actualization of the transcending dimension of the self in which it is completely non-objective and non-objectifiable. He criticizes Schleiermacher for reducing this transcending dimension of faith (man's "to be") to objectively describable states and conditions which violate not only the nature of faith but its relation to the transcendent reality grounding it. The purpose of the next chapter must be to examine whether an objective description of modes of actualized self-understanding would necessarily involve either a misunderstanding of the non-objectivity of faith or the kind of psychological subjectivizing of which Buri charges Schleiermacher. But it should be evident that the only way in which Buri can preserve the historicity of the Christian self-understanding is by some form of objective description which specifies its distinctive content. Furthermore, the status of such objective descriptions must be literal and non-symbolic in some sense. They cannot themselves be further symbolic expressions of self-understanding. As interpretations of mythological symbols expressing self-understanding and unlike the objective form of such mythology, they must refer *directly* to the non-mythological reality which myths serve to express indirectly and inappropriately. As such, their objective form must be once removed from the objective form of symbols expressing the immediate life of faith, and unless one is prepared to accept an infinite regress eventually ending again in an ineffable self and a loss of historicity, such interpretations must be more appropriate in a qualitatively different way than mythological symbols. The question is whether it is possible to preserve historicity in this way from within Buri's theology.

CHAPTER VI

EXISTENTIALIST INTERPRETATION AND OBJECTIVE DESCRIPTION

The failure of historicity in Buri's theology can be traced to the way the problem of objectivity seems to determine existentialist interpretation. As a result, the content of faith reduces to personal being in an almost entirely unspecific sense, the only relationship between Christian assertions and Christian existence is causal or even magical, and the Christian self-understanding, in effect, becomes inaccessible to theological description. These problems can be avoided only if it is possible to specify the concrete historicity of the Christian self-understanding, but this will require some qualification of Buri's restrictions on the possibilities of objectification. The task of this chapter is to examine how such qualification might be made within the bounds of existentialist interpretation. The discussion will have two aspects. First, it will be shown that a proper understanding of the non-objectivity of faith need not exclude certain kinds of objective descriptions of faith. Here the concern will be to define more carefully the nature and limits of theology as existentialist interpretation and to show what stake such a theology ought to have in the problem of objectivity. Second, the status of certain kinds of objective claims in Buri's theology will be reexamined in order to see whether Buri himself does not inadvertently confirm the thesis of this study concerning the limits of the problem of objectivity. In the concluding chapter it will then be possible to consider the systematic consequences of this thesis for the hermeneutics of a radical theology.

A. OBJECTIVE POSSIBILITY AND EXISTENTIAL ACTUALITY

1. Two Types of Limits of Knowledge

Buri argues that there are two realities which are non-objective and non-objectifiable, the intrinsic self and being-itself. It has been argued

that the failure of historicity can be overcome only by qualifying the restrictions on objectification. Since the two non-objective realities inhere
together in the reality of faith, a qualification of the limits of objectification must touch either one or both of them. While Buri bases his argument for the limits of objectification on a consideration of the limits of
knowledge, now it is important to note that these limitations apply to
and are grounded by the limits of knowledge in quite different ways.

Buri's argument (and that of Karl Jaspers on whom Buri is largely dependent at this point) for the limits of knowledge in relation to being-itself
(or being as a whole) is based on a Kantian understanding of phenomenality. Only that can become an object of knowledge which is a sensuous apprehension schematized by the categories. Knowledge is thereby
limited to specific objects or ranges of objects given in space and time.
On the assumption of this viewpoint, it is clear why the canons of the
special sciences become normative for what Buri considers warrantable
objectivity (obj-B). Being-itself or being as a whole cannot be known because neither is given as an object. Furthermore, no inferences can be
drawn from phenomenal objects concerning either being as a whole or
reality outside the possibility of temporal schematization because there is
no way to determine the reference range for such inferences.[1] Thus, the
argument for the limits of knowledge here is grounded in Buri's understanding of the conditions of objectivity as such, the subject-object relation, and leads to a rather classical understanding of the finite nature of
human rationality in relation to reality transcendent to space and time.

The argument for the non-objectifiability of the intrinsic self is different. It involves not so much the finite character of rationality in relation to the whole of being as the transcendental nature of the self. In
other words, here the argument is much more the nature of a logical
move. The pure subject cannot be objectified and thereby known because every thinking act presupposes the subject which enacts this act.
Buri connects this pure epistemological subject with his notion of the
existential self through the idea of enactment. The intrinsic self is non-
objective because it first becomes who it is in its enactment of itself.
While it may appear in its external enactments, it is never reducible to
them because, just as in the thinking act, it is always presupposed in any
objectification of itself. The pure subject in the thinking act is, thus,
merely one instance of the way the intrinsic or transcendental self may
enact itself. The non-objectifiability of the self, which can be seen most

---

[1] Cf., *DG*, pp. 20 f. (ET, 12 f.)

clearly in the instance of a transcendental reflection about the conditions of thought, must be assumed in any of its enactments. Who the self is cannot be defined in advance of its enactment, of the way it understands itself.[2] Unlike the former limitation on knowledge, however, the self is a finite reality within the spatio-temporal continuum. The conditions of its unknowability are different, therefore, from being-itself or being as a whole even though each reality is non-objective.

The limits of knowledge with one of these realities might be qualified without qualifying those for the other. In the next chapter it will become apparent that it may be important to consider reopening the question of the first limit of knowledge. But provisionally, there are good reasons why an existentialist theology is concerned to place restrictions on objective references to transcendent reality. An existentialist theology proposes to interpret all theological statements in terms of the existential reality of the self, to see the content of theological assertions as symbolic expressions for certain existential possibilities. This proposal need not necessarily be based on a classical argument for the limits of knowledge, for this understanding of faith itself seems to require a limitation on objective references to a transcendent reality. Such a theology holds that faith does not involve perpetuating any particular vision of God or the world, i.e., a metaphysical world-view; it involves, rather, an awareness of oneself in relation to God, i.e., a new self-understanding. Statements about God, thus, become statements of the *significance* of God for man, and instead of the assertion of a doctrine, the kerygma is a call to a new life, i.e., a call to give up one's former self-understanding and to accept a new one. When this existential view of faith is grounded in a rigorous analysis of the conditions of objectivity in general, the limits of knowledge become relevant, for the subject-object structure of consciousness means that references to God are epistemologically and not just existentially questionable. It then becomes evident that even the idea of the

---

[2]Cf., e.g., *ibid.*, p. 12 (ET, p. 4): "Ich denke jetzt, nicht *es* denkt in mir. Ich bin das Subjekt meines Denkens. So sehr ich mit dem, was gedacht wird und was irgendwie auch in mir denkt, verbunden bin: es gibt doch dieses Ich, das als das Denken vollzieht, und dieses Denken ereignet sich nicht, ohne dass wir dabei sind." (Buri's italics.) *Ibid.*, p. 20 (ET, p. 12): "Das subjekt, das denkende Ich, wird selber letztlich nie zum Gegenstand des Denkens gemacht werden können. Der mensch ist immer noch je das, als was er sich versteht. Er ist nicht zum vornherein in seinem Wesen festgelegt. Wissenschaftlich kann der Mensch unter bestimmten Aspekten — physiologisch, psychologisch, geistesgeschichtlich, soziologisch usw. — bestimmt werden. Aber er hat immer noch die Möglichkeit, sich in je bestimmter Weise zu verstehen und dadurch erst zu dem zu werden, was er ist."

"significance of God" (as well as "God") must be interpreted in terms of the self-reference of theological concepts to the existential dialectic.

For these reasons, there are good reasons immanent to existentialist theology for turning attention to the second limit, to the non-objectifiability of the intrinsic self. Here there is a finite reality in space and time which is also the "subject" of theological assertions in this type of theology. Are there any good reasons for qualifying the limits on objectification in relation to this reality?

2. Existentialist Theology and Qualifying the Limits on Objectification

It would seem that the intrinsic self would be a candidate for objective description simply because it is a finite reality ingredient in the world. Yet Buri argues that while it is finite, it cannot be reduced to the world or to any relation in the world. It is embodied in the world but in its intrinsic reality is transcendent of the world. Just as the pure subject can never be grasped *an sich* in its objectifications of itself in the thinking act, so the intrinsic self is never a "given" reality in those objective relations in which it embodies itself. It is always more or other than what can be described about it. It cannot be reduced to anything given because it is constituted precisely by its decisions. In the distinction first made by Kierkegaard, an objectification always works at the level of possibility whereas with the self there is a reality given only in the self-constituting enactments of itself. And there is no mediation between objective possibility and existential actuality. There is a gulf between them which cannot be crossed at the level of thought no matter how subtle and many-leveled the dialectic. It can only be bridged by the individual self in the assumption of its ownmost possibilities for itself. In Buri's terms the unconditionedness of the self cannot be reduced to the relativity of objective statements about the self. If the restrictions on objectification in relation to this reality are to be qualified, at least this much of the non-objectifiability of the self must be preserved, for it is absolutely essential to the understanding of faith in Buri and in existentialist theology in general.

But here one must examine carefully the sense in which restrictions are placed on objectifications about the self. No philosopher or theologian would argue that what he says about something can be substituted for that thing itself. It would quickly be granted that there is a difference between a conception of something and that thing itself. The two are incommensurate realities, and the difference is at least in some degree similar to that between objective possibility and existential actuality. Yet with realities other than *Existenz,* this difference does not exclude the possibility of conceptual adequacy in the description of something. Would the same not apply to *Existenz?*

Buri understands the non-objective self as an act which cannot as such be reduced to an objectification. It "is" only in its actualization of itself, and this actualization cannot be frozen into an object. This would be to lose precisely the reality of the self in its enactment. But this only confirms the above point. The reality of the self is its transcending act. But its reality as an act does not exclude the possibility of describing the act *so long as it is kept clearly in mind that there are incommensurate levels between concept and thing.* In fact, this has already been done insofar as its reality is *described* as an act.

Buri would agree that the distinction between object and description of an object holds in the immanence of the subject-object relation. Here, he would say, is the level where objective descriptions are appropriate. But the distinction breaks down with non-objective actualities. Here an objective description misconstrues the reality from the beginning by treating as objective something in principle non-objective. In other words, the two levels are incommensurate *in principle* so that the normal possibility of adequacy between concept and thing cannot come into play.

But Buri's argument does not hold. A careful analysis will show that an understanding of the transcending and non-objective nature of the self does not touch objective description at the point where the limitations on objectivity need to be qualified. At stake in the non-objectivity of the self is an understanding of the self as a being constituted by its possibility, by its decisions. In this sense, it is quite in order to say that the self cannot be reduced to objectifications about the self. No objective description of states or structures of the self can replace the responsibility for understanding himself which the individual must take upon himself *in the act by which he constitutes himself.* But precisely this understanding of the self requires a new way of *describing* the structures, states, and relations in which such a self finds itself. The special contribution of existentialist analysis from Kierkegaard's "stages" to Heidegger's "existentials" and Jaspers' "signa of existence" is to lay emphasis on the distinctive categories requisite for understanding the self once its self-making character has been recognized. The self cannot be understood on any model approaching that appropriate to the description of "objects" or things. It requires categories uniquely appropriate to a finite yet self-reflexive and self-constituting being. One among many of the features which must be built directly into such categories is precisely the difference between the categorial description and the existential process by means of which the (individual) self first constitutes itself. In other words, one of the tasks of such objective descriptions about the self is to make clear the nature of this being which does not have its being in any objectification apart from its self-constituting act. But that the self is transcending and non-objective in the one sense of having to assume its existence in the enactment of itself does not obviate the possibility of an objectifying description of that act. If this point is correct, there is a parallel here between any act and the objectification of that act. The act of running is not the same as thinking about running, but this does not mean it is not possible to think about running in a multitude of different ways.

Of course, the parallel does break down to some extent precisely because of the self-reflexive and self-constituting nature of this being. The act by which it constitutes itself is not like just any other act because it is a self-reflexive act of self-definition, of self-understanding in Buri's terms. But there is a parallel up to a point. As long as the non-objectivity of the self in the sense of its transcending self-actualization is held in view, there is no reason in principle why it should not be possible to describe the content of various historicities. It is only necessary continually to introduce the proviso that what such an objectification describes is not itself the reality. The reality itself depends on the responsible enactment of the content of various possible self-understandings. In this latter sense the self is non-objective and non-objectifiable. Because of this proviso, it was stated above that the unique categories used to describe the transcending nature of the self must incorporate this requirement for enactment into their description. Only so are they adequate to their "object." They must themselves make clear that what they say about the self is never adequate to the self in the way that the objectifications of a psychologist or sociologist might be. They are descriptions either of possibilities or of structures for possibilities which the self itself must enact. In this sense, the distinction between objective possibility and existential actuality still holds. But once it is recognized that the sense in which the self is non-objective is different from the sense in which it is possible to make objective descriptions of its transcending acts, then there is no reason why such objective description would not be possible and legitimate.[3]

---

[3]This point is nicely stated by Bultmann as follows: "Habe ich im personalen Sein — und das heisst zugleich: in personalen Verhältnissen — mein eigentliches Sein, meine

The problem with Buri's interpretation of doctrines is that he over-emphasizes the proviso without taking account of the possibility of descriptions of existential acts in view of the proviso. That is to say, the content of doctrines too often turns out to be nothing more than the statement that whatever the content is, it is one which must be enacted by the individual self. The historicity of the Christian self-understanding then ends in nothing more than the concept of historicity in general, i.e., the necessity for some concrete enactment of a responsible self-understanding. This became clear in Buri's argument that the Christological symbol is important not merely for the content but also for the form of the Christian self-understanding.[4] It indicates that the form of the Christian self-understanding is precisely the enactment of self-understanding and that whatever content it has is realized only in this transcending act. The problem arose only with the content of the actualized self-understanding which in Buri tends to reduce back either to this purely formal notion of historicity in general or to an abstract restatement of the systematic principle. From this it can be concluded that Buri does a good job of building the proviso into the categories by means of which he interprets symbols. The failure comes in his drawing back from descriptions of the content of the self-understanding enacted. But if the above argument is correct, there should be no reason why an objectifying description of *what* possibilities are enacted in various self-understandings should not be legitimate.

Great care must be taken, however, to emphasize the importance for any existentialist theology of the proviso which must accompany any such objective description. The abiding significance of the concept of existence for theology is to point to the non-objective nature of faith which indeed cannot be reduced to any set of objectively describable *Vorfindlichkeiten* or *Beschaffenheiten*. The content of the Christian kerygma and of the doctrines of the Christian faith is directed at an enactment of human existence which is not a given in human nature but al-

---

Existenz, so lässt sich also sagen, dass meine Existenz nicht objektivierbar ist. Wohl lässt sich natürlich über Existenz objectiv reflektieren, das heisst über das, was Existenz überhaupt bedeutet, über das Wesen von Existenz. Aber solche Reflexion erkennt ja eben dieses, dass Existenz je meine ist und nur je von mir übernommen oder vollzogen werden kann; das heisst aber: Existenz ist jeweils *Ereignis* in den Entscheidungen des Augenblicks. Sie ist nichts Vorhandenes, sondern je und je Geschehendes." Rudolf Bultmann, "Wissenschaft und Existenz" in *Glauben und Verstehen*, III (Tübingen: J. C. B. Mohr (Paul Siebeck), 1960), p. 117. (Bultmann's italics.)

[4] Cf., *supra*, pp. 134-136.

ways a possibility for a new self-understanding. The importance of existentialist theology is not only in having rigorously developed this concept of faith but also in having attempted to understand the content of doctrines entirely in terms of the dynamics of its enactment. Insofar as one does provide an objective description of the Christian self-understanding, this proviso must be held in view. In particular, it means that what is described must not be understood as a state or condition given as such either in human nature or in the man of faith. It is a description of a possibility which must be enacted ever anew. In speaking of the advance of Bultmann's concept of self-understanding over Schleiermacher's concept of self-consciousness, Paul Löffler has stated the point exactly:

Over against Kant and Schleiermacher, much has doubtless changed through the influence of Heidegger and existential philosophy in general in the "how" of describing God, man, and the world. Above all everything is described more as event, as momentary *(jeweiliger)* act, which maintains the *Unverfügbarkeit* of God in relation to man. In Schleiermacher, on the other hand, insofar as he communicates himself to self-consciousness, God must also be placed at its disposal.[5]

Buri is therefore correct in arguing that his understanding of the non-objective nature of faith prevents his own theology from falling prey to the "psychologism" and "subjectivism" he sees in Schleiermacher. But to the extent that theology continually holds in view the "to be" character of its subject matter, there is no reason why Buri must proceed from this criticism of Schleiermacher to the further conclusion that *all* objective descriptions of the self-understanding enacted are equivalent to reducing the content of faith to an "object" or a state present-at-hand in human existence as such.

Maintaining the distinction between objective possibility and existential actuality, thus, need not to entail the impossibility of and objective description of various existential self-understandings that might be actualized. This is true so long as the proviso (that the description of a possibility of self-understanding cannot be confused with enacting that self-understanding itself) is continually held in view and so long as the objective description adequately takes into account precisely the "to be" nature of what it describes. This conclusion is possible to the extent that it is legitimate to recognize that "objectivity" and "non-objectivity" have entirely different uses when it is said that the self is non-objective and when it is maintained that objectifying descriptions of enactments of the non-objective self are possible and legitimate.

[5]Löffler, p. 314.

3. Theology and Proclamation

The argument above can be supported from another direction by considering the distinction between theology and proclamation. While symbols for Buri are objective in form, their content resides entirely in the non-objective act of existence they occasion. In this sense, the objective forms of expressions of self-understanding act as appeals for the enactment of self-understanding. The examination of the interpretation of symbols showed the consequences to which this leads. The Christian self-understanding loses precisely the existential content this understanding of symbol is meant to provide, and the relationship between what the Christian says (i.e., the content of symbols) and the act of faith itself becomes only causal. This means that despite Buri's careful articulation of the conceptual task of theology, he in fact has no basis for a distinction between theology and proclamation. The theologian's task of interpreting symbols becomes indistinguishable from the preacher's task of calling men to a new self-understanding. This is disastrous because the preacher is dependent on the theologian for the careful statement of the content of the faith he proclaims. Yet insofar as their tasks become confused in the context of Buri's theology, neither one has any content for the self-understanding to which he calls the believer. Nothing is left but the call to a new self-understanding. There is no way of defining what among many self-understandings is being proclaimed as a possibility of faith.

Although he speaks specifically about general ethical truths contained in sayings and proverbs and not about theology, Bultmann's essay "Allgemeine Wahrheiten und christliche Verkündigung" is relevant to this problem of theology and proclamation and to the problem of acts of existence and descriptions of such acts.[6] According to Bultmann, general truths are simply generalized statements about the human condition. Bultmann says that they are general truths which any man can say to himself, be it a general piece of wisdom about the human situation, an ethical maxim, or a metaphysical world view.[7] Proclamation, to the contrary, is an address which calls the hearer to a new self-understanding and, as such, mediates an event.[8] The crucial point is that there is a con-

---

[6] Rudolf Bultmann, "Allgemeine Wahrheiten und christliche Verkündigung," in *Glauben und Verstehen*, III, pp. 166 ff.

[7] *Ibid.*, p. 167.

[8] *Ibid.*, pp. 166-168. E.g., p. 168: "'Mitgeteilt' wird nun freilich in der echten Predigt doch etwas, ein Ereignis — das Ereignis der in Jesus Christus geschehenen Offenbarung der Gnade Gottes. Aber das Merkwürdige ist, dass es statt der *geschehenen* Offenbarung eigentlich heissen muss: der *geschehenden*. Denn diese Mitteilung macht nicht ein vergan-

nection between general truths and proclamation. In the first place, proclamation itself can only be articulated in the form of discourse so that in some sense the role of address can be fulfilled only through the generalizing function of language. Just because of the nature of language, general truths, in the second place, can themselves become address:

> General truths can partake of the address character of Christian proclamation in that from time to time in a concrete situation they lose the character of general truths by qualifying the now of the one addressed. Indeed they are truths which man can and should say to himself. In actual *(faktischen)* life, however, they are often "forgotten," and what man can and should say to himself must be said to him by another in a concrete situation – *not so that he remembers a forgotten general truth as he might remember something else forgotten but to his shame, to his judgment or for his comfort or his encouragement. In short, it is said in order that he become aware of himself in the light of the truth valid for him, that thereby he is called to decision, and, yes, that thereby he is transformed.*[9]

While the relationship between theology and proclamation may not be precisely identical with this one between general truths and proclamation, this is a particularly illuminating relationship in the context of Buri's theology. Theological descriptions in an existentialist theology must have the status of general truths. As Helmut Gollwitzer has pointed out, "they differ from theoretical generalities"[10] merely in that they can be grasped "only in the event of experiencing them."[11] No matter how much emphasis is placed on the character of faith as an event or act, as soon as anything is said about it – even the statement that it is an event or act – there is a move back into the realm of general truths.

The same applies to any theological interpretation of doctrines no matter how much emphasis is placed on the fact that this content is a reality only in the non-objective act of faith. Here the meaning of proclamation is significant in emphasizing the proviso which must accompany all objective descriptions of acts of self-understanding. The non-objectivity of faith comes into play only at the point where the believer is con-

---

genes historisches Faktum bekannt; sondern das Paradoxe ist dieses, dass in dieser 'Mitteilung' sich jenes Geschehen stets neu vollzieht, indem ein historisches Ereignis als das eschatologische Ereignis verkündigt wird." (Bultmann's italics.)

[9]*Ibid.*, pp. 170 f. My italics.

[10]Gollwitzer, p. 27 (ET, p. 36).

[11]*Ibid.*, p. 70 (ET, p. 90). It should be noted that Gollwitzer is cited here only to document the point concerning the objective status of statements about existence. Gollwitzer's own criticism is not only different from the present one but far more extreme. Instead of an immament critique of existentialist interpretation, he calls into question the theological grounds and legitimacy of existentialist theology as such.

fronted with the possibility of a certain (objectively describable) self-understanding as an understanding of himself. There is always this cleavage between the objective description and its enactment. Furthermore, it is also true that proclamation is not simply constituted by converting objective descriptions of self-understanding into an indicative and imperative form of address. The proclamation is constituted by the occurrence of the event itself in the hearing of the proclaimed word. And the proviso has the purpose of pointing out that the "meaning" of the content of self-understanding (i.e., the objective description) is such that it can only first be fully appreciated in the existential act of appropriating it. The relationship is much like that between describing love or trust and being loved or trusted. The non-objectivity of existence comes into play insofar as the true "meaning" of love or trust cannot be understood from any objective description but only through handing oneself over to and suffering through the concrete acts of loving and being loved, trusting and being trusted.[12] But this does not at all mean that it is not possible to describe objectively the dynamics of love and trust. Only through acknowledging this distinction between the possibility of objective description and the non-objective act of faith itself can Buri preserve any distinction between theological interpretation and proclamation.

B. THE OBJECTIVE STATUS OF BURI'S SYSTEMATIC PRINCIPLE

It is important now to consider the objective claims in Buri's theology from the perspective of this argument. Because of Buri's understanding of objectivity, objective *Richtigkeit* as the medium of theological reflection can really perform only regulative functions. His understanding of symbols prevents such thought from defining the content of faith itself. Even after its clarifying and demythologizing functions, objective thought is only a medium since the proper "seeing" of the content of the symbol is not supposed to be an objective description but an event of revelation itself. It has now become clear that consistently carried out, this understanding of the medium of theological reflection results in a loss of content (historicity) for the Christian self-understanding and makes it impossible for Buri to carry out the task of theology on his own terms. Yet the consistency which produces this conclusion leads to a crucial anoma-

---

[12]For an illuminating discussion of this point, cf., Bultmann, "Wissenschaft und Existenz," pp. 115-120, esp. 116 f.

ly in Buri's procedure. He does not and cannot rest content merely with demythologizing and dekerygmatizing objective, mythological and *heilsgeschichtlich* doctrinal proposals in order to point toward a non-objective act of existence. In proceeding to interpret such proposals, Buri must make at least some minimal interpretive proposals of his own even if their existential actuality remains uppermost in his mind. Otherwise, his theology could be nothing more than criticisms of other positions. Some of these proposals will be examined in a moment. Here it is enough to note that insofar as he does make such proposals, he confirms the argument that there is a difference between the non-objective act of faith and objective descriptions of such acts and of the existential possibilities they embody. More important is the point made before that there must be some objective, non-mythological and non-symbolic principle for the interpretation of such doctrines. Buri's systematic principle meets this requirement and now its objective status needs to be looked at.

The systematic principle must be seen against the background of Buri's dekerygmatizing proposal. Buri rejects the kerygma as a remnant of mythology because its retention grounds the possibility for the actualization of authentic existence on an objective, non-*existentiell* event of the past. Buri's argument is that the possibility of authentic existence cannot be grounded in any objective condition outside the actualization of that authenticity itself. But it is not something achieved by human autonomy alone. In the non-objective actualization of itself, existence finds itself gifted to itself from beyond. This is not tied to any particular event although the non-objectivity of its actualization means that it must be tied to some event, i.e., it is historistic and is tied to the actualization of some event in the present historicity of the believer. Grace belongs to the non-objective actualization of existence itself. The purpose of Buri's systematic principle is to give expression to this understanding of existence. The Christian tradition can then be interpreted both as giving expression to the complex dialectic of the self which this principle involves and as being a kerygmatic historicity which elicits the actual self-understanding described by it.

It is important to recognize that for Buri and for certain other existentialist theologians, this understanding of existence as grace does not involve the reduction of the core of the Christian faith to a principle.[13] Many theologians, especially the school of neo-orthodoxy, have reacted to

---

[13]This point is argued explicitly by Van A. Harvey in his important article, "The Historical Jesus, the Kerygma, and the Christian Faith" in *Religion in Life*, XXXIII, No. 3 (Summer 1964), pp. 430 ff., esp. pp. 434, 449 f.

the nineteenth century forms of demythologizing by contrasting event or person to idea or principle. It is said that if God's unique saving act in Jesus Christ in the past is relinquished, then the distinctive content of the gospel is reduced to an idea or principle competing with other philosophical options and conceptualizing nothing more than structures given as such with man's being in the world. When the content of the gospel is reduced to a principle, the result is a loss of God's encounter with man as one who offers him grace and reconciliation. The distinctive character of the Christian faith, which is an event and, thus, a reality in the texture of human experience, is relinquished, the absolute difference between man and God is compromised, and faith is conceived as a simple human possibility. It might seem that the denial of the mythological remainder of the kerygma combined with an understanding of existence as grace among existentialist theologians involves just this reduction. Yet it can be argued that this view of the event/principle dichotomy does not adequately conceive all the options.

Buri believes that his concept of self-understanding is an alternative to the nineteenth century idea of a "Christian principle." The dialectic of gracious existence is not merely a general truth, and faith does not consist in assenting to it like assenting to a Christian world-view. The systematic principle expresses a structure of existence which is constituted only in the non-objective actualization of a self-understanding. It is not a truth about man or the world but a way of being. And faith is not acceptance of a philosophical doctrine but a response to a kerygmatic call which issues in a concrete mode of living. It is the non-objectivity of existence which allows Buri to escape the old event/principle dichotomy while at the same time denying that the reality of grace is dependent on an event of the past.

It cannot be denied that the more sensitive understanding of objectivity in relation to the concept of existence developed by existentialist philosophy has provided the means for radical theology to avoid the nineteenth century error. Yet it can also not be denied that Buri's statement of the understanding of existence elucidated by the systematic principle is an objectifying description of the structure of human personhood. The nature of existence as grace does avoid the reduction of Christianity to a principle. *But the theological description of this nature is not that actualization itself.* It is different from the forms of objectivity Buri rejects in that it is non-mythological and non-symbolic. It also includes within itself the proviso that the *reality* which it describes is a non-objective actualization. But this cannot detract from the objective status of the principle itself. Theology is not proclamation nor is it the reality of existence itself; it is the conceptually adequate description of the possibilities for existing mythologically expressed by the Christian tradition and actualized in the Christian self-understanding.

If this conclusion is correct, then precisely at the point of his systematic principle, Buri himself qualifies his own restrictions on objectivity. Only in this way can one account for some basis for the theological interpretations he does make. While existence and its relation to Transcendence are non-objective, the statement of this relationship and the non-objectivity of its enactment is an objective description in the realm of objective possibility. It is a basis for interpretation because it gives an adequate, non-mythological and non-symbolic account of the structure of faith.

This means, therefore, that Buri's understanding of objective thought *(Richtigkeit)* as the medium of theology must be qualified. It must be a medium not merely in the sense that its elucidations open up the possibility for a non-objective occurrence of revelation which cannot itself be objectively described. That is the function of proclamation in the context of existentialist theology. It must also be the medium in the sense that it describes the *content* of a particular self-understanding which is given its living expression in the life of faith itself by the mythological forms of the Christian tradition. Objective thought is still only a medium because it operates at the level of objective possibility and must never confuse itself with proclamation or with faith itself. But unlike Buri's understanding of the medium, it must issue in objective descriptions having the force of doctrinal proposals.

From the fact that Buri makes at least one objective proposal about the legitimate meaning of theological assertions when he moves beyond demythologizing to existentialist interpretation, one would expect that he might qualify his own restrictions at other points. Quite apart from the question of consistency and coherence in his total system, this would mean that at least at certain points he avoids a total loss of content in the interpretation of the Christian self-understanding. But it must also be true that by thereby avoiding the criticism above, he must also acknowledge that type of objective description which his understanding of the problem of objectivity seems to exclude and which, it is argued here, ought to be possible within an existentialist theology.

C. OBJECTIVE DESCRIPTION OF EXISTENTIAL MODES OF BEING

As was evident in the discussion of Christology, Buri's interpretations of individual doctrines is particularly detailed and rich and ranges over the entire history of theology. It is not necessary, however, in this section to go into the detail of his entire soteriology as he presents it in the second volume of his *Dogmatik*. His hermeneutical principles as well as the manner in which he applies them are clear enough for the purpose at hand. The purpose here will be, instead, to look at certain examples where Buri's critical treatment of traditional objective doctrines issues in an existentialist interpretation involving an objective claim. Part of the concern is simply to confirm the argument above. But taken in abstraction such a confirmation has little inherent interest except to document an incoherence in Buri's theology. More important is to assess the significance these objective claims have both for Buri's methodology as well as for the hermeneutical status of the problem of objectivity in radical theology in general. Since Buri's entire hermeneutical procedure is based on the dialectic of existence, each side of this dialectic in turn must be examined to see what kind of objective claim it might entail. The first side is Transcendence-relatedness.

1. The Personhood of God in the Self-Understanding of Faith

There is no question that Buri's notion of Transcendence is the crucial unclarified concept in his thought. Because of its systematic ambiguity, it is extremely difficult to mold all of Buri's statements about Transcendence and God into a single, coherent position. On the one hand, it has been argued above that Transcendence can consistently be only a limiting concept functioning within the dialectic of actualized existence. Furthermore, within certain limits, this interpretation is entirely sufficient to ground the hermeneutic Buri requires, and many of his arguments support it. On the other hand, Buri also seems to claim rather strongly throughout his theology that the Christian self-understanding involves belief in God and that God is a personal being transcendent to the world.[14] The first interpretation, which is most consistent with his hermeneutic, means that Transcendence must interpret "God" whereas, in contrast, the second, inconsistent interpretation means that the Christian concept of God must interpret "Transcendence." It will be important to show both the problems which follow from accepting this second interpretation and, in the next chapter, the limits of the first one. But for the

[14]Cf., esp. I, pp. 278 ff. Cf. also e.g., I, p. 140; II, pp. 104, 137 f.; HSRG, pp. 23-34; *DP*, pp. 153 ff.; *Gott in Amerika*, p. 249.

argument of this study, it is also significant that both of these possible meanings of Transcendence involve the kind of objective description Buri seems to rule out.

a. Transcendence as a Personal Being

What, then, can be made of Buri's statement that God is personal? Buri makes clear that this ascription of personhood is not the result of an inference, of a natural theology, or of a metaphysical system. Apparently it is an apprehension grounded alone in the act of self-understanding. Consequently, it cannot be proven but must be simply attested out of the community of faith which confesses this reality. He says, for instance, "if Transcendence is drawn into a system, then it is no longer possible at all to speak of the personhood (*Personsein*) of God but only inappropriately of God as a person (*von Gott als Person*)." (II, p. 138.) On this account, Buri seems to be making three points: (i) the reality designated "God" in the Christian faith can only be apprehended in the non-objective act of responding to the kerygma; (ii) it can be spoken about only in terms of its significance for the act of faith itself and not as a general truth; and (iii) a proper understanding of the dialectic of faith actualized in the historicity defined by the message of Jesus Christ demands that this reality be personal in nature. The following is one of the clearest examples of this combination of claims:

The hearing and the understanding of the message of God's revelation in Christ and with that the likeness of God in Christ already presuppose the possibility of human determination (*Bestimmtsein*) toward being a person. Personhood occurs, nevertheless, according to the New Testament not in the abstract sphere of such a general possibility but in the concrete historicity of the covenantal people. To this extent the likeness of God from creation can be appraised as the presupposition of the likeness of God in Christ. But for the faith which is directed toward this message and which receives it, God is not merely a general relation to Transcendence. Rather, he appears to faith as a person, and his personhood (*Personhaftigkeit*) can be articulated in mythological or speculative objectivity. In the enactment of the self-understanding defined through Christ, God is a person in such a way that his personhood (*Personhaftigkeit*) is determined through the non-objective, personal relation to Christ. If behind the statement of the likeness of God in Christ also the other statements concerning the personhood of God as the creator and the covenantal God appear possible for this faith and even if a personal relation to Transcendence is not excluded in the historicity of some other anthropology, still the Christian knows of no other personal God than the one revealed to him in Christ. (II, pp. 112 f.)

This statement entails an entirely different perspective both on Buri's hermeneutical principles and on his understanding of the problem of objectivity. This can be stated more or less as follows. Transcendence-relatedness is a limiting concept when viewed at the formal level of a philosophical description of the structure of existence. Such a description shows that the general structure of any human act of non-objective self-constitution always involves a paradoxical autonomy and determination, a determination which is perhaps best captured by such words as "gift," "call," and "claim." But because of the limits imposed by the subject-object relation and because this structure is never actualized except in a specific historicity, philosophy cannot establish the ontological nature of the other pole of the existential structure nor can it adjudicate conflicting claims as to its nature which arise from various historicities. It can only establish the formal character of the self. Transcendence is a useful limiting concept which may be used functionally to indicate this structure apart from any specific historicity. Any particular historicity, however, will give content to this concept. It will be matter for a naturalist, fate or destiny for a stoic, reason or *Geist* for an idealist, or the will to power for a Nietzsche, and for the believer who actualizes the Christian self-understanding it will become the trinitarian God. The problem of objectivity, especially the subject-object relation, will, from this perspective, still have epistemological force for a critical philosophy. But for theology, or for a philosophy which is willing to transgress the bounds of critical philosophy and make material claims from a historistic position, the problem of objectivity will have only existential force. Because, on this account, the historistic actualization of a self-understanding involves giving material, objective content to Transcendence, the problem of objectivity will simply mean (i) that such objective claims cannot be extrapolated with general validity from the existential acts in which they occur and (ii) that consequently, there is no way of adjudicating conflicting claims. To put this more directly into Buri's actual usage, the problem of objectivity now means simply that to know the Christian God, to know that God is personal in the specifically Christian sense, one must actualize existentially a belief in this God.

But examine the consequences that follow from this interpretation. In the first place, it completely undercuts Buri's entire hermeneutic, for, while it provides an existential understanding of faith, it does not justify either demythologizing or existentialist interpretation. To the extent that Buri admits in this way the single objective claim that God is personal, he cannot consistently eliminate any mythological claim, no matter how fantastic, because the principle on which he now accepts the one is the same principle on which he rejects the others.[15] This one exception implies a repudiation both of the criterion for myth and, thus, the warrant for demythologizing and of the method of existentialist interpretation according to which the contents of all doctrines are to be interpreted solely in terms of possibilities for existence.

In the second place, Buri cannot consistently maintain the distinction between the formality of Transcendence as a limiting concept and the material content of Transcendence when it is a function of a particular historicity. By this distinction, Buri attempts to tie any material content of a self-understanding to the actualization of that self-understanding itself. In this way, he seems to think that he can give at least some material content to a non-objective self-understanding (e.g., "God is personal") while at the same time preserving his criticism of objective claims. But this will not do because it runs together two different ways in which a criticism of objective claims can be made. Such claims can be criticized because of the warrants given for holding them. Here Buri might legitimately criticize various forms of natural theology and argue that the only ground for asserting one thing rather than another is the existential "leap" (the non-objective actualization of a self-understanding) which risks an understanding of oneself on this assertion. But the claim might be criticized not because its warrants fail but because of its character, i.e., *because it is objective as such.* Much of Buri's epistemology depends on this type of criticism, but in this context he seems to take it back and to claim that any objective assertion is legitimate as long as it occurs in a self-understanding. This means, however, that the *nature* of the material, objective claim cannot be tied to the non-objective historicity. For the person who actualizes the Christian self-understanding, the claim that Transcendence is a personal God cannot be limited to his historicity. Even though the grounds for asserting this claim may be a function of historicity, the claim itself is independent of any particular historicity. It is a general claim about the nature of reality and involves a denial of

---

[15]This point is particularly well illustrated by Buri's most extensive discussion of the doctrine of God to date in *DP passim*. Here Buri presents a brilliant interpretation of the trinitarian structures which he interprets existentially in terms of their symbolic importance for expressing possibilities of actualized existence. At the same time, however, he continues to maintain his claim that God is personal in the self-understanding of faith. But this is inconsistent. Buri cannot criticize the objective references of the classical trinitarian concepts and then interpret them existentially if he is not prepared to interpret existentially and without remainder the claim that God is personal. Cf., *DP*, pp. 107 ff.

all competing views. Buri cannot have it both ways. Either Transcendence is a limiting concept, or Buri *believes* that Transcendence is just one thing and not anything else. If the latter, however, then Buri has no grounds for reinterpreting the *content* of the objective theological tradition in terms of the dialectic of existence. He can only exposit its unreconstructed objective content while arguing that the only grounds for holding such things is the existential act of staking one's existence on them.

Buri goes even further sometimes and seems to make a *general demonstration* of the nature of Transcendence on the basis of the perspective gained by the Christian self-understanding. In discussing the general nature of anthropological theories, Buri argues that in every such theory a relation to Transcendence comes to expression. This occurs because any theory involves the non-objective decision of the thinker to determine his own personhood in some way. But such a decision is not merely a self-determination because the desire to define oneself is experienced as a call to self-determination.[16] As a generally describable structure of human being as such, however, Buri argues that this Transcendence relation is merely a limiting concept without content, *ein Nichts*.[17] It is only in the historicity of particular anthropologies that this Transcendence receives some particular determination. But in relation to these Buri makes the apparently *normative* and *general* statement that "where the character as person (*Personcharakter*) of Transcendence is questionable there also the Transcendence-relation of the person is questionable. Therein is documented that these anthropologies finally cannot win the entrance to

---

[16]II, pp. 100-102. "Aber es genügt nicht, nur von Bestimmung zu reden, sondern wir müssen vielmehr von einem Bestimmtsein sprechen. Unsere Bestimmung ist das, was man nur aus seinem eigenen Wesen heraus erfüllen kann, weil es sich dabei je um unsere Bestimmung handelt. Das Bestimmtsein ist die Berufung des menschlichen Seins zur Erfüllung seiner Bestimmung. Diese Berufung zur Erfüllung unserer Bestimmung gehört nicht zu dem Bereich des Je-Meinen, in dem ich meine je-meinige Bestimmung erfülle oder verfehle. Ob wir unsere Bestimmung erfüllen oder nicht — jedenfalls ist unsere Situation immer schon durch diese Berufung zur Erfüllung geprägt. Im Innewerden unserer Situation werden wir eines Bestimmtseins gewahr, das als solches nie erfasst werden kann. Darin dokumentiert sich der Transzendenzbezug der Möglichkeit menschlichen Personseins, dass dieses Berufensein nicht mehr dem Bereich des Gegenständlich-Beweisbaren angehört.... Der Mensch kann, durch diese Störung geweckt, sich aufraffen, um seiner Infragestellung zu begegnen eine Antwort zu formulieren und dadurch sein Wesen erst noch zu bestimmen. Dann zeigt sich der Transzendenzbezug in dieser seiner Selbstbestimmung darin, dass er sich zu dieser Selbstbestimmung seines Wesens berufen erfährt. Das Innewerden seiner Berufung zur Selbstbestimmung wird für den Menschen keineswegs ein Anlass zum stolzen Bewusstsein seiner Würde, sondern zu dem Bewusstsein, vor einer Frage zu stehen, die ihn bei allem seinem Selbstwerden noch übergreift." *Ibid.*, p. 101.
[17]*Ibid.*, p. 102.

human personhood which they would like to disclose." (II, p. 104.) In other words, Buri seems to be saying that a proper understanding of the non-objective dialectic in the self-determination of the person as person depends not merely on acknowledging a transcendent "other" in the determination but in understanding this "other" in personal terms.

When these statements are combined with Buri's other statements of the personal character of Transcendence when defined by the relation to Christ in self-understanding, then he seems to be asserting that not only is Transcendence defined as a personal God in the Christian faith but that this understanding of Transcendence has normative significance for a proper understanding of human nature. This conclusion is inescapable despite Buri's constant claim not to be making normative (or "absolutistic") claims but only articulating an expression of self-understanding which does not exclude other self-understandings. He seems, that is, to be defining Transcendence as God and to be making a statement about the nature of this God. It does not matter that this cannot be grounded by any kind of objective proof or general theory, i.e., that it is an expression of self-understanding. Even if its "truth" can only be apprehended in a non-objective self-understanding, the status of the expression of self-understanding is still an objective claim about the nature of Transcendence. Furthermore, to the extent that Buri seems to imply the normative significance of this claim for a proper understanding of human nature, then he is, in fact, making a *general* claim supported by something like a *proof* based on an adequate account of human nature.

As a result of his concept of self-understanding, Buri seems to think that he avoids his criticism of illicit objectifications because a personal God is known only in a non-objective act. But the argument above shows this to be a confusion. Whatever one may think of the claim that God cannot be known as personal except in the non-objective act of believing him to be personal, still an objective claim is made here which excludes other claims *on objective grounds*. On these terms, Buri is thoroughly consistent in his argument that only a personal God can account for the personal character of human existence, but this argument contradicts his criticism of natural theology and completely subverts his hermeneutical principles. Of course, it is true enough that on an existentialist conception of faith, one must say that the nature of God or the content of any other doctrine can only be known in the specific relationship to Christ. But unless the implications of this general conception of faith are specified more closely, this alone says both too little and too much for Buri's theology: too little because it does not warrant how the contents of all the doctrines defined by the relation to Christ (including the meaning of "relation to Christ") are to be interpreted, and too much because it takes no account of the problem of objective assertions as such on which Buri's entire hermeneutic depends. It must be concluded, therefore, that Buri's statements about the personal character of God in the Christian self-understanding either are confused or are inconsistent with his total theology. But the implications of "Transcendence" are systematically ambiguous, and there is another side.

b. Transcendence as a Limiting Concept

Immediately following the above statement where Buri seems to identify a personal God with Transcendence, he also seems to take it all back.

However, this personal character of the God revealed to believers in Jesus Christ represents for them no generally demonstrable theory. Rather, *it is nothing but an expression for the new being which comes to the believer in the enactment of his self-understanding in view of that message.* As such an expression of self-understanding, this personal character of the God revealed in Jesus Christ also stands in a row beside other mythological-speculative, metaphysical assertions of other anthropologies. Like them it cannot demonstrate its truth but only elucidate and attest it by coming into relation with and taking a position over against other kinds of anthropologies. (II, p. 113. My italics.)

In another context, he says:

The I and being, man and the world as a whole, have proven to be the absolute, insurmountable limits [of thought]. A thinking which is conscious of its limits deals with man and the world in the knowledge that it is a question here of something which is not merely its object. When we speak of man and of the world, we have to do with something which refers beyond *(hinausweist)* everything which can be grasped objectively about them in concepts. In the language of mythology and religion, one designates that toward which man and being refer beyond themselves as God.[18]

Given Buri's understanding of the limits of objectification, these two passages indicate (i) that the reference of God-language must remain indeterminate for objective thought and (ii) that in the historicity defined by the message of Christ, such language brings to expression only the structure of the dialectic of existence actualized in this historicity. These statements, thus, seriously qualify the first interpretation of God-language

---

[18]*DG*, p. 21 (ET, p. 13).

and confirm the earlier argument that in all consistency such language in Buri's theology could only refer to the *relationship* to Transcendence actualized in self-understanding.

This argument is given added weight by a closer look at Buri's argument that a personal Transcendence is necessary in order to preserve personal being. Speaking of naturalism which denies both Transcendence and the personhood he finds indispensable, Buri says that a relation to Transcendence still comes to expression: "In the place of a spiritual Transcendence [i.e., in contrast to idealistic anthropologies which Buri argues are also inadequate because of a false objectivity], they absolutize some immanent conceptual or causal interconnection which then assumes the role of a Transcendence. This wins *a personal character* through the fact that in assuming a naturalistic anthropology and in the personal self-understanding which thereby comes to expression, something final (*ein Letztes*) is affirmed in a decision." (II, p. 103. My italics.) If this is what Buri means by the personal character of Transcendence in any anthropology, then he is only expressing the idea of his systematic principle that the personal character of man is always actualized dialectically in relation to a transcendent "other". "Personal character of Transcendence" means no more in this case than the *personal form* of the relationship in which the dialectic occurs. It is personal because the true meaning of personhood comes to expression in it. But this says nothing about the *nature* of this "other."

It needs to be noted that this reduction of God-language to the dialectic of the self is not necessarily a loss within the context of Buri's theology nor does it necessarily imply a "practical atheism." In the first place Buri vigorously rejects Herbert Braun's existentialist interpretation of "God" purely in terms of the dialectic of "I may" and "I ought" in man's relations with others.[19] Braun argues that the significance of New Testament discourse about God is exhausted by the self-understanding of the man of faith who "experiences life ever and again in being upheld from beyond himself."[20] Trust in the "I am" of the Fourth Gospel means to trust "the from-without-ness of my being maintained and upheld" and to confess "that life ever comes to me from beyond, from outside myself."[21] Despite this emphasis on the "beyondness" of grace, its cash value

[19]HSRG, pp. 7 and 27.

[20]Herbert Braun, "Vom Verstehen des Neuen Testaments" in *Gesammelte Studien zum Neuen Testament und seiner Umwelt* (Tübingen: J. C. B. Mohr (Paul Siebeck), 1962), p. 298. Cited in Gollwitzer, p. 26 (ET, p. 36).

[21]Braun, "Vom Verstehen . . . ," p. 296. Cited in Gollwitzer, p. 70 (ET, p. 90).

comes to be nothing more than the beyondness of "I may" and "I ought" experienced in the dialectic of relating to other men. "God" becomes "a particular kind of cohumanity,"[22] "the point where the moment in its fullness is accepted and lived."[23] In Braun's case, the existentialist proposal to interpret all theological assertions as expressions of self-understanding ends with the loss of all real transcendence except the transcendence of the non-objectivity of other selves. And for this reason, Buri rejects it. One might want to argue that Braun's reduction of Transcendence to the transcendence of other selves is the only fully consistent meaning to be attributed to Transcendence once Buri has placed such severe restrictions on objectification. It might at least be argued that Buri has no defense against this reduction. But Buri consistently rejects this alternative *because it makes an objective identification of Transcendence.* On Buri's terms Transcendence cannot be identified with anything immanent to the subject-object structure. Since that which is "world" is qualified for man totally by this structure, Transcendence must be transcendent of the world. But this negative statement and this alone is all that Buri's epistemology legitimately allows him to say. This being the case, his hermeneutic permits articulating only the kind of *relationship* to this other demanded by a proper understanding of human personhood (i.e., the systematic principle) and actualized in particular self-understandings.

But once world and object transcendence is acknowledged in this way, there is, in the second place, no reason not to proceed to interpret "God" and "personal" in terms of the dialectic of the self without implying an ontological description of the nature of this reality. In a recent article, Schubert Ogden has distinguished the two questions: How does God himself function in human life? and "How does the word 'God' function in human language, in which our life and experience are somehow represented?"[24] In relation to this second question, Ogden argues that the question whether "God" is "real" becomes meaningless once the function of the word "real" is properly understood. The word "real" always presupposes "some mode of reasoning, some context of meaning, some way of taking account of things through questions and answers, even to ask about its reality with any sense."[25] Presupposing "the mode of

---

[22]Braun, "Die Problematik einer Theologie des Neuen Testaments" in *Gesammelte Studien...*, p. 341. Cited in Gollwitzer, p. 66 (ET, p. 85).

[23]Braun, "Die Problematik...," p. 339. Cited in Gollwitzer, p. 66 (ET, p. 85).

[24]Schubert M. Ogden, "How Does God Function in Human Life?" in *Christianity and Crisis*, XXVII, No. 7 (May 15, 1967), p. 106.

[25]*Ibid.*, p. 107.

reasoning proper to religion" "God" is simply the synonym for whatever that reality is which sustains the basic confidence in the worth of life which Ogden argues is the center of religion.[26]

Ogden does not share Buri's reservations about the extent to which determinate knowledge of this reality can be attained, and in the next chapter it will be shown that there are definite limits to Buri's concept of Transcendence. *But these are not limits that can be consistently affirmed within Buri's system as it now stands.* Granted his epistemology and his understanding of the dialectic of existence, Buri needs and can have nothing more than this argument for the "reality" of whatever it is that does ground the dialectic. Within these restrictions he is free to interpret God-language entirely in terms of the dialectic of existence without the loss of Transcendence. But he is not free to make ontological claims about the nature of Transcendence – even from within self-understanding. He can only show how the word "God" functions *in the self-understanding* actualized as a response to the Christian message. In this sense the statement "God is personal" expresses (i) the actualization of one's own personhood in relation to the reality which sustains the act of self-understanding itself and (ii) the fact that this relationship can be adequately articulated only by the use of such personal "analogies" or "symbols" as "being called," "being claimed," "being held responsible," "being gifted to oneself."

This is the only interpretation of Buri's use of "God" and "personal" that is consistent with his epistemology. But more important for the thrust of the present argument, even this interpretation of God-language entirely in terms of the dialectic of existence is an objective description of the structure of the dialectic. The description is not the act of faith or the dialectic of existence itself although the descriptive statement takes account of the existential and, therefore, non-objective nature of the dialectic's actualization. Thus, on either interpretation of God-language in Buri's theology, there is an apparent qualification of his understanding of objectivity. It is either an objective, general, and normative claim about the nature of the transcendent reality to which the self is related, or it is an objective characterization of the self's relationship to some reality which in itself remains unknown and indeterminate.

2. Self and World in the Self-Understanding of Faith

Despite the importance of the meaning of "God" in Buri's theology,

[26]*Ibid.,* Cf., also, p. 106.

the most important area for the possibility of objective descriptions is on the other side of the dialectic. This is because the actual content of the Christian self-understanding must be specified by various existential possibilities actualized as a response to the Christian kerygma. To the extent such specifications occur, they will be objective in form. Almost all of Buri's interpretations of doctrines reduce to the formality which has such debilitating consequences for his theology. But at certain isolated points, he cannot avoid a material specification. The final concern of this discussion will be to examine the consequences these objective claims have on the method of existentialist interpretation. In particular, once it becomes clear that the limits of objectivity must be qualified in relation to the self, it will be important to examine whether this qualification does not imply objective claims about the world independent of the self. Should this be the case, then obviously far-reaching rethinking is required concerning the hermeneutical scope of the problem of objectivity for an existentialist theology. First it is necessary to examine the kinds of claims Buri is forced to make.

Four examples will be discussed. The first two are the doctrines of Christ's rule of the world and eschatology. These are selected because, in their mythological form, they have particularly strong objective force which makes it difficult to understand them solely in terms of an existential dialectic. They will be presented with little special comment, but it will be evident that objective claims about the self are made. In support of this conclusion, two additional doctrines, justification and predestination, will be analyzed. All of the examples are taken from the last section of Buri's second volume. Having treated theological anthropology (and in its compass, the person of Christ) and the doctrine of sin, he turns to the doctrines of reconciliation and the new being. He organizes this interpretation of the work of Christ and its appropriation in faith around the traditional symbols of the threefold offices of Christ. The first example is taken from the traditional doctrine of the *regnum potentiae* which constitutes one part of the kingly office of Christ. The second example, eschatology, is structured by the *regnum gloriae* as the culminating phase of Christ's kingly work and by the doctrine of sanctification in the *ordo salutis* as the fulfillment of this office in faith.

a. Christ's Rule of the World

The kingly office is important in the total perspective of Christ's work because it expresses the extension of his work beyond his life and the fulfillment in the world of the reconciliation accomplished by his life, death, and resurrection. As Buri says:

Insofar as believers, for whom Christ intercedes with the Father, are not in heaven but on earth, it cannot be merely a question of an inner-divine event in this account of Christ's merit. The reconciliation which has occurred is valid for them in their mortal being in time. It must take effect in their being as reconciled men.... Without this effect in time, the saving work of Christ would be incomplete; it would not have attained its purpose. *As reconciled the faithful represent the sphere of dominion of the reconciler.* (II, p. 416. My italics.)

Buri goes on to note that the existential significance of the mythological image of Christ's exalted glory and rule is to give expression to the fact that reconciliation, experienced in the dialectic of faith as the significance of the prophetic and priestly offices, is not limited to an isolated point of the self but must express itself in the world.[27] Traditionally the exercise of this kingly office was divided into three parts. There was Christ's participation, after his accomplishment of reconciliation and in view of it, in God's rule of the entire world (the *regnum potentiae*); there was rule over the church (the *regnum gratiae*); and there was his glorified rule in heaven with the Father, an office which receives its fulfillment in Christ's return at the end of time to lift this world into the perfection of his glory (the *regnum gloriae*).[28]

As Christ's participation in the overall rule of the world, the traditional *regnum potentiae essentiale sive naturale* indicated that God's rule of the world was now defined by Christ's work of reconciliation. In contrast to the *regnum gratiae* where this work becomes specifically visible to the eyes of faith in the church, the *regnum potentiae* was taken to mean that Christ fulfills his kingly office in the whole world so that "the believers' trust in his dominion as redeemer is not disillusioned through the course of the world." (II, p. 420.) However, despite the functional similarity of this doctrine to the doctrine of providence, the latter doctrine was developed independently of Christology under creation. This created the problem in traditional theology of there tending to be two doctrines of *Weltherrschaft*. The one based on the doctrine of creation tended to a "rationalization and naturalization" of God's rule since it was grounded on arguments of a natural theology and of general human and cultural experience. The other tended toward a *Heilsgeschichte* grounded on a supernaturalistic understanding of God's saving acts.[29]

[27]II, p. 419.
[28]Cf., *ibid.*, pp. 417, 429.
[29]*Ibid.*, pp. 421 f.

It was Ritschl, Buri says, who first pointed the way to a solution. Ritschl took his point of departure from nineteenth century materialism and naturalism which had dissolved what remained of the notion of God's providence in idealism after its mythological, *heilsgeschichtlich* form had become problematic in the Enlightenment. He suggested that the fundamental reason for questioning God's rule in the world does not first lie in arguments about the nature of the world but in the nature of sinful man himself. As Buri paraphrases Ritschl's argument: "How should one who has not acknowledge (*anerkannt*) God's will in his life recognize (*anerkennen*) this will in the world? The sinner cannot know God's will in the world because he does not want to acknowledge its dominion for himself." (II, p. 422.) In this way, Ritschl was able to ground the doctrine of providence in Christology. He argued, as Buri says, that "only by bringing into order our personal relation to God which has been clouded by sin can the relation of our world to God also come into order again. The world receives another appearance for him who allows himself to be led through Christ to say yes to God in his conscience and to experience God as that one who accepts and forgives sinners." (II, p. 422.)

The error Buri sees in Ritschl is that he tried to elevate this idea into a religious world-view. Ritschl correctly set faith off from the sciences of the *Erkennbar-Wirklichen*.[30] But in rejecting a scientific or metaphysical world-view, Ritschl proceeded to erect a religious world-view not different in principle from the former except that it was grounded in a questionable concept of faith. And when this concept of faith was called into question by advances in historical-critical research into the historical Jesus, the basis for Ritschl's theology began to crumble. As Buri says, "Ritschl confused the enactment of faith with its psychological and historical explanation and foundation." (II, p. 423.) But Buri is in fundamental agreement with Ritschl that the doctrine of Christ's saving work must precede the doctrine of creation. Against Ritschl's "pseudoscientific Christology of experience and history," he asserts that it must be "a doctrine of the saving work of Christ which allows itself to be understood out of the co-enactment of the self-understanding of faith attested in it." (II, p. 423.) In other words, Buri proposes that the Christologically grounded doctrine of creation and providence must be existentially interpreted in terms of the non-objective act of self-understanding.

Yet Buri goes on to attempt to make the difficult transition from mere inwardness to a relation to the world which he seems to have made im-

[30]*Ibid.*, p. 423.

possible by his rejection of Ritschl's "religious world-view." Buri says that "in this sphere of faithful self-understanding, the high-priestly saving work is by no means related merely to the inwardness of the soul and its relation to God" but that "reconciliation takes effect in the spatio-temporal being of the believer." (II, pp. 423 f.) In explanation, Buri seems simply to say that this relation to the world cannot be rationally or scientifically *grounded:*

As the unconditionedness of the enactment of faith, which cannot be grasped psychologically, corresponds to the once-for-all-ness of the saving work of Christ which bursts through everything historical *(der alle Historie sprengenden),* so the reality of the world-dominion of Christ cannot be justified in any way by science or a world-view. Its origin and sphere is faith. But genuine faith is not worldless and timeless. It occurs in history, and Christ rules in it in space and time... as the one exalted to the right hand of God. (II, p. 424.)

This relation to the world is grounded, then, in the non-objective experience of reconciliation.

From this perspective, Buri now states precisely the content of this faithful relation to the world. In so doing he confirms the argument about objective description of existential possibilities.

As in this self-understanding of faith everything is included which belongs to the believer, i.e., his entire world, so also is this entire world included in reconciliation. It thereby appears to faith as a reconciled world. As for those powers which still stand in conflict with this appearance of the reconciled world, *faith begets a confidence (Getrostheit) given with its reconciliation.* However, this confidence of faith can be explained and grounded neither psychologically nor cosmologically. As much as it takes effect in space and time, as much as it encompasses the spatio-temporal objectivity of our outer and inner world, still as an account of the enactment of faith, it is not the same type as this objectivity. It can neither be deduced out of it nor explained with its help. Corresponding to the transcending essence of faith, it transcends every such attempt. The world of faith is not to be understood in terms of the objectivity of a *Heilsgeschichte* independent of faith. (II, p. 424. My italics.)[31]

It is important to note here that, at least on superficial examination, no claim is made about the world. "Confidence" can be viewed simply as a subjective disposition without the correlative claim that the world itself has been reconciled or that the world supports this confidence. If this is not the case, then Buri's criticism of Ritschl is confused. He criticizes him both for a "religious world-view" (a claim about the nature of the world) and for the way he grounds this claim (a conception of faith based

---

[31]The connotations of *Getrostheit* are more complex than the English word "confidence." They also suggest comfort, solace, and trust.

on an objective, historical-critical relation to Jesus). But again, these two criticisms are separable. If by "confidence" Buri means to make a claim about the nature of the world, the objective claim is formally identical with the "religious world-view" he rejects in Ritschl even though he does not make the mistake of grounding it in a false conception of faith. Thus, "confidence" can consistently refer only to an existential possibility. But in this sense, even as a subjective state alone, it is the objectively describable content of the Christian self-understanding and represents an alternative to other possible modes in which the existential dialectic of freedom and responsibility might be actualized.

b. Eschatology

Although a special section of his system will be devoted to it, Buri finds it impossible to complete his soteriology without reference to the eschatological significance of Christ's work. This is expressed in terms of the *regnum gloriae* of Christ's kingly office and the final phase of sanctification. Buri, of course, rejects every objective interpretation of eschatology.[32] He asserts in fact that, in either of their two forms (as descriptions of a realm beyond time or a cosmic apocalypse), they accomplish precisely the opposite of what they intend: "the final event (*Endgeschehen*) does not become visible in its eternality as the wholly-other which annuls space and time; it becomes, rather, a kind of impoverished imitation of. our world and history in which the essence of eschatology signifying the end of spatiality and temporality is completely betrayed." (II, p. 512.) Consequently, it must be interpreted existentially in terms of the non-objective enactment of faith. Then eschatology gives expression to the paradox of faith which is, according to Buri, structurally the same as the myth of the incarnation.[33] On the one hand, it signifies the unconditionedness of faith which is a transcendence of everything objective and thus a transcendence of the spatio-temporal world. On the other hand, it signifies the correlate of the *Getrostheit* of the *regnum potentiae* in the *hope* of faith as it works itself out in objective relations in space and time. These two sides of the paradox will be taken up in order.

Faith is, Buri says, in essence eschatological. By this he means that "it finds itself in a world whose objectivity becomes transparent to it for the

---

[32]Cf., II, pp. 430, 511 f.
[33]*Ibid.*, pp. 431 f.

non-objective truth to know itself called by God to responsibility." (II, p. 431.) This "eschatological situation" of faith refers to its unconditionedness. Buri proceeds to equate the mythological concepts of the incarnation and its expression in Jesus's proclamation of the coming eschaton with the unconditionedness of faith here and now:

> The unconditionedness in which faith enacts its self-understanding corresponds to the nearness of the last things proclaimed in the prophecy of Jesus. In the self-understanding of faith enacted on the basis of the message of salvation, this concretely material (dinghaften) nearness becomes the unconditionedness of personal being before the God revealed in Christ. Here occurs what is meant by the phrase "incarnation of the Word of God" insofar as the reality of this phrase is disclosed to the self-understanding directed toward it. The once-for-all-ness of the incarnation can be legitimately asserted nowhere else than out of the unconditionedness of faith. (II, p. 431.)

This incarnation is preserved by the paradox that the unconditionedness of faith as a transcending of objectivity is actualized in the objectivities of time. The eschatological situation is defined, therefore, not merely by "the near expectation or unconditionedness of the last things" but also by "its appearance in time in awaiting the consummation." (II, p. 431.) Existentially interpreted this means that eschatology is structured in the act of faith as hope:

> In distinction from the enactment of self-understanding in time in which the consummation in the appropriation of the message is always before one (aussteht), the concept of the regnum gloriae now becomes important as the goal of the hope of faith. Time thereby also gains positive significance as the possibility of the confirmation of this hope which must occur not through inaction but in continually new hearing, understanding, and attesting of the message. (II, p. 432. My italics.)

Because the actualization of the content of every doctrine is subject to the relativity of time, every doctrine is eschatological in this sense of being defined by hope. The mythological imagery of Christ's return at the last judgment serves to give it expression. But this imagery is misleading if it is allowed to suggest only the future. Existentially interpreted, it is important to emphasize the eschatological dimension of every enactment of faith.[34] As Buri articulates the cash value of his own interpretation:

> Only for him who makes the objective misunderstanding of an ostensible possession of faith [out of this imagery] or for him who conversely absolutizes his

---

[34]Ibid., pp. 432 f.

non-believing, objective knowledge is it a question here of projections of unfulfilled wishes and needs into a beyond. For him, on the contrary, who understands himself in his faith related to the message of Christ as a being in the world and as a part of the body of Christ, the *eschatological images of the Christian tradition represent assertions of hope constituting the legitimate understanding of time...* Hope is no flight from the present into a chimerical distance. *In hope, rather, the present is taken seriously in its lack of fulfillment – but taken with such seriousness that the shortcomings of the present which are taken up into faith disclose this hope for the future as its fulfillment.* (II, p. 434. My italics.)

Unconditionedness and hope are, hence, the existential significance of the *regnum gloriae*. But in addition to its symbolic significance for the work of Christ, eschatology is also important for the *ordo salutis*. Here eschatology gives expression to the ultimate goal of sanctification in the final judgment and glorification of believers. And it is, again, the traditional mythological imagery which serves to express this existential significance. As Buri expresses his own interpretation, it can again be seen that in fact he is making a doctrinal proposal. In the images of the *glorificatio* of the believer in the *regnum Christi,* the mythological assertions of faith bring to expression

that personhood finds its perfection to the extent that therein becomes visible that it is impossible to describe personhood in an objective-conceptual manner. In the judgment which befalls each of faith's objectifications, there results at the same time the recognition of this standing in judgment as an awareness of the authenticity of human personhood which knows itself here called to responsibility before its personal Transcendence. The *glorificatio* represents for the Christian faith the consummation of that which occurs to it in every moment in the enactment of its self-understanding. . .: the fulfillment of its being determined *(Bestimmtseins)* to the likeness of God in Christ as the annulment *(Aufhebung)* of the perversity *(Verkehrt-seins)* of sin which consists of the self-assertive desire-to-be-like-God. In the annulment of this perversion of the *Imago Dei,* the correcting and comforting reconciliation of the sinner with God occurs. That is the salvation which occurs in every act of self-understanding. The grace which God gives to his children who are elected, justified, and sanctified in Christ is, in this way, glorified in the believer who enacts this act. As men of grace *(als Begnadete),* we are also glorified men just as grace is glorification. . . . (II, p. 513.)

This is a capsule summary of Buri's entire understanding of existence as grace. The paradigm of sin follows from the necessity given with finite existence itself of living in an objective world. The objectifying powers of consciousness with their capacities for control, manipulation, and exploitation are what is mythologically meant by the desire to be like God, for man inclines always to understand himself entirely in terms of an objectified world that falls before his consciousness and, thus, to absolutize himself and his world. From this all other meanings of individual sins follow. At the same time, sin is not merely a tragic fate given with human finitude as such. Insofar as the person hears himself called to responsible existence amidst the relativities of his objective world, he realizes that his situation can be assumed in freedom and responsibility. He also realizes that he is called to live in this situation in freedom and responsibility.[35] Because this awareness is an acknowledgement of the limited nature of the objective structures of finitude, the awareness itself is already a freedom "from" those structures at the same time that it is a freedom "in" them. For Buri it is the classic instance of Paul's "in but not of the world." In this way man's free assumption of his sinful existence is at once an understanding of himself as grace. All of this is brought to expression through the *regnum gloriae* in the *glorificatio* of sanctification. The significance of giving it an existentialist interpretation is that the mythological symbol and the understanding of both sin and grace are collapsed into the single, unitary act of self-understanding. The judgment and the glorification in the last judgment become symbols for actualized modes of existence possible at every moment.

c. The Self in Objective Description of the Christian Self-Understanding

It is now possible to comment on these two examples. The first thing to be noted should be obvious, namely, that Buri's specification of the abstract dialectic of grace by the historicity of the Christian faith does result in objective descriptions of possibilities of existence. Both "confidence" and "hope" are objective statements of such possibilities. And even though one side of eschatology, "unconditionedness," is meant to point to the non-objectivity of these contents in their actualization, the statement that this is the meaning of the eschatological imagery is not itself the unconditioned actualization of faith but is an objective statement of what faith is like. The symbols of the last judgment and glorification then show how unconditionedness is actualized in freedom "from" and freedom "in" the world whose modalities are structured by man's objectifying consciousness. To be sure, Buri continually interjects the proviso that these contents have no objective status in themselves apart from the actualization of faith. This proviso is important because, in-

---

[35]Cf., *ibid.*, pp. 212-260 for Buri's discussion of the doctrine of sin.

deed, it is the center of existentialist interpretation. It makes possible the decisive move from the content of doctrines as objective states of affairs to that content as the dialectical structure of acts of existence. In this sense, faith and its content are non-objective. But all the emphasis placed on this proviso cannot avoid the conclusion that the existentialist interpretation of the mythological symbols in terms of the existential structure of the self is an objective description of possibilities of existence actualized in a particular historicity. Nothing more nor less than the difference between theology on the one side and faith and proclamation on the other is at issue here.

The conclusion should be clear now that at any point where Buri specifies the concrete historicity of the Christian self-understanding some form of an objective statement of a possibility of existence will be made. A further illustration of this point is Buri's doctrine of justification. The existential possibility which is its cash value correlates closely with "confidence" and "hope." Turning to his own interpretation after his usual sketch of the problematic situation of this doctrine, he remarks:

The case is different when the justification of the sinner is no longer articulated in the sense of such objectifications. By justification we mean a reality which occurs in the enactment of the self-understanding of faith related to the message of Christ's vicarious fulfillment of the law. He who knows himself called to account through the unconditionedness of God's command, which can only be met by Christ's perfect fulfillment of the law, knows himself at the same time guilty before God. The recognition of being guilty leads, however, beyond sin to a new trust in being accepted by God. In this self-understanding, one cannot speak of a meritorious co-operation with grace. The awareness of being accepted cannot be worked out as a result of the insight and effort of the good will but has the character of an unmanipulative *(unverfügbaren)* gift of grace. In this knowing-oneself-accepted *(Sich-angenommen-wissen)*, the likeness of God in Christ and therewith our personhood becomes an event. In that, the possibility is opened for us that we can accept ourselves. The so described way to the occurrence of becoming a person is articulated – in a conceptual objectification of the significance of Christ for this way – in the doctrine of Christ's fulfillment of the law. The articulation of this fulfillment of the law by Christ as something vicarious that has happened for us brings to expression that our trust in being accepted by God is not grounded in our natural creaturehood *(Wesen)* but first becomes possible out of the relation to the proclamation of this new possibility which must always first become reality. (II, pp. 501 f.)

Buri cannot avoid using the mythological language of the Christian tradition in his own exposition of the existential content of doctrines, but his general principles as well as the way he gradually builds upon prior interpretations in his system make it obvious that his use of the traditional objective forms is always intended to point reflexively back to their existential content. With this in mind, it is clear enough from this passage that justification with all of its supporting objective assertions refers solely to an existential possibility. Thus, "knowing-oneself-accepted" describes a disposition or state of the self and not an objective state of affairs apart from the self. The proviso is particulary important in this passage because Buri indicates that "knowing-oneself-accepted" cannot be extrapolated from just any actualization of freedom and responsibility, and by implication, there are other modes in which they could be actualized. Nevertheless, while this content is one that has no status in the self apart from an existential process of becoming, the *description* of it as the content of this particular doctrine is an objective description of an existential possibility.

Aside from their objectivity, the second thing that must be noted about such descriptions is also expressed by this passage. In proceeding to interpret symbols, it has been argued, Buri does more than allow them to become transparent to a non-objective act of self-understanding which cannot be objectively articulated. At certain places, such interpretations involve objective descriptions of possibilities of existence. The argument is that they must, indeed, have this status if there is to be any possibility for Buri to specify the historicity of the Christian self-understanding. If this argument is correct, then it must be concluded that correlated with their objectivity is also their status as *doctrinal proposals* or *proposals for belief*. Even though the content of doctrines which Buri specifies does not have the same meaning as the traditional meaning of "doctrine," this content is, nevertheless, an alternative, objective proposal concerning the true content, significance, or meaning of the more traditional doctrines which are interpreted. They replace the more or less direct and obvious meaning of mythological proposals for belief by drawing an indirect interpretation from them which is hermeneutically grounded on a systematic principle. While such interpretations replace the mythological content with another one, they do not replace the objectivity of the mythological content with something non-objective – at least, not at the level of theological reflection.

Buri, of course, makes allowance for this to some extent. He continually emphasizes that the only form in which theology can be done is the objective form of scientific discourse. This also accounts for his claim that only mythological imagery is adequate for giving expression to faith. While theology itself must examine the traditional mythological imagery critically in order to elucidate the non-objective act of faith, the immediate life of faith must receive expression through this imagery because its non-scientific status peculiarly adapts the imagery to give expression to the non-objectivity of faith. But in his historical-critical discussions of doctrines in which he tries to balance competing claims to the point where they elucidate the act of faith itself, Buri continually draws back from the conclusion that his own interpretations are equally objective proposals. At these points he simply emphasizes the non-objectivity of the act of faith. But when the *regnum potentiae* was discussed, it became obvious that there is a certain confusion in Buri's argument because this emphasis really only applies to *how faith is grounded*.[36] That is, he only emphasized that the content of faith cannot be established by an objective proof. This type of argument applies, however, only to *the grounds of certitude* on the part of the faithful man, and in this Buri is surely right. But what he cannot deny is the objective status of his own proposals.

Buri's emphasis on the objective form of theological discourse does not, therefore, really take the nature of his own proposals into account. While objective discourse is necessary for theology, Buri continually indicates that *for the true content of faith* it really has no higher status than mythological imagery. Its critical and scientific self-consciousness does give it the advantage in the discussion of such imagery. But at the point of faith itself, its objective form makes it equally as dangerous. For this reason Buri severely criticizes those nineteenth century theologians who attempted to give a scientific, *begriffliches* restatement of the *Vorstellungen* of traditional religion. And his point is, of course, that they failed to take seriously enough the non-objectivity of faith. Thus, when Buri uses objective discourse in his theology, he insists that, like the symbol, it can only elucidate faith but not express it. Yet if the above argument is correct, he really is making new doctrinal proposals on the basis of an ostensibly sounder account of faith. Furthermore, to the extent that such proposals are objective, they cannot be reduced to myth or symbol. That is, to a much higher degree they must be sounder, more literal statements of the *real* content of faith. Otherwise, as *interpretations* of myths and symbols they would themselves be mythological or symbolic and would, thus, require further interpretation.

This argument does not necessarily obviate Buri's criticism of mythological proposals on the basis of a false objectivity. Granted his understanding of the limits of knowledge *and* of the nature of faith, he can

---

[36] Cf., *supra*, pp. 206 f.

still argue that an objectifying interpretation of the mythological content of faith is illicit. And he can still justify this interpretation on the basis of non-objectivity because of the proviso which must accompany even the conclusion concerning the objective status of his own proposals. He can still, that is, argue that the content of faith must be interpreted entirely in terms of the non-objective dialectic of the actualization of faith in the self. But he cannot deny that the *theological interpretation* of that dialectic will be an objective description of its structure having the form of more adequate doctrinal proposals.

This point can be illustrated by another example where Buri clearly replaces one objective doctrinal proposal with another. The example here is from his discussion of predestination and election. Just as the "being accepted" of justification correlated with "confidence" and "hope," this doctrine correlates with the "unconditionedness" of faith in the interpretation of eschatology.

Election does not result from a decree of God temporally preceding His creative works. This temporal determination of predestination as the beginning of the ways of God with man is a *mythological expression for the all-encompassing, unconditioned validity of the consciousness of the believer that this election is not at his disposal but stands exclusively in God's power and will.* The kind of event encompassing the whole being of the believer which occurs to him and which can be articulated as calling and illumination, re-birth and conversion and the unconditionedness with which he personally participates in it are *brought to expression in the Christian faith in the assertion that the believer knows himself elected from eternity* by God to the likeness of God in Christ.... *As the resolution of God from eternity, election functions only in the enactment of the self-understanding of faith. The from-eternity of election occurs in faith, but not in a divine decree posited in a causal-logical conceptuality at the beginning of the temporal series.* The self-understanding of faith itself transcends every conceptuality; it thereby transcends that classification in a temporal causal series. *In this transcending, eternity occurs to the faithful self-understanding as the unconditionedness of decision. Eternity becomes real in time through the seriousness, encompassing the whole being of the believer, with which this decision is taken. The unconditionedness in the decision of the self-understanding of faith . . . is that alone which corresponds to the eternity of predestination.* (II, pp. 490 f. My italics.)

Here Buri rejects an objectifying interpretation of election and predestination and then interprets it existentially in terms of his concept of unconditionedness. It should be clear not only that this is an *objective description* of the genuine significance of this doctrine – even though this unconditionedness is something which must be enacted and cannot be caught by a concept – but also that in its objectivity his interpretation is a *doctrinal proposal* for the true content of this doctrine.

This becomes even more obvious when Buri treats the various scholastic distinctions which have grown up around this doctrine. The notions of a *vocatio generalis* and *specialis* are particularly interesting because it is around this distinction that the arguments for and against double predestination have been fought. Again Buri emphasizes that insofar as such distinctions have any meaning at all, they cannot refer to various aspects of God's will or to various classes of men; they can serve a legitimate theological function only to the extent that they help clarify the unitary act of self-understanding itself. Buri goes on to say:

On the basis of this clarification, it is not possible in the Christian faith (either out of scripture or one's own self-understanding) to speak of those who are called and those who are not called in the sense of a divine decree conceived from eternity. Such an objective, double predestination contradicts both the universalistic places in the scriptures and the situation of decision actualized in the enactment of faithful self-understanding. This situation excludes such an objectively present-at-hand determination. But at the same time, the Christian will also know himself called in no other way than through a *vocatio* by the message of God's saving work in Christ which befalls him in just this particular way. The universality of the divine message of salvation only occurs in such historicity. Universality and particularity are not matters of a self-contained *decretum aeternum dei*. This theologoumenon is, rather, an assertion of the self-understanding of the Christian faith in the enactment of which the believer experiences himself elected by God. That the possibility of such a self-understanding rests from eternity on a divine order is nothing else but an expression for the unconditionedness in which faith knows itself responsible for its decision. The "from eternity" represents, in truth, not an assertion concerning the temporal point of the *vocatio* – which always occurs only in the moment of understanding oneself in terms of the saving message – but one concerning its unconditioned character. Other than in its unconditionedness there is no eternity for us. The essence of eternity consists, rather, in this unconditionedness. Faith is not in a position to understand the universality and particularity of the divine saving decree in relation to humanity otherwise than in the sense of the universal offer of salvation to all men and the still open decision to be enacted just by them. Faith knows of a condemnation (*Verworfensein*) only in the light of its situation of decision, as the destiny (*Bestimmung*) obviously not desired for it by God, in its understanding of itself in terms of the message of salvation. Condemnation comes to nothing not in the condemnation of Christ, as Barth contends, but in faith's own self-understanding defined by the message of Christ. That in this special instance God has not desired condemnation is not to be read off of an objective fact of salvation. The event of salvation occurs in the enactment of faithful self-understanding which is beyond the opposition of subjectivity and objectivity. As the non-condemnation by God is an expression for the Transcendence-relation of this self-understanding, so the election in Christ represents its historicity. (II, pp. 495 f.)

This passage is interesting not merely because it substantiates the argument that Buri's existentialist interpretations issue in doctrinal proposals but also because his proposal takes the form of a more or less classical dogmatic possibility. First, Buri rejects the doctrine of double predestination. Then, he rejects a straightforward universalism according to which all men will be saved. He must reject it because a universalism could only be articulated in an objective mythological form. He does, however, accept the quasi-universalistic position that the offer of grace is made to all men and that there are no objective reasons of principle why it cannot be accepted by all men (i.e., the Armenian position). In his terms, he endeavors to interpret the relationship between *vocatio generalis* and *specialis* so that the dialectic of universality and particularity has no status outside the internal dialectic of self-understanding. But he can achieve this only by allowing universality to mean the *objective doctrinal proposal* that the possibility for actualizing the existential possibilities of authentic human personhood is a possibility in principle and in fact for every man. *Vocatio specialis* or particularity then defines the historicity in which these possibilities are actualized, in the Christian self-understanding by the fact that the man of faith can express his "election to salvation" only as a response to the Christian kerygma.

It must be emphasized again that the proviso is still in force. Buri is talking here not about an objective state of affairs but about the understanding of existence which comes to expression only in a non-objective act of self-definition. But it is also necessary to emphasize that, at the level of theology, he is making a general and objective description of the nature of this non-objective actualization. And this description, in his view, has a more adequate conceptual status than the mythological and symbolic classical forms it interprets.

d. Self and World in the Self-Understanding of Faith

Before the implications of this argument for the hermeneutics of a radical theology are discussed, one further question must be addressed. An existentialist theology attempts to interpret all theological claims having an objective status about reality independent of the self as expressions of self-understanding and, thus, as statements about the self. The argument of this study has shown that while such interpretations may indeed succeed in interpreting all theological statements as assertions having the force of self-involving[37] statements about the self, the interpretations will

---

[37]The concept of self-involving language is taken from Donald Evans' extensive analysis

themselves be objective descriptions about the self making doctrinal proposals. Insofar, however, as the limits of objectivity in relation to interpretations of non-objective acts of self-understanding are thus qualified, the question becomes relevant whether it is not necessary also to qualify the extent to which theological statements can be limited to the self. If theological interpretations of self-understanding are objective in form, then can this objectivity be limited to the self alone since it is precisely the problem of objectivity (i.e., the attempt to avoid objectivity) that provides the major warrant for the restriction of theological assertions to the existential self? One must carefully note that within an existentialist theology such reference beyond the self would have to be a function of the primary reference to the non-objective dialectic of the self. It is necessary, in other words, to maintain the basic existentialist insight about the primary force of theological assertions. A reference to the world could legitimately arise only out of the dialectic of existence itself. But the question is still relevant whether some form of minimal objective claim about the world is co-implied with the objective status which must be assigned to theological descriptions of possibilities of existence.

Buri rather consistently tries to avoid this conclusion. He attempts to reduce everything to the non-objective actualization of the self. Aside from such examples as those discussed above (and from which Buri hesitates to draw the proper conclusions), the only exception seems to be the ambiguous status of Transcendence and God in his system. But even here it has been argued that these references can also consistently be interpreted in terms of the dialectic of the self, the only external reference being an indeterminate "whence" of the possibility of existence as grace.

But for other reasons than this, caution must be exercised in raising this question. This becomes evident when it is realized how difficult it is to formulate precisely the question to which an answer is being sought. The question might take at least four different forms. (i) It might be the historical question whether the force of classical Christian theological claims has intended to speak about the world independent of the self. (ii) Or it might be the more systematic question whether the force of religious language allows for any meaningful reference beyond the self. (iii)

in *The Logic of Self-Involvement* (London: SCM Press Ltd., 1963). Evans defines self-involving language as a language in which there are "logical connections between a man's utterances and his practical commitments, attitudes, and feelings." (*Ibid.*, p. 11.) This definition applies to the conception of theological language in a fully consistent existentialist theology such as Buri's because it is assumed that the very *meaning* (and not merely the appropriation) of theological assertions must be approached through the existentiality of faith itself.

Another possibility is the descriptive question whether Buri himself intends to make any claim about the world arising out of the self-understanding of faith. (iv) And finally, there is the additional systematic question whether the existentialist concept of self-understanding implies certain claims about the world.

Despite their importance, the first three can be set aside within the limits of this study. The first question is set aside, at least provisionally, by Buri's argument that in their traditional form, theological claims are mythological and that a proper understanding of the non-objectivity of faith demands a symbolic interpretation pointing entirely to the existential self. The second question has created considerable controversy in contemporary analytic approaches to religious language, but its resolution must await a more complete analysis of the logic of religious language than is presently available. Ordinary language analysis has succeeded brilliantly in discounting the old positivistic argument that religious language is nonsense. But while there is agreement over the meaningfulness of religious language in the context of religious usage, there is still considerable obscurity and controversy over the relationship between such usage and reference beyond the self – both as regards the actuality of such reference and its intelligibility. Concerning the third question, it seems that, at least in intention, Buri attempts to restrict theological claims to the non-objective enactment of self-understanding. But it is precisely the argument that his understanding of the problem of objectivity must be qualified which forces the further question concerning how far this qualification extends. Thus, the relevant problem is the systematic question of the range of objective description within existentialist interpretation, and the larger issues concerning whether Christians *have* historically made objective claims about the world or whether, given the logic of religious language, religious people not only do but *ought* to make such claims can initially be set aside.

Even with this limitation, it must be emphasized that the question is logical and not psychological. Presupposing, that is, the existentialist account of religious language, the question is not whether religious people still intend existentially interpreted language to refer to the world. This question is irrelevant to the problem of the logical status of objectivity in existentialist interpretation itself. And this latter question is the one that must be pressed. Does not the qualification on the limits of objectivity, which must now be admitted to be necessary, also qualify the limitation of the reference of theological language to the self which is the touchstone of existentialist theology?

Buri attempts to avoid such qualification because of the problem of objectivity. He fears that if theological language, in either its mythological or its existentially interpreted forms, makes a reference to the world, such a reference will misconstrue the significance of such language for faith. Instead of having its entire significance in the non-objective life of the believer, the content of faith will have the status of an objective picture of the world which can be accepted or rejected quite apart from the unconditionedness of *living* as a faithful or unfaithful man. Epistemologically he bases his argument for this understanding of faith on his analysis of the limits of knowledge and objectivity in relation to the world as a whole. Without undercutting his concept of the non-objectivity of faith, however, it is possible to qualify his notion of the limits on objective description of existential acts (i.e., in terms of existential possibilities). It would seem that the same argument might hold concerning the manner in which the world is disposed for faith. Just as the structure of faith can be described within the proviso of the non-objectivity of faith itself, so it would seem that the nature of the world *for faith* could be described without implying the reduction of faith to nothing more than an intellectual world view. Of course, Buri's conception of the subject-object relation means that objective theological claims about the world are restricted for slightly different reasons than those restricting the content of assertions to the self. An argument for the legitimacy of objective statements about the one would not, therefore, be an argument for the legitimacy of objective statements about the other. For this reason, it will be necessary to examine the implications of the subject-object relation for this argument more closely in the next chapter. Here, however, it is enough simply to examine the logic of Buri's claims themselves.

Three of the four examples discussed in the last several pages were chosen with this point in mind. Buri's existentialist interpretation of doctrines in terms of "confidence," "being-accepted," and "hope" all seem to imply certain attitudes toward the world.[38] Initially, the interest in discussing these doctrines was directed toward showing how Buri does in fact provide certain objective descriptions of structures of actualized existence. Now it must be noted that, insofar as these are the ways in

---

[38]It will be noted that one of the objectively describable, existential possibilities in faith, namely "unconditionedness," has been omitted from this list. Although "unconditionedness" can be described objectively as an element in existential self-actualization, it cannot, on existential grounds alone, be interpreted as implying directly any claim about the world. On Buri's terms, "unconditionedness" does not have to refer to any reality other than the self that is unconditioned in the moment of its self-actualization.

which the existential self is structured in the Christian self-understanding, then certain claims are also implied about the way the world is disposed toward man. The non-objective actualization of one's actual living as "confidence" implies a world ultimately worthy of such confidence. "Being-accepted" implies that such a world structures this confidence in a certain way. In the Christian self-understanding, according to Buri, "hope" correlates with "confidence" and "being-accepted," but the kind of telos the existentially interpreted concept of "hope" gives to "confidence" and "being-accepted" implies a world in which such an actualization of existence is meaningful. Just as descriptions of structures of self-understanding have an objective status that does not qualify the non-objectivity of faith itself, so also these implications of those structures are objective statements about the world even though they need not be a fullblown metaphysical system or world-view. They are at least minimal claims about the constitution of the world.

Buri's objection to this interpretation will not actually stand up under the argument that it is possible to separate objective descriptions of non-objective enactments from those enactments themselves. The only argument Buri ever presents to support his objection is one concerning the grounds of faith. As this was quoted above, he says:

> As the unconditionedness of the enactment of faith, which cannot be grasped psychologically, corresponds to the once-for-allness of the saving work of Christ which bursts through everything historical, so the reality of the world-dominion of Christ cannot be justified (ausweisen) in any way by science or a world-view. Its origin and sphere is faith. (II, p. 424.)

This is the characteristic manner in which Buri justifies the move to the non-objectivity of faith throughout his theology. But this argument applies only to the grounds for the certitude of faith. It says nothing about what might be believed or implied by faith. Alone it does not, therefore, touch the argument that certain objective claims about the world might nevertheless arise out of the non-objective enactment of faith.

There need be no dispute with Buri's argument that such encompassing claims about the world cannot be justified on objective grounds. Whatever one might think of his argument concerning the limits of knowledge at this point, he is certainly correct about the nature of faith. *That* one actualizes a self-understanding which is disposed toward the world in a certain way and which understands the world disposed toward the self in a certain way cannot be grounded or justified by any scientifically objective schema. To put this more theologically, that God

justifies a man *by* faith is not something that can be justified by a justification *of* faith. But this need not mean that in his non-objective self-understanding a man does not understand the world in a certain way.
Again theologically, it does not mean that it is not possible to describe
objectively what is meant by justification by faith. A self-involving
interpretation of such concepts as "confidence," "being-accepted," and
"hope" implies that the man of faith believes the world to be a certain
way even if it is impossible ever to justify such claims rationally and
objectively.

It might be objected that such concepts as "confidence," "being-accepted," and "hope" should be seen in an existentialist theology only in
terms of their reference to the dialectic of the self. The problem is whether such a limitation can be clearly expressed. The logic of such concepts seems to make it impossible to limit them to the self. They do refer to the self insofar as they say something about certain attitudes or
dispositions of the self and do not directly make a claim about the
world. But can an attitude of confidence be limited to the self alone?
Does it not imply a disposition toward the world? One would not have
confidence or hope in the sense Buri means unless he thought the world
(or a person) were such as to support such confidence. This is true despite the fact that confidence and hope themselves are only subjective
states. It might be said of such existential possibilities that the self acts *as
if* the world were worthy of confidence and hope and as *if* the self were
accepted. But even this much would be an objective statement of the nature of the world toward which faith relates in an "as if" fashion. One
would act toward the world "as if" the world were worthy of confidence
instead of despair, "as if" the world offered intelligible grounds for the
continuity of action throughout an entire lifetime ("hope"), and "as if"
the world came to the self in such a way (perhaps not objectively evident) that one's actions were freed from the involution upon self which
sees the only ground for human action in self-serving motives and which
breeds isolation, hate, and insecurity ("being-accepted").

Furthermore, there is the question whether an "as if" interpretation of
faith is at all consistent with Buri's understanding of the unconditionedness of faith. The correlate of an "as if" confidence, trust, hope, or awareness of acceptance is qualification, reservation, and hedging, and these
are precisely the attitudes that are incommensurate with the totality and
unconditionedness of faith. I would appear, then, that even the unconditionedness of faith has implications for the nature of faith's beliefs once
it is granted that existentialist interpretation cannot exclude such beliefs.

Faith is peculiarly total in two directions – in the totality with which faith makes its commitments and in the totality of its understanding of things entire which support them.

It must be acknowledged that faith can have an "as if" status in one sense. In relation to a justification of faith, it can be said that faith relates to the world "as if" the world were such and such. There is no way to establish objectively that the world is *in fact* such and such. But this applies only to the grounds for the certitude of faith. It does not deny that the faithful man *believes* the world to be such and such. It is difficult to see how even an exhaustive existentialist interpretation can exclude such beliefs as correlates of actualizing certain existential possibilities. If this is the case, then the non-objectivity of faith need not be inconsistent with certain minimal, objective claims about the world.

This argument rests on the conclusion about the necessity of qualifying the limits of objectivity in relation to the self. Once it is granted that objective descriptions of the structure of faith are possible and legitimate, then it becomes possible to examine whether some such actual descriptions do not also imply reference to the world. This conclusion is legitimate to the same extent that the one about objective descriptions of the self is also legitimate. In neither case would it mean a false understanding of faith as something other than the event of enactment. It applies, rather, to the content of that enactment. Faith can still be understood as the event of self-understanding, as the response to a new offer of life which can be actualized only in the here and now of living out that response. In this sense faith is not constituted by a world view. But this does not mean that faith, the actualization of certain existential possibilities, is not constituted by an ultimate confidence in the final nature of things. Nor does it mean that the theologian cannot go some distance in specifying the beliefs in the final nature of things in terms of the structures of self-understanding disposed toward it. The event of actualizing a self-understanding involves some belief in the final nature of reality even though an extensive metaphysical discussion of this reality might be irrelevant to the theological task of expositing the self-understanding of faith. The question of metaphysics will be one of the topics to be addressed in the last chapter.

CHAPTER VII

RADICAL THEOLOGY AND THE PROBLEM
OF OBJECTIVITY

It is now time to sort out the significance this analysis of Buri has for the hermeneutics of a radical theology. Acknowledging the pervasiveness of the so-called problem of objectivity in existentialist theology, this study began with the question in what sense the problem of objectifying thinking and speaking can be the central hermeneutical problem for a radical theology when it must be recognized that theological language will inevitably be objectifying. Buri is of paradigmatic importance here because he self-consciously adopts the hermeneutical centrality of the problem of objectivity but clearly recognizes that all theological thinking and speaking will be objective in character. At the same time he does not equivocate on what the problem is by reducing it to something else, namely, to the problem of the canons for assessing scientific knowledge. In order to show how objectivity as such is a problem for theology he must show how the conditions of objectivity are wider than the conditions of scientific knowledge alone. This he does through his analysis of the subject-object relation. From this perspective, it becomes evident that the two primary realities with which the content of theological assertions has to do, the existential actualization of faith and the transcendent ground of faith, transcend the subject-object relation and are non-objective. It becomes possible in this way both to criticize objective theological assertions *because of their objectivity* and to show how the non-objective character of faith qualifies what the theologian says objectively (when a critical awareness of the subject-object structure is present) so that his own objective assertions do not fall prey to the same shortcomings which force him to reject the criticized forms.

But it also became evident that, carried through to its end, Buri's view of the problem of objectivity has debilitating consequences. He cannot meet one of his principal hermeneutical requirements, namely, that the content of any particular faith be specified by its historicity. The most he can say is that whatever the content of a specific faith is it will be non-objective, and to a large extent, this is in fact what his interpretation of the content of Christian affirmations turns out to be. The meaning found in the affirmations which express the Christian self-understanding is no content at all but a purely formal statement about the character of any self-understanding whatsoever.

For this reason, it was argued that the content of the Christian self-understanding could be specified only by describing objectively the existential possibilities which constitute it and which differentiate it from other possible self-understandings. But this specification has now turned out to involve making objective assertions about the existential self and, in some sense, the world as a whole, precisely the two realities which are non-objective according to Buri. Furthermore, the non-objectivity of these two realities is the source of the clarity with which Buri is able to show why objectivity as such is a theological problem. To argue for the necessity of speaking about these realities objectively would seem, therefore, to involve the complete destruction of just those hermeneutical principles which make possible the existentialist interpretation in the first place. Existentialist interpretation is both possible and necessary because objectivity as such is a problem for the meaning of theological assertions; but the success of existentialist interpretation seems to demand a form of objective description which calls into question the reason objectivity as such is a problem.

Thus even at this stage, it seems as though there is as much confusion about the status of the problem of objectivity as there was at the beginning, and the reason for this confusion derives from nothing less than the greater clarity which marks Buri's analysis of the problem. To what extent, then, is the problem of objectivity even relevant to a radical theology? It should be obvious by now that this question can be answered only by separating out several different layers in the hermeneutics of a radical theology in which objectivity and non-objectivity play different roles at different points.

A. THE SIGNIFICANCE OF EXISTENTIALIST INTERPRETATION
FOR A RADICAL THEOLOGY

A first step in this sorting out can be taken by asking the direct question why the method of existentialist interpretation has proved so fruitful for those who are concerned to develop a radical theology. The answer lies in the extraordinary hermeneutical potential of the idea of existential possibilities. If traditional theological assertions can be interpreted as expressing various possibilities of existence, then a host of theological and philosophical problems with the meaning of religious language are not so much solved as made irrelevant. For one thing, the entire problem of verification, a problem which has plagued modern theology, is, at least at a certain level, entirely transformed. If the traditional theological language is not about the world but about various possibilities of existing, then it cannot be falsified. One cannot falsify a particular possibility of existing; one can simply refuse to accept it as a possibility for oneself. Here the problem of verification is reduced to a question of which description of existential possibilities is most adequate to the existential content of a particular tradition and whether all of these possibilities are consistent with one another.

For another thing, interpretation in terms of existential possibilities frees the content of the Christian faith from dependence on any particular conceptual schema for interpreting the world. This, indeed, may be said to be the epistemological significance of the doctrine of justification by faith, for the Christian is freed even from the law which hinges his salvation on appropriating a particular conceptual schema.[1] He is asked, instead, whether he is prepared to understand himself in a particular way, to actualize his existence according to possibilities that are offered to him as possibilities of life in contrast to those which are only isolation, hatred, and death. In no sense then does the kerygma of the Christian faith require of a man that he reject that way of looking at the world which he finds appropriate for his time. This means that at a time when the process of secularization has made the understanding of the kerygma in terms of the mythology of the so-called traditional Christian world-view both questionable and irrelevant for modern man, the content of "religion" or Christianity can and does impinge on his existence as directly as ever it did. Every man is "religious" in the sense that existentially he gives an answer to the question how he shall understand himself, for no matter how a man expresses his way of looking at his world conceptually, he actualizes himself moment by moment according to various existential possibilities for understanding himself, and there are on-

---

[1]Cf., Rudolf Bultmann, "Zum Problem der Entmythologisierung" in Hans Werner Bartsch (ed.), *Kerygma und Mythos,* II (Hamburg: Herbert Reich Evangelischer Verlag, 1952), p. 207 f.; ET, Fuller and Bartsch (eds.), *Kerygma and Myth,* pp. 210 f. And Van A. Harvey, "The Nature and Function of Faith" in Dean Peerman (ed.), *Frontline Theology* (Richmond: John Knox Press, 1967), pp. 109 f. & 115 f.

ly so many options available to human beings in which these actualizations can take place – love, openness, and trust, for example, in contrast to hatred, closing, and fear.

This account of the fruitfulness of existentialist interpretation could be extended in many further directions, but these are sufficiently obvious from the literature of the movement to require no additional documentation. What needs to be noted here is that, up to a certain point, the significance of the existential method can be established without appeal to the merely gnoseological problem of objectivity. It is entirely possible to provide such justification on the basis of substantive issues surrounding the nature of faith and the content of the Christian message. The crux of such a theology depends on the proposal to interpret all theological statements in terms of existential possibilities. This proposal, in turn, depends on a certain conception of both faith and the Christian message. The Christian message, it can be said, is best understood not in the first instance as information about historical or metaphysical facts but as the call to and offer of a new life. Faith is thereby best understood not as neutral acceptance of certain information but as the appropriation, in a continual act of becoming, of a new self-understanding. It can then be claimed that the concept of existence provides the most adequate philosophical clarification for the articulation of the content of faith and unfaith, i.e., for describing various existential possibilities. Although this justification of existentialist interpretation is sketched here only in the most provisional and rudimentary way, it is important to see that it still offers grounds for demythologizing and for an alternative to a cosmological interpretation of doctrinal content. On this account, the Christian and Biblical traditions must be interpreted in terms of their significance for faith, i.e., in terms of the self-understanding of faith, and any meaning of theological assertions which cannot be reduced to an expression for existential possibilities must be strictly said to be irrelevant or even falsifying for the nature of faith.

The primary problem in appealing to the problem of objectivity as a warrant justifying existentialist interpretation is that the concept of "objectivity" alone is too broad to discriminate among the various criteria for criticizing unacceptable positions and the criteria for an alternative. It excludes too much. In the above argument concerning the necessity for objective descriptions of existential possibilities, for example, the status of objectivity in the description of the content of faith is formally identical with its status in the rejected cosmological and mythological interpretations. It is the same, that is, in terms of the general conditions of objectivity as such, the subject-object structure. The problem of objectivity alone and without distinctions and qualifications cannot, therefore, be the *differentia* between the method of existentialist interpretation and some other rejected alternative. The reasons given for undertaking existentialist interpretation must rest instead on substantive issues definitive for any theology whatsoever.

Yet if it is possible to defend existentialist interpretation by a consideration of these substantive issues – as was suggested above – nevertheless it is also true that in some sense the problem of objectivity is crucially relevant to an existential method. The only point is that its relevance cannot be properly conceived if "objectivity" is a univocal concept excluding everything and nothing. It must be possible to see "objectivity" as an umbrella concept for a number of different issues not all of which are relevant in the same way and at the same point and not all of which exclude the possibility of some form of objective theological discourse.

Viewed in this light, distinctions can be made among three different ways in which the problem of objectivity has been relevant for Buri and for radical theologians in general. (i) In the first place, the problem of objectivity is the foundation for the existential understanding of faith, for only by distinguishing between objectivity and non-objectivity is it possible to understand faith itself as the actualization of existential possibilities. The existential encounter with reality is entirely different from that type of encounter in which the world is objectively known, believed or described.

(ii) This understanding of faith then has hermeneutical significance because it requires a particular way of interpreting the mythological statements in which all religious traditions have historically articulated themselves. Objectivity is relevant here because it is the objective understanding of such myths which makes it impossible to discern their religious significance, the way they express existential possibilities, once the concept of myth itself has been acknowledged and explored after the rise of the modern scientific self-consciousness. This hermeneutical significance of the existential understanding of faith is not immediately apparent and was a long time in being recognized, for one might acknowledge that faith itself is non-objective and still want to say that the ground and the content of this existential act is a mythological, objective state of affairs, e.g., the objective fact that God became man at a particular time and place in the past. The failure to recognize the hermeneutical force of his non-objective understanding of faith is what accounts for the anomaly which runs throughout Kierkegaard's thought. As Van A. Harvey states it: "Despite Kierkegaard's insistence on faith as a passion and his polemic against objectification and belief, his own view basically hangs on the identification of faith with propositional belief, although in this case the proposition is claimed to be an absurd one. But, it may be asked, what is saving about believing an absurdity?"[2] It is the merit of Buri and, with somewhat less consistency, Bultmann to have recognized the hermeneutical force of the existential understanding of faith. Once, that is, one fully appreciates that faith is a non-objective process of becoming, then the content of theological assertions must be totally appropriate to the nature of faith. No religious statement can be religiously significant if its content cannot be exhaustively interpreted in terms of the existential possibilities available to the self in any present moment. In sum, the problem of objectivity is relevant both to the conception of faith underlying existentialist interpretation and to the hermeneutic which follows from that conception of faith and which makes possible a critical understanding of mythological language.

(iii) Confusion arises with a third way in which the problem of objectivity is taken to be relevant. Most of the thoroughgoing existentialist theologians, especially Buri and Bultmann, find it impossible not to extend the critical understanding of objectivity which makes possible an interpretation of mythology *to every objective statement about the world and God without exception.* This seems cogent because the existential concept of faith relies on an analysis of the general conditions of objectivity as such. It then follows that the warrants for interpreting myths seem to depend on a conception of the thinking and speaking which occurs in myth but which is far wider than myth itself. But inevitably something goes wrong at this point. Either, in the case of Buri, it is only possible to say that whatever faith is it is an existential process, and the content of faith thus becomes entirely vacuous, or, in the case of Bultmann and others, a hidden concept of objectivity is smuggled in through the back door, and the grounds for accepting one and rejecting the other, *if appeal is still made to the problem of objectivity alone,* become confused. The question, then, is whether the relevance of the problem of objectivity in the first two senses can be analyzed in such a way that it does not draw the third meaning in its train.

That it can has already been demonstrated in this study. In the last chapter, it was shown that existential possibilities as they cohere together

[2]Harvey, *The Historian and the Believer,* p. 286.

in a particular religious tradition can be described objectively without disputing either the sense in which faith itself is non-objective or the way in which the non-objectivity of faith makes the problem of objectivity relevant to the hermeneutical question.

It is now important to notice that this point has logical significance which goes beyond the particular subject matter in question, i.e., the self in its non-objective dimension. It is not, that is, the nature of the self which warrants the legitimacy of objective description but the logical structure of the problem of objectivity itself. Both the nature of faith as well as the content of theological assertions are misconstrued unless the content of those assertions is interpreted in terms of the non-objective actualization of existential possibilities, and for this interpretation, it is important to make the proper distinctions between objectivity and non-objectivity. But once the non-objectivity of faith itself is recognized, i.e., the fact that it is an existential process of becoming actualized non-objectively in terms of existential possibilities, and once the proviso concerning its non-objectivity is incorporated into the very interpretation given to theological doctrines, then there is absolutely no reason why such existential possibilities, as well as the proviso, cannot be described objectively. The non-objectivity of the actualization of faith's content, so important for getting straight how that content can be interpreted properly, simply does not exclude the legitimacy of describing existential possibilities objectively. But if this is the case, then it is not the self which warrants objective description but the logical structure of the problem of objectivity in the different levels at which it is and is not relevant to the problem of the objectivity of theological language. It follows, consequently, that the principle which permits the objective description of the existential self, of existential possibilities, cannot be used to exclude objective statements about the world or God. If, without violating the canons according to which the problem of objectivity is relevant to the foundations of an existentialist theology, it is possible to make objective statements at one point, it ought to be possible according to the same principle at any other point. The problem of objectivity alone, at least, cannot be used to warrant the illegitimacy of objective statements about realities other than the self.

It might be said, of course, that these further objective assertions are illicit because the existential method does not permit objective description of anything beyond existential possibilities, i.e., references to the self. But in the last chapter, there was reason to question whether existential possibilities can be so restricted. In some sense existential possibilities seem to imply beliefs about the world. In any case, the problem of objectivity cannot warrant their exclusion. At purely logical level quite apart from the substantive question of their nature and their legitimacy, the same principle which allows objective description of existential possibilities without detriment to the hermeneutical scope of the non-objectivity of faith also allows objective statements about the world and God.

It is one thing, however, to argue from a purely formal point of view that such statements ought to be legitimate and quite another thing to show how such statements should appear in an existentialist theology. The problem of objectivity is still relevant to them, for it dictates the understanding of faith and its content which, in turn, leads to a critical awareness of the objective forms that are accepted. If objective statements are uncritically admitted without considering the total context of objectivity and non-objectivity in an existentialist theology, then, again, the basis for demythologizing is undercut. It is still necessary to discriminate among objective statements about the world and God which are all formally objective but some of which are inappropriate. And in an existentialist theology the basis of this discrimination will be a function of the way he content of faith is understood. It will, thus, be a function of the existentialist conception of the problem of objectivity. The question, then, is what qualifications and restrictions does the legitimate function of the problem of objectivity in an existentialist theology place on objective statements about the world and God. To answer this question, it is necessary to return to the general conditions of objectivity.

B. ONTOLOGY AND THE SUBJECT-OBJECT STRUCTURE

It has been argued that Buri brings a certain amount of clarity into the discussion of objectivity and non-objectivity because he specifies the general conditions of objectivity as such. This he does through his analysis of the subject-object structure. Without some such encompassing thesis concerning what constitutes objectivity in the widest sense, it is doubtful that the problem of objectivity can be given the hermeneutical status it has occupied in existentialist theology. The subject-object structure, however, has force in two different directions, an existential and an epistemological, and it is extremely important to recognize this. Existentially the subject-object structure is the basis for Buri's understanding of the non-objectivity of faith, and it is, thus, the foundation for his primary hermeneutical proposal. Epistemologically it is the basis for an argument concerning the limits not only of knowledge but also of reference (since according to Buri's view not even the reference of beliefs about the world as a whole or God can be made intelligible to say nothing of justifying them as knowledge). Now these two implications of the subject-object structure are separable. In the last section, it became clear that there is nothing in the existential force of the problem of objectivity alone which excludes objective statements about self, world or God. In contrast, the epistemological force of the problem does exclude them. Thus, if the epistemological force of the subject-object structure is the necessary and sufficient condition of the existential view of faith (i.e., of the existential force of the subject-object structure), then such statements are out of place in principle. Still it is important to recognize that they are excluded for epistemological reasons, not existential ones. So the question is whether the subject-object structure needs to have the epistemological implications Buri draws from it.

Nevertheless, this question must be phrased very carefully. The abstract problem of the limits of knowledge is of no interest in and of itself. It becomes relevant in this context only if it is a function of an adequate existentialist interpretation. Consequently, the way it is approached must still be controlled by the problem of objectivity as it is relevant at the existential level. The epistemological implications of the subject-object structure must, therefore, be viewed from the perspective of existential possibilities. This means not just that ontological claims about the world and God are appropriate only if they are directly a function of existential possibilities. It also means that the nature of such claims and the way they are justified must be strictly controlled by the requirements of such possibilities. Hence, even if Buri's interpretation of the subject-object structure must be seriously revised, the problem of objectivity will still qualify the ontological claims that are made. With this in mind, there are two levels at which Buri's restrictions on ontological claims may be called into question.

The first of these arises at the level of existential possibilities themselves. This level may be called the immediate dimension of the religious life.[3] It is immediate because the actualization of existential possibilities is, strictly speaking, independent of any particular conceptual statement about reality. The possibilities are called existential for no other reason than that they arise from an immediate response to the way reality is encountered. Even at this level, however, it was shown in the last chapter

[3] Cf., Harvey, "The Nature and Function of Faith," pp. 111 f.

that such possibilities imply beliefs about the nature of reality which make the actualization of certain possibilities appropriate in contrast to others. If one is careful not to misconstrue it, it might even be said that a person actualizes certain possibilities *because* he believes that reality comes to him in such and such a way. Again, it must be emphasized that holding in view a conceptual statement of these beliefs is not a condition for actualizing the possibilities. This would be a failure to remember the reversal which is always required by the relationship between objective claims and existential possibilities. The existential possibilities which are the content of Christianity are possibilities for human existence irrespective of whether one appropriates the assertions of the Christian tradition. But even if the actualization of the possibilities does not depend on an explicit statement of certain objective beliefs, nevertheless, the possibilities imply beliefs which are objective claims about the nature of reality and which can be explicated objectively.

In the last chapter, the beliefs implicit in the existential possibilities of "confidence," "hope," and "being-accepted" were examined. Do these beliefs violate the restrictions on the structure of consciousness? It is difficult to see how they do. Buri's analysis of the limits of knowledge really only succeeds in calling into question world-views which seek to describe in detail the structure of being as a whole or being-itself. According to his view of the subject-object relation, these are illicit because it is impossible to adduce the rules of reference or the reference range for the application of object concepts immanent to the subject-object relation to reality transcendent to it. But the objective claims on which existential possibilities depend are not of this type. Instead of describing a world-view in detail, they are simply claims about how being comes to the self such as to support the actualization of various possibilities. They are, consequently, highly general and unspecific. To say, for example, that reality is such that confidence and hope are not illusory and that one is ultimately accepted is to make an objective claim about the trustworthiness of being, but it is not to give an objective description of the structure of being. The same thing could be said of any claim about the world which is implicit in other existential possibilities. The reason for this is that no existential possibility, taken solely in the immediate dimension of the religious life, depends on or gives expression to any specific world-view. The objective belief claims which can be extrapolated from existential possibilities are specific enough, however, to say something rather than nothing – which is to say that they exclude and deny other objective claims about the world which are implied by contrasting existential possibilities.[4] The point of this is that Buri's position on the limits of knowledge, and consequently on the limits of objective statements about being as a whole and being-itself, operates to exclude a type of objective claim that is entirely irrelevant to the objective beliefs which occur in the immediate dimension of the religious life. His criticism of world-views simply does not apply in this case.

It is important to recognize that the extrapolation of these belief claims occurs already at the level of theology. This is another way of saying that the actualization of existential possibilities is not itself a function of holding in view any particular objective assertions. A religious man may actualize certain existential possibilities in a fully appropriate way all the while that he articulates his self-understanding with a totally naive and direct confession of the traditional Christian language. Theological interpretation, however, will show that the content of this objective language is itself the structure of the existential possibilities that are actualized. Only at this point will it then become relevant to examine the ontological beliefs which are implicit in the existential possibilities and which are, in turn, also implicit in the traditional language. The actual explication of these beliefs occurs, in other words, at the level of theology. This means that being able to give an account of these beliefs in just these terms is not a condition for the actualization of the Christian self-understanding. It also means that the religious man may "understand" the traditional mythological language of the Christian tradition, in the sense that this language is *used* (not interpreted) as an expression for the existential content of the Christian faith, without being able or needing to give this theological account of it.[5]

Once it is clear that the explication of these belief claims is already a matter of theological interpretation, it also becomes clear that there is another level at which Buri's restrictions on objective claims must be questioned, and at this second level it is no longer possible to sidestep a direct confrontation with the epistemological problem of the limits of knowledge and reference. This is the level at which it is appropriate to ask for a philosophical account of the unspecific belief claims that are operative in the immediate dimension of the religious life, and, unlike the former level, it will involve a description of the structure of being or

---

[4]For an extremely suggestive exploration of this point, cf., Peter Berger, *A Rumor of Angels* (Garden City, New York: Doubleday and Co., Inc., 1969), pp. 61-119.

[5]This may seem strange, but it is nothing other than the existentialist version of the relation that has always obtained between faith, the pre-theological witness to faith, and theology.

what Buri calls a world-view. If it is granted that the immediate dimension of the religious life implies beliefs about the nature of reality but not a world-view, then it is appropriate to ask how reality must be structured such that those beliefs are not illusory. It is appropriate, in other words, to ask for an account of the ontological content of both the existential possibilities of the Christian self-understanding and the traditional mythological language (the content of the latter, of course, appropriately qualified by the hermeneutical disclosure of an existentialist interpretation).

It is important to recognize that there is no *existential* reason for prohibiting this further theological endeavour. Existentialist theologians such as Buri and Bultmann often suggest that there is such a reason because they seem to think that an ontological account of the content of faith will transform faith itself into ontology and thereby ignore the existentiality of faith which is crucial both for its nature and its content But it is now clear enough from the analysis of this study that such a conclusion results from a confusion over how the problem of objectivity is relevant at different levels in an existentialist theology. There is no inherent conflict between the existential actualization of faith and objective belief claims that are either implicit in that actualization or are made on the basis of the perspective on reality from which faith is actualized. There need be no presumption that faith itself is reduced to an ontology. This is especially true, when, as is necessary in an existentialist theology, the proviso concerning the existentiality of faith directly influences the interpretation by means of which the content of faith is articulated. Furthermore, it has been found necessary to make a distinction between the immediate dimension of the religious life at which point an elemental loyalty is actualized existentially and the belief claims implicit in that loyalty even at the level of immediacy. If this distinction can be granted, then there is no existential reason to prohibit the rationalization of these immediate commitments by ontology and metaphysics.

If there are, thus, no existential objections to questions of ontology in theology, then, again, the problem comes down to the epistemological limits of the subject-object structure. Since consciousness is confined to this structure, the only way to develop an ontology is by the imaginative extension of particular symbols and objects to generalized structures characteristic of being as a whole. This means that an ontology within the epistemology of the subject-object structure will depend heavily on an adequate theory of analogy, and interestingly enough, Buri and Bultmann give almost no sustained attention to the question of analogy. It is relevant, therefore, to examine whether their primary criticism of objectivity, i.e., the criticism of myth, entails a rejection of all ontological claims as such, especially those that might be made on the basis of an appropriate theory of analogy.

Their most basic criticism of mythological objectivity arises from a theological motive. They argue that myth falsely objectifies that which is not an object by speaking of the divine and unworldly in human and worldly terms. Granting the Kantian epistemology which is normative for them, all human thinking and speaking falls within the relational limits of the subject-object structure, and it can, therefore, claim no absolute reference to being-itself. But this argument does not actually justify the conclusions concerning all forms of objective thinking and speaking which they draw from it because it only means that *all* human thinking and speaking about the divine and unworldly – not just the mythological – will be in human and worldly terms. So defined, the problem is no different from the classical problem of referring to transcendent reality. Theologians have always recognized the limited nature of human categories and their inappropriateness for making any direct or literal reference to ultimate being, but, instead of ruling out such reference altogether, they have sought adequate rules by means of which finite categories can refer indirectly to this reality. The option is not: either a false objectivity in mythology or no reference at all and instead a non-objective, existentialist interpretation. Such a dichotomy will not work because it has been demonstrated above that non-objectivity is not an exhaustive *differentia* of existentialist interpretation. The real option at this point is: either an inadequate objectivity in mythology or an adequate objective reference on the basis of a criticism of mythology and a sounder understanding of the way *any* human language whatsoever may refer to the divine and unworldly.

The same point can be made by examining more closely what it might mean to say that the divine and unworldly is non-objective. It may be non-objective in the sense that it is not an "object" or "thing" (Bultmann's meaning sometimes). It may be non-objective in the sense that it is never given as an object in the subject-object structure but is the source and ground of that structure and of all finite reality (Buri's meaning and Bultmann's wider meaning). Or it may be non-objective in the sense that is it difficult or impossible to specify rules of reference for finite categories so that reference to it in "human and worldly" terms can have no "absolute" or "scientific" justification (Buri's meaning sometimes).

In none of these cases can the problem of speaking about transcendent reality be ruled out on the basis of the problem of objectivity alone. The first two meanings simply define the classical problem traditionally treated under the question of analogy. Neither of these senses say that objectifications of this reality are ruled out as such but only that all human thinking and speaking about this reality confronts the problem of speaking about the divine and unworldly in adequate human and worldly terms. The issue they present is *more or less adequate objectification,* not no objectification at all. And as has been noted, the third meaning deals with the grounds for the certitude of faith but not with *what* faith says. It may be impossible to justify the content of faith (the third meaning), and, indeed, it may be impossible even to specify the reference range and the rules for referring to the divine and unworldly (the first and second meanings), so that the meaning, in addition to the justification, is problematic. But the problem of objectivity *alone* cannot absolve the theologian from the most arduous attempts at such specification nor can it rule out the possibility of making distinctions between more and less adequate solutions to the problem.[6]

[6]It is interesting that Jaspers has received a good deal of attention, both sympathetic and critical, from thinkers congenial to Thomist philosophy and theology. There is general agreement among these readers of his thought that the weakest link in his assumption about the nature and consequent limits of knowledge is his failure to give any attention to the concept of analogy, a concept that his scepticism about "absolutistic" systems need not exclude at all. The possibilities in his thinking for developing concepts of continuity between analogical levels of being (instead of his emphasis on the *Zerrissenheit* of being for objective knowledge) are most clearly suggested by Ludwig Armbruster, S.J. in his book, *Objekt und Transzendenz bei Jaspers: Sein Gegenstandsbegriff und die Möglichkeit der Metaphysik* (Innsbruck: Verlag Felizian Rauch, 1957), pp. 106-136. (Cf., also, Julian Hartt, "God, Transcendence and Freedom in the Philosophy of Jaspers" in *The Review of Metaphysics,* IV, No. 2 (December 1950), p. 256; James Collins, "An Approach to Karl Jaspers," in *Thought* (1945), pp. 690 ff.; J. B. Lotz, "Analogie und Chiffre," in *Scholastik* (1940), pp. 40, 53 ff.) Lotz and Collins have noted that ultimately the reason Jaspers never seems to give consideration to the possibilities of analogical thinking resides in the Kantian phenomenalism he presupposes. Because of this phenomenalism he assumes the impossibility of arriving at a concept of being-in-itself and settles for an existential *Vergewisserung* as the only access to the fullness of being. This phenomenalism thus passes by from the beginning the Thomist argument that being is not a concept at all but the fullness posited in the judgment of existence. Collins articulates this most clearly. Noting that there are two strands in Jaspers' thought, one which sees the object of knowledge as an appearance and another which sees it as a mode of being, Collins goes on to say: "Yet, granted that what we know in the world is a determinate mode of being and not being as such or in its fullness, there is no evident need to equate determinateness or particularity with phenomenality. From the fact that our initial knowledge is particularized, it does not follow that it must also be phenomenal and in no way manifestive of being. A *determinate* mode of being is still a mode of *being* and gives knowledge of appearance. Such knowledge is not formally metaphysical, but it can

There is nothing about the subject-object structure which in and of it-self rules out ontological claims so long as these claims are based on a theory of analogy which is cognizant of this basic character of consciousness. The theological problem of objectivity which Buri draws from his analyses of the subject-object structure and the limits of knowledge is almost entirely a function of a proper understanding of the existentiality of faith, not of the intrinsic limits on ontological claims as such. And where it is more than this, his analysis will simply not bear the weight he wants to ascribe to it. This is the case provided that the role of ontology in theology is strictly controlled by the existentialist interpretation of faith.

This is not the place actually to develop a theory of analogy which would meet these conditions. The only concern here is to show how the problem of objectivity is and is not relevant to an existentialist theology, and it must be concluded that, for all its hermeneutical scope, the problem of objectivity does not permit an existentialist theology to avoid the hard classical questions which surround the problem of giving an ontological account of the referential force of religious symbols. It will be ap-

provide a basis for the metaphysical judgment that separates being-as-such from any of its particular, sensible modes." James Collins, "Jaspers on Science and Philosophy," in Paul A. Schilpp, ed., *The Philosophy of Karl Jaspers* (New York: Tudor Publishing Co., 1957), p. 139. Cf., Lotz, p. 54.

Another possible line of criticism of Jaspers' and Buri's denial of ontology and metaphysics has received little attention in relation to their thought. This would be the notion of a "descriptive metaphysics" represented by such thinkers as Dorothy Emmet, W. H. Walsh and the movement of process philosophy. The value of this position is that it takes systematic account of the revolution in our understanding of knowledge and the world effected by the development of the special sciences — a development which has, quite appropriately, so deeply impressed Jaspers and Buri. Such a position would agree with them both that "being as a whole" is not a legitimate object of knowledge and that we have no cognitive access to super-sensible realms (although it might not base this latter judgment on a phenomenalism). But it would argue that these denials do not exclude the possibility of developing generalized concepts from mundane experience which account for everything that happens and thereby help us "to see things entire" in fresh and imaginative ways. As Walsh has pointed out, the canons of assessment for such a metaphysics must be admittedly weaker than the mathematical ideal that has usually guided metaphysicians, perhaps approaching the ways in which disputes are carried on in literary criticism. (Cf., Walsh, pp. 171-184.) But there is no intrinsic reason why Jaspers and Buri, with their evident openness to a pluralism of rational criteria in various disciplines, should be closed to the possibilities of such a metaphysics. Sometimes one receives the impression that Jaspers and Buri have reacted so strongly to the rationalistic imperialism of Hegelian metaphysics and positivistic scientism that they decide the question of metaphysics too quickly and without sufficient consideration of all the options.

However, for vigorous and brilliant defenses of the contrary position to that argued in this note, that is for defenses of positions which in major thrust, if not in detail, are parallel to Jaspers and Buri, cf., Preller, and Robert C. Neville, *God the Creator: On the Transcendence and Presence of God* (Chicago: University of Chicago Press, 1968).

propriate here, however, to mention briefly some of the implications an ontology will have for existentialist interpretation.

The first of these concerns the way in which an ontology must take its departure from and be controlled by the interpretation of existential possibilities. A major thesis of this study has been that mythological objectivity must be interpreted exhaustively in terms of existential possibilities. This still holds as a first order procedure for solving the problem of theological interpretation. But this might suggest that it is not the mythological assertions that refer (except self-referentially) but only the existential possibilities, and this would surely be to misconstrue the way mythological language functions in the ordinary religious life. Ultimately it would seem that there must be some more intimate relationship among the referential implications of mythological symbols in their own right, existential possibilities, and an ontological account of those possibilities than has been suggested here – although it still might be necessary to go through something like the steps in the argument of this study to appreciate the complexity of that relationship fully. There must, in other words, be some more direct relationship between mythological references and the ontology which interprets the referential implications of existential possibilities.

Here it is worth considering that the number of existential possibilities in terms of which human beings can actualize their existence is limited. The remarkable diversity that characterizes the human species arises, in contrast, from the infinite number of ways these possibilities can be actualized in an individual life and from the differing images and symbols which are built up into myths in order, among other things, to interpret the limited number of existential responses. But how does one account for the variety in these interpretations? If it is granted that the actualization of existential possibilities is a response to reality, then it is reasonable to assume that images and symbols and thus myths arise from features in reality which are taken to be especially important for individuals making the response. But if this is the case, then the relationship between myths and existential possibilities is exactly parallel to the relationship between existential possibilities and an ontology which interprets them since within the subject-object structure an ontology can be developed only by an imaginative analogical extension of some objects and relations which are deemed especially important. The distinction between the immediate dimension of the religious life, at which level the mythological symbols function, and an ontological explication of existential possibilities still holds. But in this case, the ontology is directly related to the same general features of experience which initially elicited the myth-ological symbols, and the same judgments of importance guide each of them. In this way, one can account for an analogy of reference between the myths which express a religious tradition and an ontology which in-terprets that same tradition on the far side of demythologizing and exis-tentialist interpretation.[7]

Of course, the warrants by means of which an ontology is judged must be independent of any special appeal to a particular religious tradi-tion. But this is beside the point because it is not a special appeal to a religious tradition which is at stake but judgments of importance con-cerning paradigmatic features of experience which are taken to illumi-nate being as a whole. And at this point there is a real parallel between mythological symbols which articulate the immediate dimension of the religious life and ontological description.

The real question concerns how different judgments of importance and hence differing mythological systems and ontologies can be assessed. One should not be misled by the methodological nature of the present discussion into thinking that the objective concepts and relations which express the judgments of importance are themselves simple and abstract. The features of experience which are taken to be paradigmatic by a reli-gion or an ontology as well as the responses to those features may be ex-tremely complex. Consequently, the objective symbols or concepts may also be complex and, in this sense, have a wide scope of application. As a result, judgments of importance can be assessed by the classical criteria of coherence, logical consistency, adequacy of interpretive scope, and ap-plicability to concrete instances.[8] But this helps only up to a certain point because there may be conceptual schemes (either religions or ontologies) which meet these criteria internal to themselves but are mutually exclu-sive.[9] Ultimately there may be no resolution to this problem, no way to gain a standpoint from which a judgment could be made. It goes far, however, in explaining the immense appeal that certain impressive

---

[7]For the general line of argument developed here, I should like to acknowledge the influence in his teaching and writing of Van A. Harvey, in particular, *The Historian and the Believer*, pp. 258-265. The position here is not, however, identical with Harvey's position, and he is, of course, not to be held responsible for it.

[8]Cf., Alfred North Whitehead, *Process and Reality* (New York: The Macmillan Compa-ny, 1957 (1929)), pp. 4-6. For a commentary on these criteria, cf., Ivor Leclerc, *White-head's Metaphysics: An Introductory Exposition* (New York: The Macmillan Company, 1958), pp. 33-40.

[9]Cf., H. A. Hodges, *Languages, Standpoints and Attitudes* (London: Oxford University Press, 1953).

religions and ontologies have had on the minds of men throughout the ages. Furthermore, to put the question at the level of assessing some few perduring options in man's history runs the danger of overlooking how many options can be excluded by the above criteria. It may also overlook the really crucial point that a great deal of assessment is possible concerning the most adequate account of the referential implications of any particular judgment of importance internal to a religious tradition or an ontology.

For the present purposes, it is enough to recognize that there can be an analogy of reference between the mythological language which expresses the immediate dimension of the religious life and an ontology which explicates it fully. Once it is clear that both myths and ontologies arise from judgments of importance concerning paradigmatic features of experience, then there is nothing intrinsically question-begging about using the historistic form of certain existential possibilities as a departure for ontology. This is extremely important, however, because nothing less than the cognitive value of existentialist interpretation is at stake. Unless something like the relationship here suggested obtains among mythological objectivity, existential possibilities, and ontological explication, it is difficult to see how the existential method can avoid a totally noncognitive interpretation of religious language in which statements about existential possibilities are nothing more than statements about attitudes and commitments.

A second point concerns the theory of analogy required by the subject-object structure. One of the reasons Buri denies the possibility of objective claims about being-itself or being as a whole is the unstated assumption that ultimate reality, because it is "transcendent" in some sense, must be an exception to the basic principles by means of which mundane experience is organized immanent to the subject-object structure. From a Kantian perspective, it then immediately follows that ontology is impossible. But the movement of "descriptive metaphysics" in contemporary philosophy has shown beyond dispute that an adequate ontology does not require this assumption and that, indeed, it is the bane of much classical metaphysics.[10] It is now important to note that an ontology based on the subject-object structure also requires the rejection of

[10]Cf., Walsh, pp. 34-47, 154-198; and Whitehead, p. 521. Preller and Neville, of course, argue the opposite case, namely, that the principles of ultimate reality must be exceptions to other metaphysical principles. But interestingly enough, each of them indirectly confirms the above argument because they conclude, unlike the more classical metaphysical tradition, that the exceptional character of the principles of ultimate reality makes it impossible to speak about it.

this assumption. Within the subject-object structure an ontology is possible only by the analogical extension of certain paradigmatic features and relations to account for the structures of being as a whole. No ontological reality, therefore, can be an exception to the principles which apply generally to all structures immanent to the subject-object relation. To affirm otherwise would either make ontology impossible or require a standpoint transcendent to the subject-object structure. But neither of these affirmations is necessary as soon as it is recognized that no ontology is adequate if it must be salvaged by appeal to metaphysical entities which are exceptions to its basic principles.[11]

This means that the purpose of an ontology is not, as Van A. Harvey nicely put it, "the construction of a world behind the world but the systematic description of the structures of existence as they are implicitly affirmed in certain basic forms of human thought and action."[12] On this basis it is necessary, of course, entirely to rethink such questions as the meaning of transcendence or of contingency and necessity, for much of the classical theistic tradition in the West has answered them by making exceptions to its basic metaphysical principles. But contemporary descriptive metaphysics has shown not only that this rethinking is possible but also that many of the conundrums of classical metaphysics evaporate when this is done.[13] What is more important for the purpose here is the correlation between the theory of analogy which is required by the subject-object structure and by existentialist interpretation. The ontology to which existentialist interpretation leads is obviously one for which it would be arbitrary and question-begging to posit a "world behind the world" as an explanation. The question is purely a descriptive one: to give an ontological explication of the referential implications of certain existential possibilities. But now it appears that the analogical limits imposed on an ontology within the subject-object structure exactly meet the theological conditions imposed on an ontology demanded by existentialist interpretation. So, from still another direction, there is reason to question whether Buri's restriction on objective ontological claims is really demanded by the overall thrust of his hermeneutic.

Finally, combining these two points leads to a third which involves returning for the last time to Buri's concepts of God and Transcendence. *Given Buri's principles as he sees them*, Transcendence must be nothing

[11]Cf., Whitehead, p. 521.

[12]Harvey, "The Nature and Function of Faith," p. 112. Cf., the chapter in Walsh entitled "Metaphysics as News from Nowhere," pp. 34 ff.

[13]Cf., e.g., Leclerc, pp. 38 f., 178, 189-208.

beyond a limiting concept, and "God" must be interpreted exhaustively in terms of existential possibilities. It was shown in the last chapter that this position does not actually entail a "practical atheism" – an atheism would involve transgressing the limiting concept as much as would its opposite – but it does involve ruling out an entire realm of theological investigation in which it is impossible even to ask the question. And it is an important realm, for quite apart from the specific question of God, it is precisely this realm which is involved in an interpretation of the ontological ground and meaning of those existential possibilities which are taken to constitute a truly fulfilled humanity. It also makes extremely problematic the adequacy with which existentialist interpretation can claim to interpret the intention of God-language in mythological utterances – even if the problem of objectivity may require judging the actual form of mythological utterances inadequate. In other words, Transcendence as a limiting concept reaches its own limits, not, in the first instance, because it rules out references to God but because it necessarily leaves the question of the ontological ground of existential possibilities hanging in the air.

This need not be the case, however. It is now evident that the ontological question is not merely possible and legitimate but also necessary within the hermeneutics of existentialist interpretation. This is not to say that the limiting concept ceases to function. Strictly speaking, the interpretation of existential possibilities cannot move beyond the limiting concept. Such interpretation departs from certain paradigmatic features of human experience – in Buri's case, the experience of freedom and responsibility – and finds at a purely existential level that such experiences are not intrinsically self-positing. But at this level, existentialist interpretation warrants no move beyond a phenomenological description of the dialectical structure of the paradigmatic experience. No ontological reference as such is given with the dialectical structure of existential possibilities; if it is there, it is implicit only and requires ontological explication. The criticism of Buri's own attempts to go beyond the limiting concept at the immediate level of self-understanding still holds, therefore. The point, however, is that the basis of the existentialist interpretation, the limiting concept, does admit of ontological explication on the far side of existentialist interpretation, and in this sense, the question of God can be addressed theologically from within the existential method.

The two former points are relevant to how this is to be done. First, the "God" concept will be a function of the ontological requirements of the analogical principles by means of which the ontological references implicit in existential possibilities are developed. There can be no special pleading or jumps to concepts of God that are not directly required by the explanatory principles which give a generalized account of everything that happens. This means that classical meanings of various aspects of God-language, where they are relevant at all, must be interpreted according to the internal logic of these principles themselves.

At the same time, second, the theory of analogy will arise from judgments of importance concerning certain features of human experience to which the existential possibilities are responses and which are expressed traditionally in terms of mythological symbols. Buri develops his paradox of grace, for instance, out of an analysis of the paradigmatic experience of freedom and responsibility. In order to develop a full ontology it would be necessary to extend the base of this central response to the human situation and see if the same donative character of existence is not also exemplified in such other paradigmatic features as the experiences of transiency and flux, of suffering and death, and of guilt, forgiveness and community.[14] But in each of these cases, the judgment of importance, i.e., the donative character of existence, at the ontological level would develop a response to experience analogous to the same judgment of importance reflected in the mythological symbols which are interpreted in terms of existential possibilities. Thus, even though the meaning of God would be a function of explanatory principles in the ontology, there would again be a direct relation to the referential implications of mythological symbols as they function in the immediate dimension of the religious life to express a self-understanding. In this way, one can account theologically for the continued use of the traditional language in confession and proclamation while also showing how mythological references, existential possibilities, and ontological references are more intimately related than Buri's principles seem to allow. And the crucial mediating link is the notion that religious language is ultimately unintelligible unless, at all of the various levels at which it functions, it intends to make claims about the nature of the world man believes he lives in.[15]

It must be emphasized that raising the question of God in this way is

[14]Buri himself has in places taken the first step toward this extended application of the paradigmatic response to broader ranges of experience. Cf., e.g., *DP*, pp. 81-97, 103-106. But again, he always leaves the question of ontological reference essentially unclarified. Cf., *Ibid.*, pp. 122-128, esp. 124.

[15]This point is nothing but the full extension of Bultmann's statement that the intention of demythologizing and existentialist interpretation is to interpret the mythological tradition, not to eliminate it. Bultmann, "Neues Testament und Mythologie," p. 24 (ET, p. 12).

not a retreat from the earlier criticism of Buri's attempt to say that God is personal. On Buri's terms, this statement must either be a remnant of mythological symbol which apparently does not require demythologizing or a direct ontological claim arising from a self-understanding. Buri leaves it unclear which of these he intends, but each of them is inconsistent with the demands of his own principles. The claim can only be intelligible as an ontological explication of the referential implications of both demythologized mythological symbols and their existential possibilities, but Buri will not admit the possibility or legitimacy of such explication. The anomalies in Buri's concept of Transcendence – both its function as a limiting concept and its place in interpreting "God" – can be dissolved only if it is admitted that the problem of God is an ontological problem which is not excluded by the existential method.

C. EXISTENTIAL LANGUAGE IN ITS LARGER LINGUISTIC CONTEXT

In conclusion, it is necessary to return to a point too briefly mentioned above and to make a few suggestions about the most promising line of advance beyond Buri and Bultmann in the method of existentialist interpretation. In order to justify the possibility of ontological reference without destroying the hermeneutical force of the existential method, it was necessary to distinguish between three different levels at which religious language can function: mythological symbols, the immediate dimension of the religious life where the mythological language functions existentially, and ontological explication of the referential implications in the former two. It is clear enough that mythological symbols can be interpreted exhaustively in terms of existential possibilities (even if, in the final analysis, there is something like an isomorphic relation between mythological references and the ontological interpretation of existential possibilities), and it is also clear that ontological explication must take its point of departure from existential possibilities. The connecting link here is the fact that existential possibilities are responses to features of reality which are articulated by judgments of importance in mythological symbols. But it has been emphasized repeatedly that holding in view a particular world-view is not a condition of actualizing existential possibilities. This means that religious language as it functions in the immediate dimension of the religious life has a certain independence of both uninterpreted mythological symbols and ontology. It has a logic of its own. But it is a logic which in some sense includes reference beyond the

self since it is evident that certain existential possibilities imply such reference.

Once the status of the problem of objectivity has been clarified in the
various ways discussed above, the most important further task for the method of existentialist interpretation will have to be the examination of how
existentially interpreted language functions in the larger context of reference beyond the self. Certainly, at the same time that the place of ontology
in such a theology must be recognized, the actual function of religious language at the immediate level does not involve developing such an ontology – few religious men are theologians. It will not do to reply that the
mythological symbols explain this function. Prior to being interpreted existentially they are hermeneutically opaque, and their interpretation involves existential possibilities the referential implications of which are precisely what is in question. In other words, if existentialist interpretation is
to claim to be an interpretation and not a translation of religious language, then it must show how that language functions referentially, but not
mythologically, in the religious life itself. A reference to the world ingredient in the religious uses of language as it emerges from an existentialist
interpretation will not be of the same type as an ontology (although ontological explication will show that they are ultimately references to the
same thing), and the relationship between the two needs to be clarified.
This will involve a more extensive analysis than is presently available of
the referential implications of existential language in its immediate religious usage.

Existentialist interpretation is one way in which religious language can
be interpreted as self-involving. As noted above, a self-involving language
is one in which, directly embedded in the language itself, there are "logical connections between a man's utterances and his practical commitments, attitudes, and feelings."[16] Language can have many other functions
than that of registering facts. It can have "preformative" uses, for instance, in which linguistic acts actually "do" or "accomplish" something.
Many non-reportive functions of language have self-involving force. Self-
involving language, including some performative usages, can, in its religious dimension, have a series of complex functions involving expressions of attitude, valuational judgments of large scope, commitments to a
way of life, and an inner rapport with such a context of self-involvement
for an understanding of the language.[17] An example of the importance of

[16]Evans, p. 11.
[17]Cf., *Ibid.*, pp. 110-114 *et passim*.

the self-involving analysis of religious language is the way it shows that a statement like "God created the world" in its properly religious usage is only superficially similar to the factual statement "Jones built a house."[18] The self-involving analysis of such a religious statement is, thus, quite similar to that of an existentialist interpretation of creation language. The purpose is to show that religious language is not like factual reporting language about cosmological facts but functions in a complex way to order a religious perspective and a way of life.

Yet, various self-involving interpretations of religious language on the part of a group of Anglo-Saxon analytic philosophers have shown that, in exceedingly complex and far from clear ways, self-involving language also has some reference to the world.[19] The statements, for instance, "I look on God as a shepherd" or "I look on God as a loving father" do function in a total complex of religious language in such a way that, while they are not like the metaphysical statement "God is a person," they do have some further reference than subjective states of the self. Parallel with this, this study has shown that existentially interpreted doctrines indicating existential possibilities imply some reference to the world. Such existential modes as "confidence," "hope," and "being accepted" are very much like attitudes involving a perspective on things entire when they function in an existentially interpreted religious context. And doctrines which give expression to such modes of existence in the immediacy of the religious life as Buri interprets it seem to function as a self-involving language giving expression to a complex context of religious self-involvement.

The clarification of the problem of objectivity demonstrates that an existentialist theology need have no fear of talking about beliefs about the world involved in an existentialist interpretation of religious language. At the same time, the proper understanding of religious language

---

[18]*Ibid.*, p. 11.

[19]The beginnings of further reflection about the self-involving force of religious language have been made by a few Anglo-Saxon analytic philosophers of religion. Some of the most important contributions are: Evans; I. M. Crombie, "The Possibility of Theological Statements" in Basil Mitchell, ed., *Faith and Logic* (London: George Allen and Unwin, 1958); Ronald W. Hepburn, "Scepticism and the Naturally Religious Mind" in Hepburn, *Christianity and Paradox* (London: C. A. Watts and Co., Ltd., 1958); Alasdair MacIntyre, "The Logical Status of Religious Belief" in S. E. Toulmin, R. W. Hepburn, and A. MacIntyre, eds., *Metaphysical Beliefs* (London: SCM Press, 1957); and R. W. Braithwaite, *An Empiricist's View of Religious Belief* (London: Cambridge University Press, 1955). The most important of these for the particular problem adumbrated here is Evans' analysis of "onlooks" and his application of this analysis to the causal language about creation. Cf., Evans, pp. 124-141, 220-252.

from an existentialist point of view does have some stake in avoiding the cosmological or speculative interpretation of its language in its *religious use*. What is needed, then, is a more extensive analysis of self-involving language from an existentialist perspective in order to show how such language does refer beyond the self without any loss of the total existential context of such language. This is not the ontological task, but the ontological task depends upon it, for an ontological interpretation of a particular self-understanding is appropriate only when the full richness of the existential response to reality in that self-understanding is fully comprehended.

The question of such self-involving reference of language in its properly religious and existential context is so complex and many-faceted that, as Bultmann said when he first made his programmatic proposal, the completion of its analysis could well occupy a full generation of scholars. But with existentialist interpretation in some senses having reached its systematic completion in Bultmann's *Theologie des Neuen Testaments* and Buri's *Dogmatic als Selbstverständnis des christlichen Glaubens,* the next task for a radical theology must involve this further analysis of existential language in its larger linguistic context. This study of the problem of objectivity in Buri has attempted to provide the necessary conceptual clarification for this next step in the project of existentialist interpretation of the Christian faith. Only when it is completed will it be appropriate to proceed to the further problem of developing an adequate ontology. On these two together depend the full promise of a radical theology equal to the religious situation of our time.

A SELECTED BIBLIOGRAPHY

PRIMARY SOURCES

A. BOOKS

Buri, Fritz. *Die Bedeutung der Neutestamentlichen Eschatologie für die neuere protestantische Theologie. Ein Versuch zur Klärung des Problems der Eschatologie und zu einem neuen Verständnis ihres eigentlichen Anliegens.* (Dissertation, University of Bern), Zürich: Niehans, 1934.

–. *Bildnerische Kunst und Theologie.* Basel: Basilius Presse, 1965.

–. *Christian Faith in Our Time.* Translated by Edward Allen Kent. New York: The Macmillan Company, 1966.

–. *Christlicher Glaube in dieser Zeit.* Bern: Verlag Paul Haupt, 1952.

–. *Clemens Alexandrinus und der paulinische Freiheitsbegriff.* Zürich: Verlag Max Niehans, 1939.

–. *Denkender Glaube. Schritte auf dem Weg zu einer philosophischen Theologie.* Bern: Verlag Paul Haupt, 1966.

–. *Dogmatik als Selbstverständnis des christlichen Glaubens.* Erster Teil: *Vernunft und Offenbarung.* Zweiter Teil: *Der Mensch und die Gnade.* Bern: Verlag Paul Haupt, 1956 and 1962 respectively.

–. *Das Dreifache Heilswerk Christi und seine Aneignung im Glauben.* Hamburg: Herbert Reich Evangelischer Verlag, 1962.

–. *Gott in Amerika. Amerikanische Theologie seit 1960.* Bern: Verlag Paul Haupt, 1970.

–. *How Can We Still Speak Responsibly of God?* Title essay translated by Charley D. Hardwick. Philadelphia: Fortress Press, 1968.

–. *Das lebendige Wort.* Hamburg: Herbert Reich Evangelischer Verlag, 1957.

–. *Der Pantokrator. Ontologie und Eschatologie als Grundlage der Lehre von Gott.* Hamburg: Herbert Reich Evangelischer Verlag, 1969.

–. *Die Reformation geht weiter.* Bern: Verlag Paul Haupt, 1956.

–. *Thinking Faith. Steps on the Way to a Philosophical Theology.* Translated by Harold H. Oliver Philadelphia: Fortress Press, 1968.

–. *Theologie der Existenz.* Bern: Verlag Paul Haupt, 1954.

–. *Theology of Existence.* Translated by Harold H. Oliver and Gerhard Onder with an introduction to the English edition by Fritz Buri. Greenwood, S.C.: The Attic Press, 1965.

–. *Unterricht im christlichen Glauben.* Bern: Verlag Paul Haupt, 1957.

B. ARTICLES

Buri, Fritz. "Abschied von der Umschau." *Schweizerische theologische Umschau,* 28 (Nov./Dez., 1958).

–. "Der alte und der neue Glaube." *Schweizerische theologische Umschau,* 15 (Okt., 1945).

–. "Christus gestern und heute." *Schweizerische theologische Umschau,* 18 (Dez., 1948).

–. "Entmythologisierung oder Entkerygmatisierung der Theologie." *Kerygma und Mythos.* Bd. II. Herausgegeben von Hans-Werner Bartsch. Hamburg: Herbert Reich Evangelischer Verlag, 1952.

–. "Ernst Blochs 'Prinzip Hoffnung' und die Hoffnung im Selbstverständnis des christlichen Glaubens." *Reformatio,* XV. Jahrgang. Heft 4 (April, 1966).

–. "Der existentielle Charakter des konsequent-eschatologischen Jesus-Verständnisses Albert Schweitzers im Zusammenhang mit der heutigen Debatte zwischen Bultmann, Barth und Jaspers." *Ehrfurcht vor dem Leben: Eine Freundesgabe zum 80. Geburtstag Albert Schweitzers.* Herausgegeben von Fritz Buri. Bern: Verlag Paul Haupt, 1955.

–. "Freies Christentum – noch oder wieder Avantgarde." *Schweizerische theologische Umschau,* 27 (Juni, 1957).

–. "Gott und seine Schöpfung für das Selbstverständnis des christlichen Glaubens." *Theologische Zeitschrift,* 19 (1963).

–. "Die hermeneutische Funktion der Lehre vom prophetischen Heilswerk Christi." *Der historische Jesus und der kerygmatische Christus.* Herausgegeben von Helmut Ristow und Karl Matthiae. Berlin: Evangelische Verlagsanstalt, 1960.

–. "Kierkegaard und die heutige Existenzphilosophie." *Theologische Zeitschrift,* 7 (1951).

–. "Die Menschlichkeit Gottes als Symbol des Glaubens." *Schweizerische theologische Umschau,* 27 (Jan./Feb., 1957).

–. "The Problem of Non-Objectifying Thinking and Speaking in Contemporary Theology." Translated by Harold H. Oliver. *Distinctive Protestant and Catholic Themes Reconsidered.* (Vol. III: *Journal for Theology and Church.* Edited by Robert W. Funk in association with Gerhard Ebeling.) New York: Harper and Row, Publishers, Inc., 1967.

–. "Das Problem der ausgebliebenen Parusie." *Schweizerische theologische Umschau,* 16 (Okt./Dez., 1946).

–. "Das Problem der Prädestination." *Schweizerische theologische Umschau,* 13 (Juni, 1943).

–. "Das Problem des ungegenständlichen Denkens und Redens in der heutigen Theologie." *Zeitschrift für Theologie und Kirche,* 61, Heft 3 (Nov., 1964).

–. "Das Selbstverständnis des christlichen Glaubens als Prinzip der Dogmatik." *Theologische Zeitschrift,* 10 (1954).

–. "Sich selber geschenkt werden: Karl Jaspers zum 80. Geburtstag am 23. Februar, 1963." *National-Zeitung Basel, Sonntagsbeilage,* Nr. 91 (24 Februar, 1963).

–. Sünde und Versöhnung als Grundbegriffe einer theologischen Anthropologie." *Schweizerische theologische Umschau, 25 (Juli, 1955).*

–. "Theologie der Existenz." *Kerygma und Mythos.* Bd. III. Herausgegeben von Hans-Werner Bartsch. Hamburg: Herbert Reich Evangelischer Verlag, 1954.

—. "Theologie der Existenz." *Schweizerische theologische Umschau,* 24 (Jan., 1954).

—. "Theologie und Philosophie." *Theologische Zeitschrift,* 8 (1952).

—. "Theologie zwischen – oder mit Jaspers und Heidegger." *Schweizerische theologische Umschau,* 30 (Juli, 1960).

—. "Thesen zur Christologie der Dogmatik als Selbstverständnis des christlichen Glaubens." *Schweizerische theologische Umschau,* 28 (Juli/Aug., 1958).

—. "Toward a Non-Objectifying Theology." *Christianity and Crisis,* XXVII, No. 7 (May 1, 1967).

—. "Über Orthodoxie und Liberalismus hinaus." *Theologische Zeitschrift,* 16 (1960).

—. "Von Harnack zu Bultmann und weiter." *Schweizerische theologische Umschau,* 21 (Feb., 1951).

—. "Vom Sinn der Geschichte." *Schweizerische theologische Umschau,* 10 (Juni, 1940).

—. "Zehn Thesen zum Thema Gotteswort und Menschenwort." *Kirchenblatt für die reformierte Schweiz,* 122. Jahrgang, Nr. 12 (9. Juni, 1966).

—. "Zum Problem der Heilstatsache." *Schweizerische theologische Umschau,* 28 (Juli/Aug., 1958).

—. "Zur Diskussion des Problems der ausgebliebenen Parusie: Replik." *Theologische Zeitschrift,* 3 (1947).

—. "Zur Grundlegung einer Theologie der Existenz bei Paul Tillich." *Schweizerische theologische Umschau* (Jaspers-Nummer), 22 (Feb., 1952).

C. UNPUBLISHED MATERIAL

Buri, Fritz. "Zum Verhältnis von philosophischem und christlichem Glauben." Unpublished essay read before the *Übung* on Karl Jaspers' *Philosophische Glaube angesichts der Offenbarung,* University of Basel, Summer semester, 1963.

SECONDARY SOURCES

A. BOOKS

Armbruster, Ludwig, S. J. *Objekt und Transzendenz bei Jaspers. Sein Gegenstandsbegriff und die Möglichkeit der Metaphysik.* Innsbruck: Verlag Felizian Rauch, 1957.

Baillie, Donald. *God Was in Christ.* New York: Charles Scribner's Sons, 1948.

Barth, Karl. *Der Römerbrief.* Dritter Abdruck der neuen Bearbeitung. München: Chr. Kaiser, Verlag, 1924.

Bartsch, Hans-Werner (ed.). *Kerygma und Mythos.* II and III. Hamburg: Herbert Reich Evangelischer Verlag, 1952 and 1954 respectively.

Berger, Peter L. *A Rumor of Angels. Modern Society and the Rediscovery of the Supernatural.* Garden City, N.Y.: Doubleday and Co., 1969.

—. *The Sacred Canopy. Elements of a Sociological Theory of Religion.* Garden City, N.Y.: Doubleday and Co., 1967.

Bollnow, O. F. *Existenzphilosophie*. Stuttgart: W. Kohlhammer Verlag, 1955.

Braithwaite, R. W. *An Empiricist's View of Religious Belief*. London: Cambridge University Press, 1955.

Braun, Herbert. *Gesammelte Studien zum Neuen Testament und seiner Umwelt*. Tübingen: J. C. B. Mohr (Paul Siebeck), 1962.

Bultmann, Rudolf. *Existence and Faith*. Translated and introduced by Schubert M. Ogden. New York: Meridian Books, Inc., 1960.

–. *Glauben und Verstehen*. Dritter Band. Zweite unveränderte Auflage. Tübingen: J. C. B. Mohr (Paul Siebeck), 1962.

–. *Theology of the New Testament*, 2 Vols. Translated by Kendrick Grobel. New York: Charles Scribner's Sons, 1951.

Cox, Harvey. *The Secular City*. New York: The Macmillan Co., 1965.

Cullmann, Oscar. *Christus und die Zeit. Die urchristliche Zeit- und Geschichtsauffassung*. Zollikon-Zürich: Evangelischer Verlag, erste Auflage, 1946.

Diem, Hermann. *Dogmatics*. Translated by Harold Knight. Philadelphia: The Westminster Press, 1959.

–. *Theologie als kirchliche Wissenschaft. Handreichung zur Einübung ihrer Probleme*. Band II: *Dogmatik: Ihr Weg zwischen Historismus und Existentialismus*. Dritte Auflage. München: Chr. Kaiser Verlag, 1960.

Emmet, Dorothy. *The Nature of Metaphysical Thinking*. London: Macmillan and Co., 1945.

Evans, Donald. *The Logic of Self-Involvement*. London: SCM Press, Ltd., 1963.

Fackenheim, Emil L. *Metaphysics and Historicity*. Milwaukee: Marquette University Press, 1961.

Fuller, Reginald H. (ed. and tran.) with Hans-Werner Bartsch. *Kerygma and Myth*. New York: Harper and Brothers, 1961.

Gilkey, Langdon. *Naming the Whirlwind. The Renewal of God-Language*. New York: The Bobbs-Merrill Co., 1969.

Gollwitzer, Helmut. *The Existence of God as Confessed by Faith*. Translated by James W. Leitch. London: SCM Press, 1965.

–. *Die Existenz Gottes im Bekenntnis des Glaubens*. München: Chr. Kaiser Verlag, 1963.

Hart, Ray L. *Unfinished Man and the Imagination*. New York: Herder and Herder, 1969.

Harvey, Van A. *The Historian and the Believer*. New York: The Macmillan Co., 1966.

Heidegger, Martin. *Sein und Zeit*. Neunte unveränderte Auflage. Tübingen: Max Niemeyer Verlag, 1960.

Hepburn, Ronald W. *Christianity and Paradox*. London: C. A. Watts and Co., Ltd., 1958.

Hodges, H. A. *Languages, Standpoints, and Attitudes*. London: Oxford University Press, 1953.

Jaspers, Karl. *Einführung in die Philosophie*. München: R. Piper and Co., Verlag, 1953.

–. *Existenzphilosophie*. Zweite Auflage vermehrt um ein Nachwort. Berlin: Walter De Gruyter and Co., 1956.

–. *Philosophie*. Band I: *Philosophische Weltorientierung*. Band II: *Existenzerhellung*. Band III: *Metaphysik*. Dritte Auflage. Berlin: Springer-Verlag, 1956.

–. *Der philosophische Glaube.* München: R. Piper and Co., Verlag, 1946.

–. *Der philosophische Glaube angesichts der Offenbarung.* München: R. Piper and Co., Verlag, 1962.

–. *Reason and Existence.* Translated and introduced by William Earle. New York: The Noonday Press, 1955.

–. *Vernuft und Existenz.* München: R. Piper and Co., Verlag, 1960.

–. *Von der Wahrheit.* München: R. Piper and Co., Verlag, 1947.

Jaspers, Karl, and Bultmann, Rudolf. *Die Frage der Entmythologisierung.* München: R. Piper and Co., Verlag, 1954.

Jørgensen, Poul Henning. *Die Bedeutung des Subjekt-Objektverhältnisses für die Theologie. Der Theo-Onto-Logische Konflikt mit der Existenzphilosophie.* Hamburg: Herbert Reich Evangelischer Verlag, 1967.

Kierkegaard, Søren. *Concluding Unscientific Postscript.* Translated by David F. Swenson and Walter Lowrie. Princeton: Princeton University Press, 1941.

–. *The Sickness unto Death.* Translated by Walter Lowrie. Garden City, N.Y.: Doubleday and Co., 1954.

Knudson, Robert Donald. *The Idea of Transcendence in the Philosophy of Karl Jaspers.* J. H. Kok, N.V. Kampen, 1958.

Leclerc, Ivor. *Whitehead's Metaphysics. An Introductory Exposition.* New York: The Macmillan Co., 1958.

Lohff, Wenzel. *Glaube und Freiheit: Das theologische Problem der Religionskritik von Karl Jaspers.* Gütersloh: Carl Bertelsmann Verlag, 1957.

Long, Eugene Thomas. *Jaspers and Bultmann. A Dialogue between Philosophy and Theology in the Existentialist Tradition.* Durham, N.C.: Duke University Press, 1968.

Macquarrie, John. *The Scope of Demythologizing.* London: SCM Press, Ltd., 1960.

Neuenschwander, Ulrich. *Protestantische Dogmatik der Gegenwart und das Problem der biblischen Mythologie.* Bern: Verlag Paul Haupt, 1949.

Neville, Robert C. *God the Creator. On the Transcendence and Presence of God.* Chicago: University of Chicago Press, 1968.

Noller, Gerhard. *Sein und Existenz: Die Überwindung des Subjekt-Objektschemas in der Philosophie Heideggers und in der Theologie der Entmythologisierung.* München: Chr. Kaiser Verlag, 1962.

Ogden, Schubert M. *Christ without Myth.* New York: Harper and Brothers, Publishers, 1961.

–. *The Reality of God and Other Essays.* New York: Harper and Row Publishers, 1966.

Ott, Heinrich. *Geschichte und Heilsgeschichte in der Theologie Rudolf Bultmanns.* Tübingen: J. C. B. Mohr (Paul Siebeck), 1955.

Preller, Victor. *Divine Science and the Science of God. A Reformulation of Thomas Aquinas.* Princeton: Princeton University Press, 1967.

Robinson, James M. *A New Quest of the Historical Jesus.* London: SCM Press, Ltd., 1959.

Robinson, James M. and Cobb, John B., Jr. (eds.). *New Frontiers in Theology.* Vol. I: *The Later Heidegger and Theology.* New York: Harper and Row, Publishers, 1963.

–. *New Frontiers in Theology.* Vol. II: *The New Hermeneutic.* Harper and Row, Publishers, 1964.

Schleiermacher, Friedrich. *The Christian Faith*. Translated by H. R. Mackintosh and J. S. Stewart. Edinburgh: T. and T. Clark, 1928.

—. *Der christliche Glaube nach den Grundsätzen der Evangelischen Kirche im Zusammenhange dargestellt*. Zwei Bänder. Siebente Auflage auf Grund der zweiten Auflage und kritischer Prüfung des Textes. Herausgegeben mit Einleitung, Erläuterungen, und Register von Martin Redeker. Berlin: Walter De Gruyter and Co., 1960.

Schlipp, Paul Arthur (ed.). *The Philosophy of Karl Jaspers*. New York: Tudor Publishing Co., 1957.

Schmidhäuser, Ulrich. *Allgemeine Wahrheit und existentielle Wahrheit bei Karl Jaspers*. Bonn: Dissertation der rheinischen Friedrich Wilhelms-Universität, philosophische Fakultät, 1953.

Walsh, W. H. *Metaphysics*. London: Hutchinson University Library, 1963.

Welte, Bernhard. *Der philosophische Glaube bei Karl Jaspers und die Möglichkeit seiner Deutung durch die thomistische Philosophie. Symposion: Jahrbuch für Philosophie*, II. Freiburg: Verlag Karl Alber, 1949.

Whitehead, Alfred North. *Process and Reality*. New York: The Macmillan Co., 1929.

B. ARTICLES

Allen, E. L. "A New Liberal Theology: Fritz Buri of Basel." *Religion in Life*, XXX, No. 2 (Spring, 1961).

Allison, Henry E. "Christianity and Nonsense." *The Review of Metaphysics*, XX, No. 3 (March, 1967).

Collins, James. "An Approach to Karl Jaspers." *Thought*, 20 (1945).

Crombie, I. M. "The Possibility of Theological Statements." *Faith and Logic*. Edited by Basil Mitchell. London: George Allen and Unwin, 1958.

Hartt, Julian. "God, Transcendence and Freedom in the Philosophy of Jaspers." *The Review of Metaphysics*, IV, No. 2 (December 1950).

Harvey, Van A. "The Historical Jesus, the Kerygma, and the Christian Faith." *Religion in Life*, XXXIII, No. 3 (Summer, 1964).

—. "The Nature and Function of Faith." *Frontline Theology*. Edited by Dean Peerman. Richmond, Virginia: John Knox Press, 1967.

Heidegger, Martin. "Brief über den 'Humanismus'." In Heidegger, Martin, *Platons Lehre von der Wahrheit*. Bern: Francke, 1947.

Lotz, J. B. "Analogie und Chiffre." *Scholastik*, 15 (1940).

MacIntyre, Alasdair. "The Logical Status of Religious Belief." *Metaphysical Beliefs*. Edited by S. E. Toulmin, R. W. Hepburn, and A. MacIntyre. London: SCM Press, Ltd., 1957.

Mackey, Louis. "Kierkegaard and the Problem of Existential Philosophy." *The Review of Metaphysics*, IX (March and June, 1956).

Neuenschwander, Ulrich. "Zu Buris Dogmatik als Selbstverständnis des christlichen Glaubens." *Schweizerische theologische Umschau*, 26, Nr. 5/6 (Dezember, 1956).

Ogden, Schubert M. "How Does God Function in Human Life?" *Christianity and Crisis*, XXVII, No. 7 (May 15, 1967).

Oliver, Harold H. "Fritz Buri: A Chronology of His Theologizing." *The Journal of Bible and Religion*, XXXIV, No. 4 (Oct., 1966).

Schmidt, Erik. Review of *Dogmatik als Selbstverständnis des christlichen Glaubens. Erster Teil: Vernunft und Offenbarung* by Fritz Buri. *Theologische Literaturzeitung*, 82. Jahrgang, Nr. 10 (Okt., 1957).

—. Review of *Dogmatik als Selbstverständnis des christlichen Glaubens. Zweiter Teil: Der Mensch und die Gnade* by Fritz Buri. *Theologische Literaturzeitung*, 89. Jahrgang, Nr. 1 (Jan., 1964).

Tillich, Paul. "Mythus und Mythologie." *Die Religion in Geschichte und Gegenwart*. Bd. IV. Herausgegeben von H. Gunkel and L. Zscharnack, Tübingen: J. C. B. Mohr (Paul Siebeck), 1927-1932.

Walker, William O., Jr. "Demythologizing and Christology." *Religion in Life*, XXXV, No. 1 (Winter, 1965-66).

GENERAL INDEX

258

94